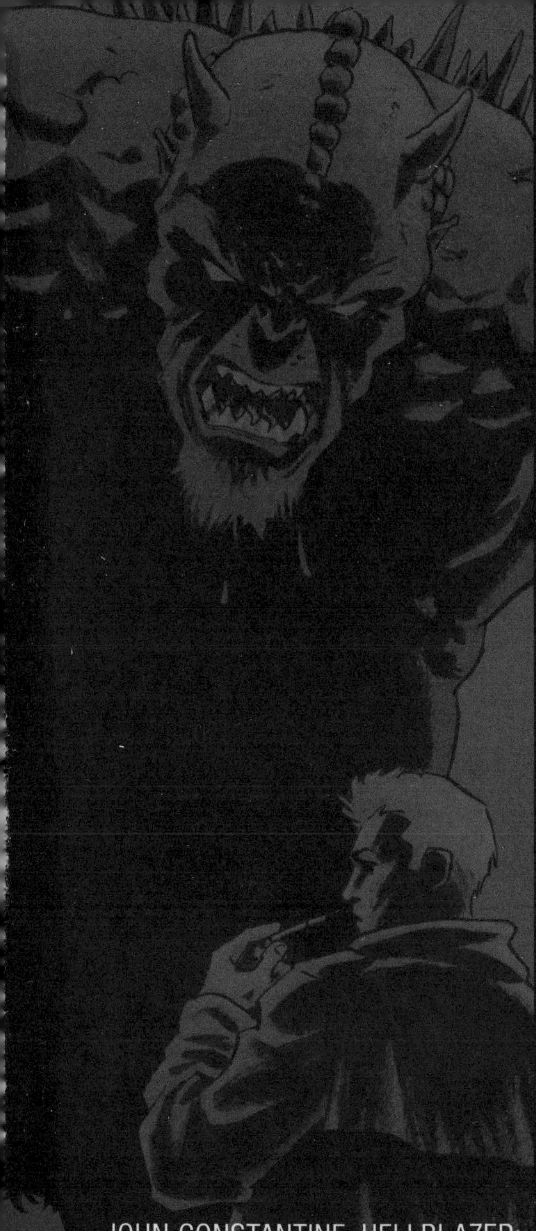

JOHN CONSTANTINE, HELLBLAZER: CHAS-THE KNOWLEDGE

JOHN HELLBLAZER:
HELLBLAZER CHAS-THE KNOWLEDGE

Simon Oliver
Writer

Goran Sudžuka
Artist

Matt Hollingsworth
Colorist

Clem Robins
Letterer

Glenn Fabry
Original Series Covers

Chas created by
Jamie Delano & John Ridgway

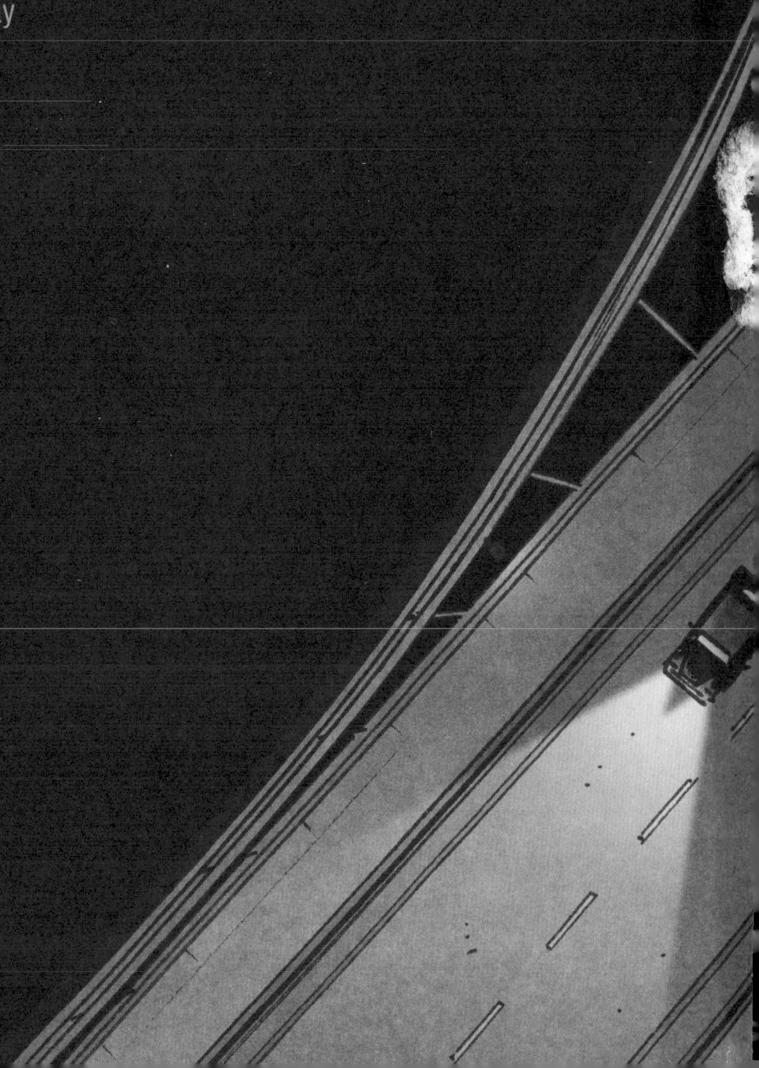

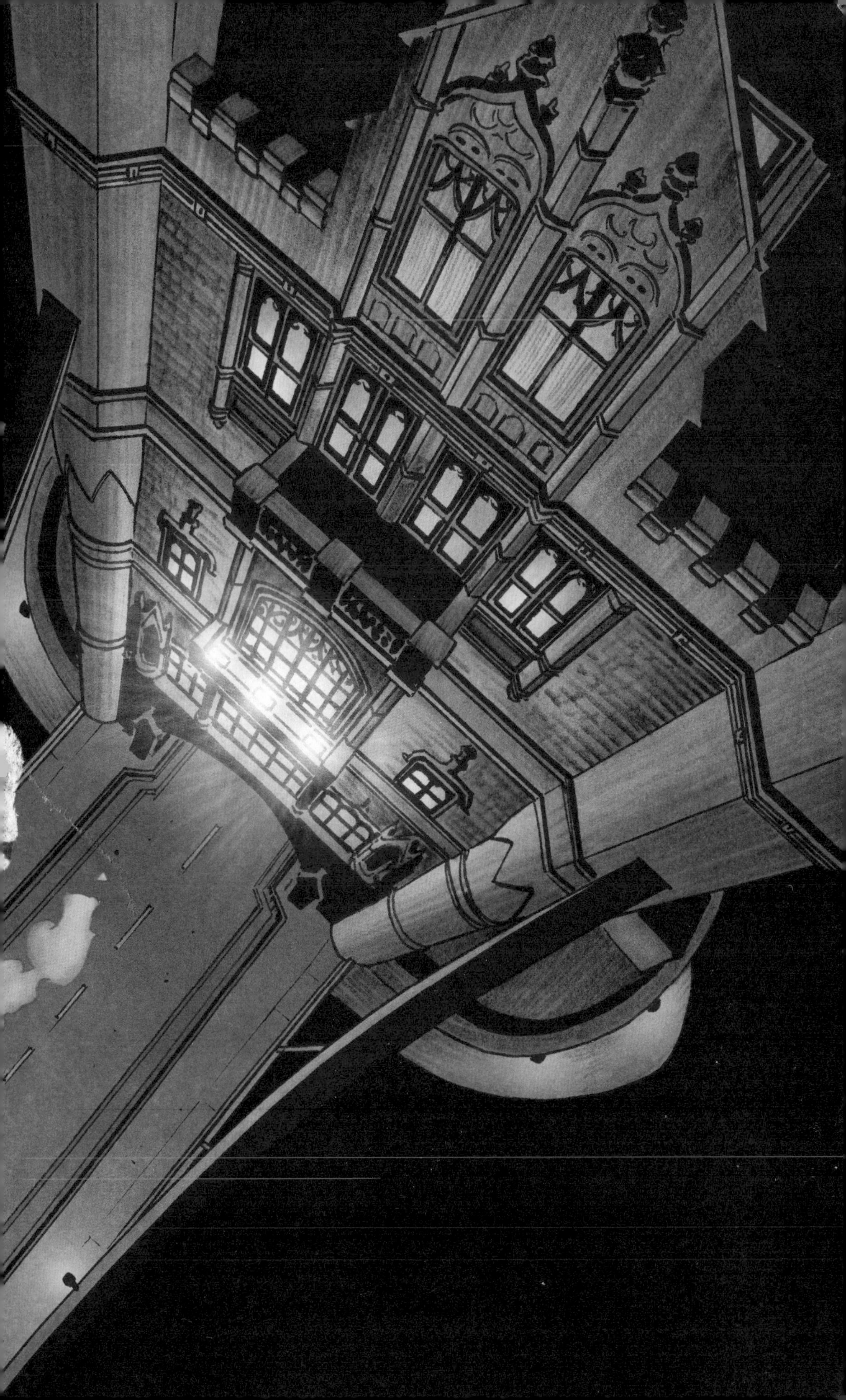

Karen Berger	Senior VP-Executive Editor
Jonathan Vankin	Editor-original series
Mark Doyle	Assistant Editor-original series
Bob Harras	Editor-collected edition
Robbin Brosterman	Senior Art Director
Paul Levitz	President & Publisher
Georg Brewer	VP-Design & DC Direct Creative
Richard Bruning	Senior VP-Creative Director
Patrick Caldon	Executive VP-Finance & Operations
Chris Caramalis	VP-Finance
John Cunningham	VP-Marketing
Terri Cunningham	VP-Managing Editor
Amy Genkins	Senior VP-Business & Legal Affairs
Alison Gill	VP-Manufacturing
David Hyde	VP-Publicity
Hank Kanalz	VP-General Manager, WildStorm
Jim Lee	Editorial Director-WildStorm
Gregory Noveck	Senior VP-Creative Affairs
Sue Pohja	VP-Book Trade Sales
Steve Rotterdam	Senior VP-Sales & Marketing
Cheryl Rubin	Senior VP-Brand Management
Alysse Soll	VP-Advertising & Custom Publishing
Jeff Trojan	VP-Business Development, DC Direct
Bob Wayne	VP-Sales

Cover illustration by Glenn Fabry

JOHN CONSTANTINE, HELLBLAZER: CHAS-THE KNOWLEDGE

DC Comics, 1700 Broadway, New York, NY 10019
A Warner Bros. Entertainment Company.
Printed in Canada. First Printing.
ISBN: 978-1-4012-2127-0

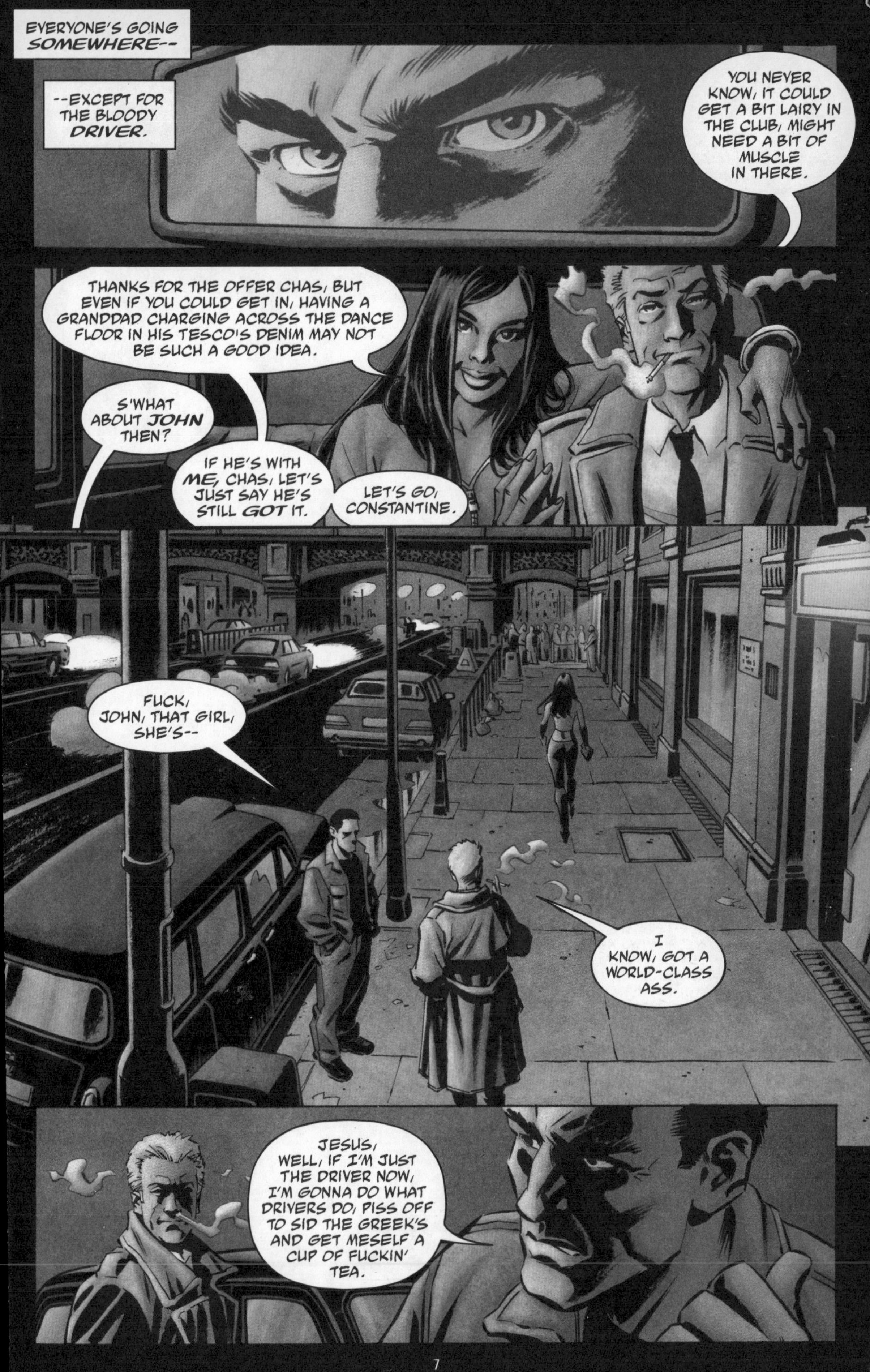
EVERYONE'S GOING SOMEWHERE--
--EXCEPT FOR THE BLOODY DRIVER.
YOU NEVER KNOW, IT COULD GET A BIT LAIRY IN THE CLUB, MIGHT NEED A BIT OF MUSCLE IN THERE.
THANKS FOR THE OFFER CHAS, BUT EVEN IF YOU COULD GET IN, HAVING A GRANDDAD CHARGING ACROSS THE DANCE FLOOR IN HIS TESCO'S DENIM MAY NOT BE SUCH A GOOD IDEA.
S'WHAT ABOUT JOHN THEN?
IF HE'S WITH ME, CHAS, LET'S JUST SAY HE'S STILL GOT IT.
LET'S GO, CONSTANTINE.
FUCK, JOHN, THAT GIRL, SHE'S--
I KNOW, GOT A WORLD-CLASS ASS.
JESUS, WELL, IF I'M JUST THE DRIVER NOW, I'M GONNA DO WHAT DRIVERS DO, PISS OFF TO SID THE GREEK'S AND GET MESELF A CUP OF FUCKIN' TEA.

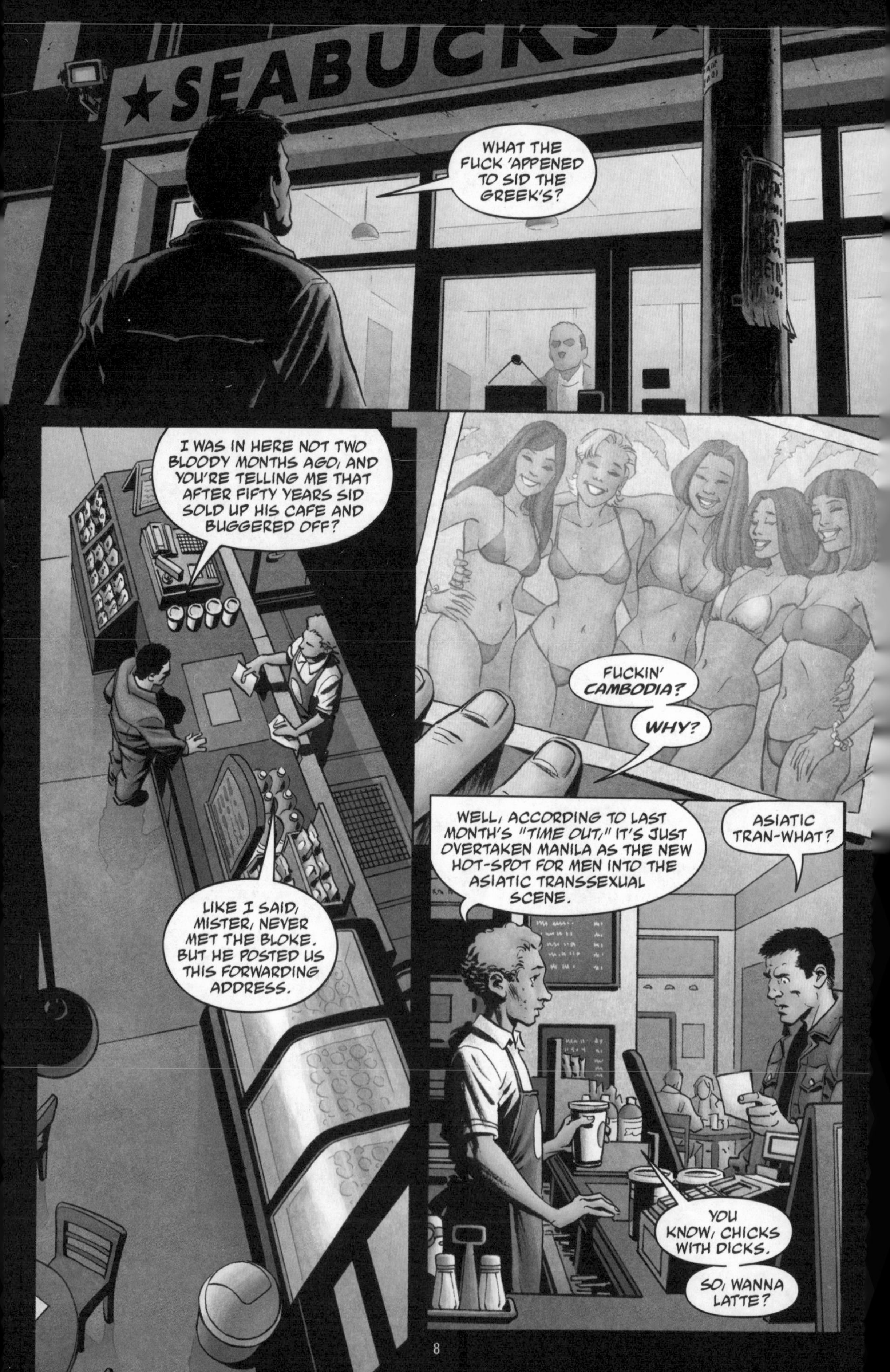
SEABUCKS
WHAT THE FUCK 'APPENED TO SID THE GREEK'S?
I WAS IN HERE NOT TWO BLOODY MONTHS AGO, AND YOU'RE TELLING ME THAT AFTER FIFTY YEARS SID SOLD UP HIS CAFE AND BUGGERED OFF?
LIKE I SAID, MISTER, NEVER MET THE BLOKE. BUT HE POSTED US THIS FORWARDING ADDRESS.
FUCKIN' CAMBODIA?
WHY?
WELL, ACCORDING TO LAST MONTH'S "TIME OUT," IT'S JUST OVERTAKEN MANILA AS THE NEW HOT-SPOT FOR MEN INTO THE ASIATIC TRANSSEXUAL SCENE.
ASIATIC TRAN-WHAT?
YOU KNOW, CHICKS WITH DICKS.
SO, WANNA LATTE?

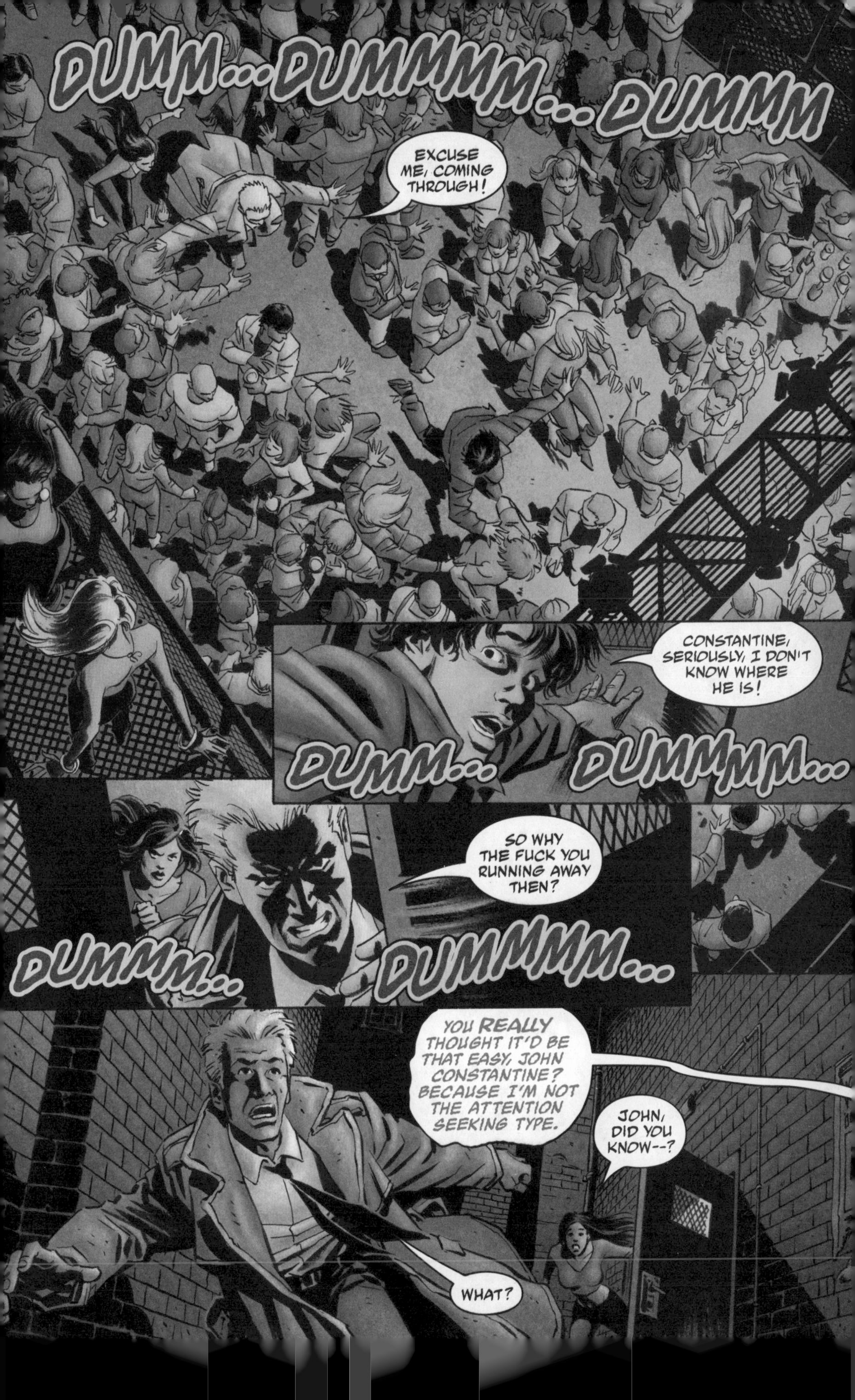
DUMM...DUMMMMM...DUMMM
EXCUSE ME, COMING THROUGH!
CONSTANTINE, SERIOUSLY, I DON'T KNOW WHERE HE IS!
DUMM.. DUMMMM..
SO WHY THE FUCK YOU RUNNING AWAY THEN?
DUMMM.. DUMMMM...
YOU REALLY THOUGHT IT'D BE THAT EASY, JOHN CONSTANTINE? BECAUSE I'M NOT THE ATTENTION SEEKING TYPE.
JOHN, DID YOU KNOW--?
WHAT?

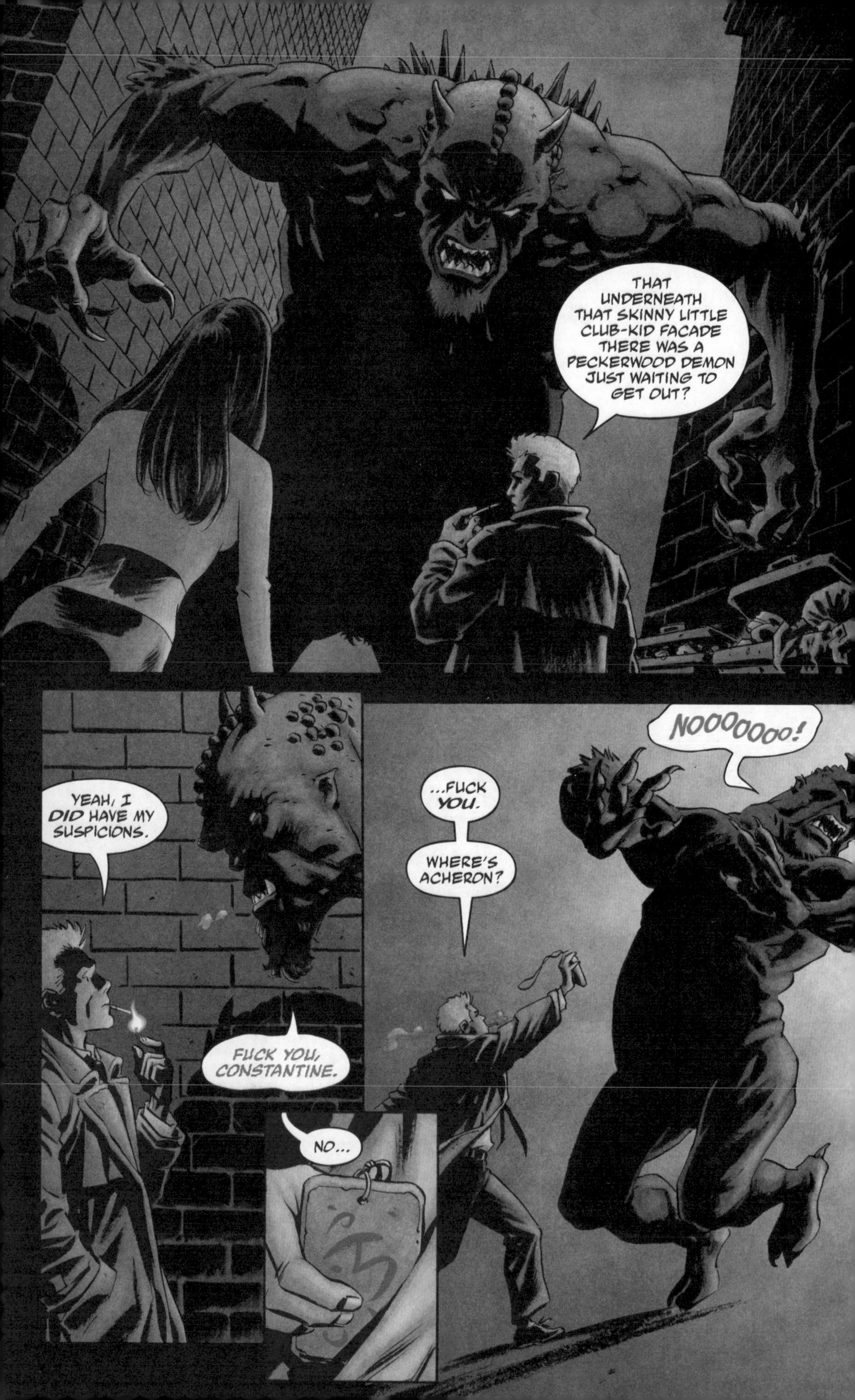
THAT UNDERNEATH THAT SKINNY LITTLE CLUB-KID FACADE THERE WAS A PECKERWOOD DEMON JUST WAITING TO GET OUT?
YEAH, I DID HAVE MY SUSPICIONS.
FUCK YOU, CONSTANTINE.
NO...
...FUCK YOU.
WHERE'S ACHERON?
NOOOOOOO!

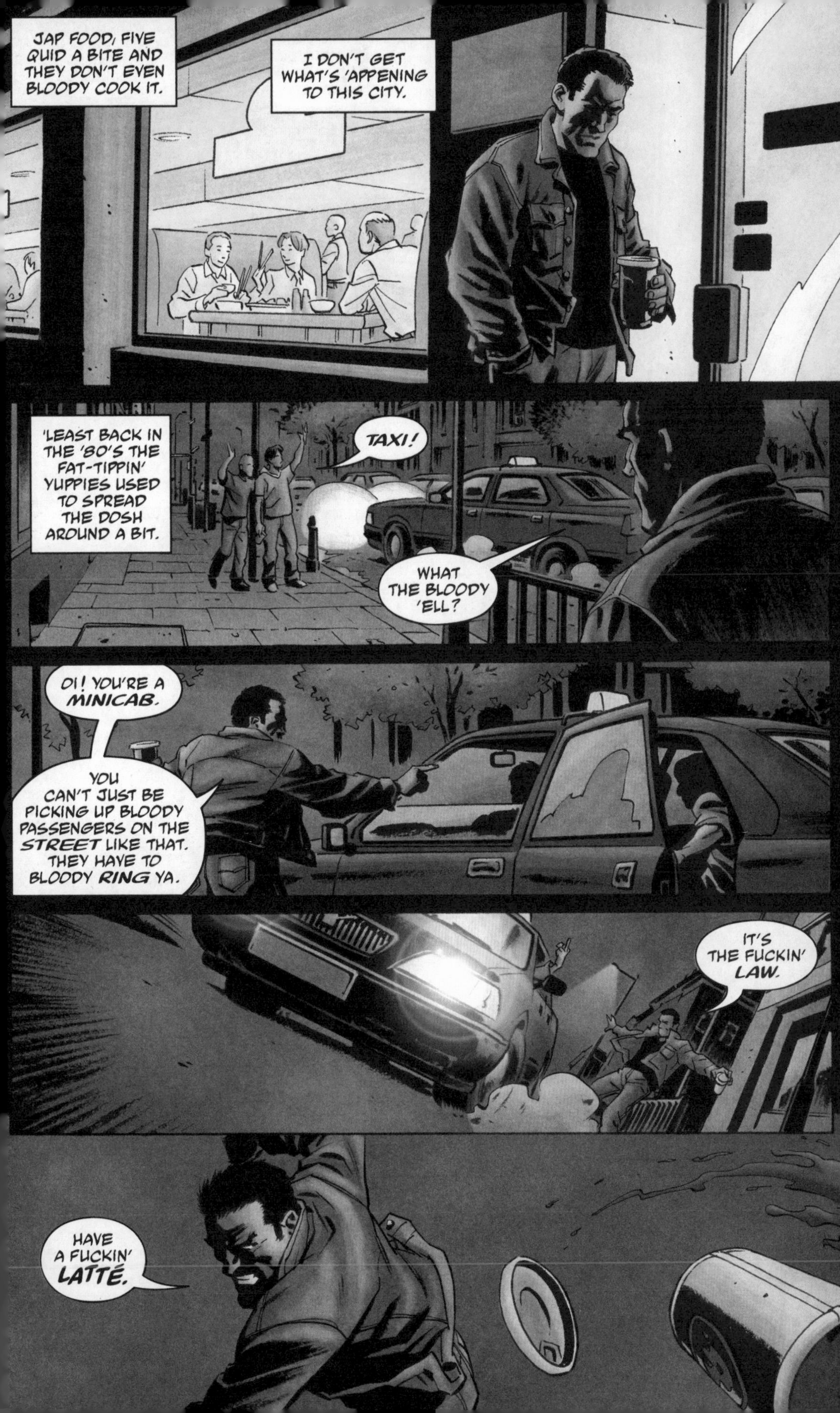
JAP FOOD; FIVE QUID A BITE AND THEY DON'T EVEN BLOODY COOK IT.
I DON'T GET WHAT'S 'APPENING TO THIS CITY.
'LEAST BACK IN THE '80'S THE FAT-TIPPIN' YUPPIES USED TO SPREAD THE DOSH AROUND A BIT.
TAXI!
WHAT THE BLOODY 'ELL?
OI! YOU'RE A MINICAB.
YOU CAN'T JUST BE PICKING UP BLOODY PASSENGERS ON THE STREET LIKE THAT. THEY HAVE TO BLOODY RING YA.
IT'S THE FUCKIN' LAW.
HAVE A FUCKIN' LATTÉ.

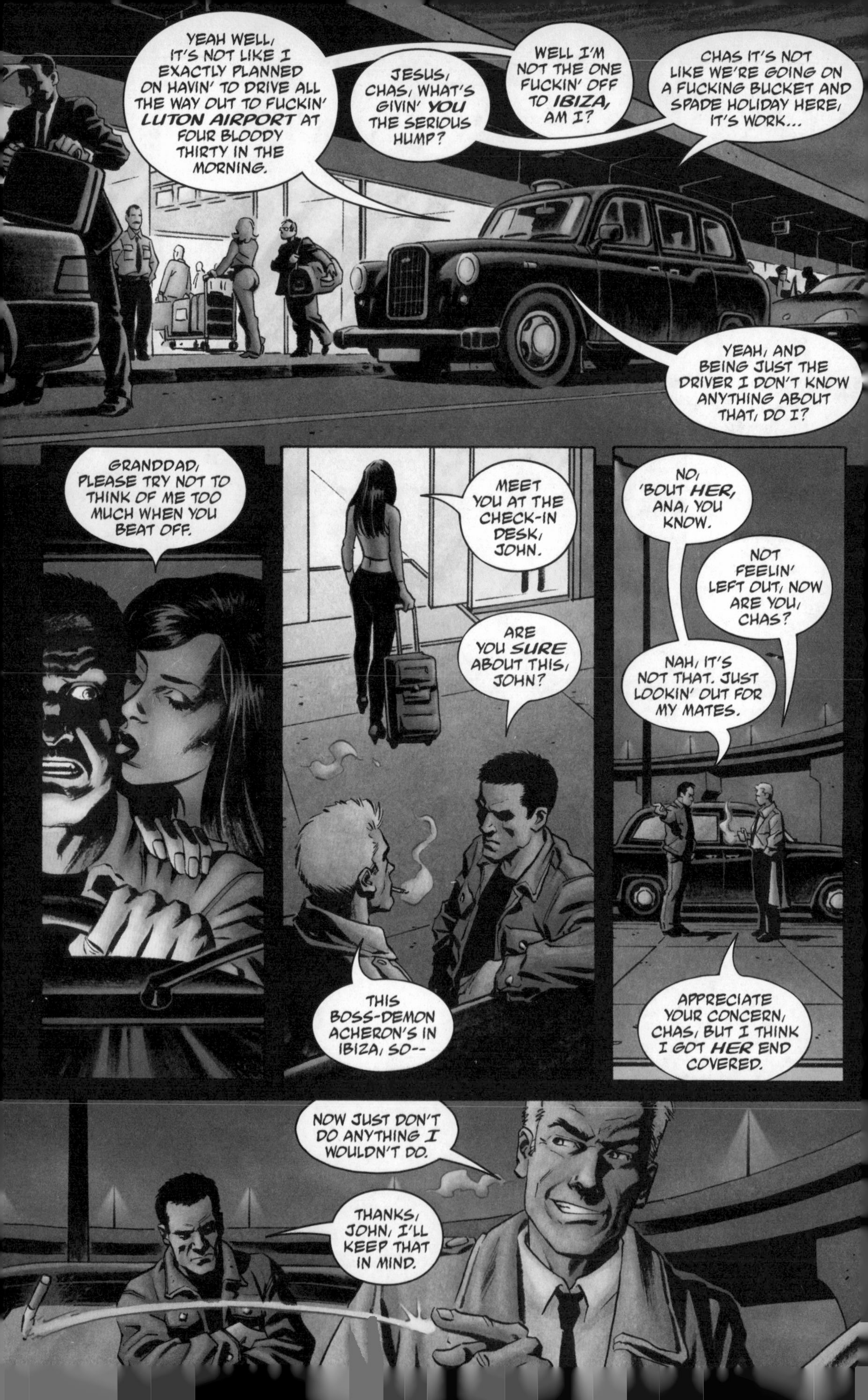
YEAH WELL, IT'S NOT LIKE I EXACTLY PLANNED ON HAVIN' TO DRIVE ALL THE WAY OUT TO FUCKIN' LUTON AIRPORT AT FOUR BLOODY THIRTY IN THE MORNING.
JESUS, CHAS, WHAT'S GIVIN' YOU THE SERIOUS HUMP?
WELL I'M NOT THE ONE FUCKIN' OFF TO IBIZA, AM I?
CHAS IT'S NOT LIKE WE'RE GOING ON A FUCKING BUCKET AND SPADE HOLIDAY HERE, IT'S WORK...
YEAH, AND BEING JUST THE DRIVER I DON'T KNOW ANYTHING ABOUT THAT, DO I?
GRANDDAD, PLEASE TRY NOT TO THINK OF ME TOO MUCH WHEN YOU BEAT OFF.
MEET YOU AT THE CHECK-IN DESK, JOHN.
ARE YOU SURE ABOUT THIS, JOHN?
THIS BOSS-DEMON ACHERON'S IN IBIZA, SO--
NO, 'BOUT HER, ANA, YOU KNOW.
NOT FEELIN' LEFT OUT, NOW ARE YOU, CHAS?
NAH, IT'S NOT THAT. JUST LOOKIN' OUT FOR MY MATES.
APPRECIATE YOUR CONCERN, CHAS, BUT I THINK I GOT HER END COVERED.
NOW JUST DON'T DO ANYTHING I WOULDN'T DO.
THANKS, JOHN, I'LL KEEP THAT IN MIND.

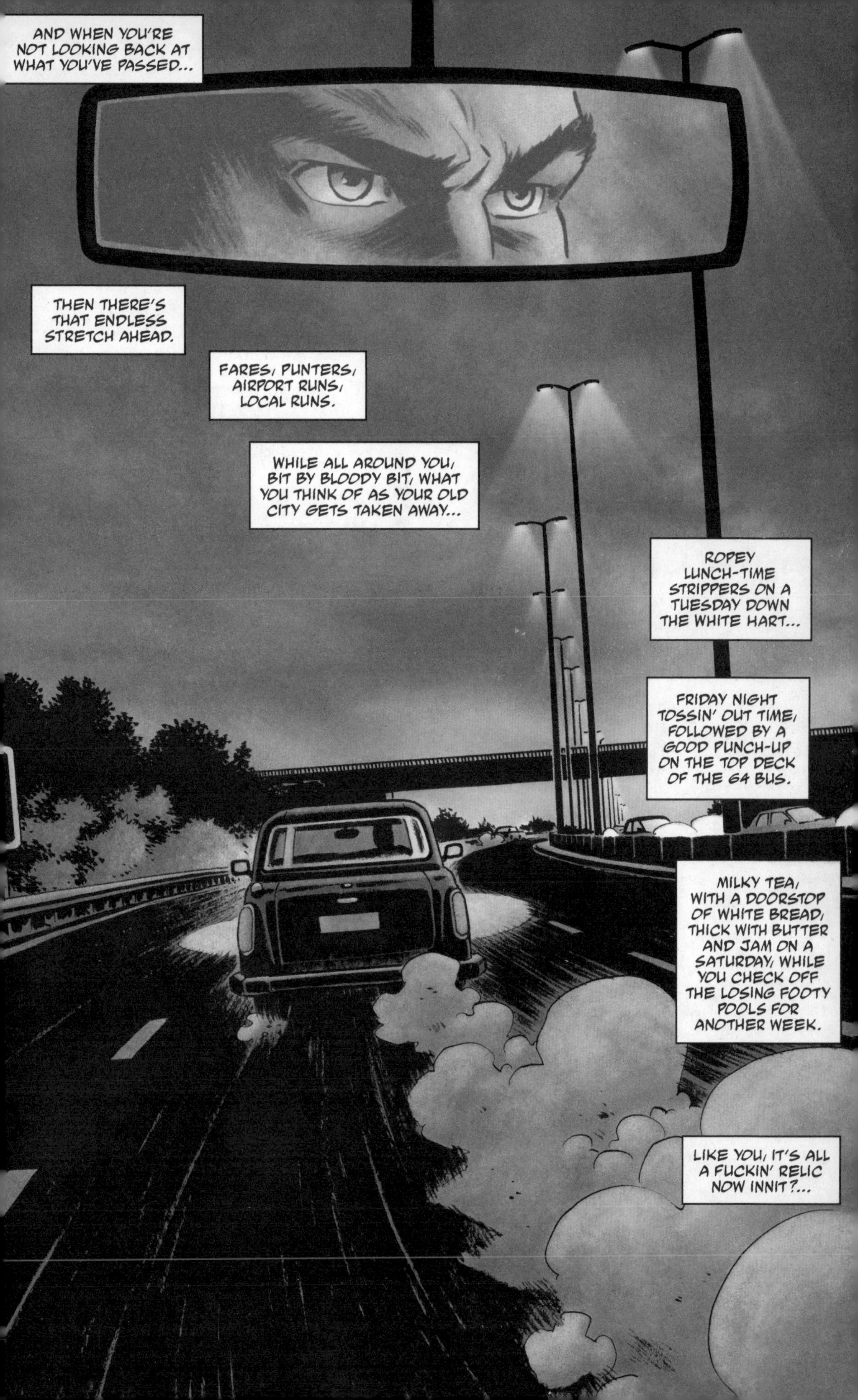
AND WHEN YOU'RE NOT LOOKING BACK AT WHAT YOU'VE PASSED...
THEN THERE'S THAT ENDLESS STRETCH AHEAD.
FARES, PUNTERS, AIRPORT RUNS, LOCAL RUNS.
WHILE ALL AROUND YOU, BIT BY BLOODY BIT, WHAT YOU THINK OF AS YOUR OLD CITY GETS TAKEN AWAY...
ROPEY LUNCH-TIME STRIPPERS ON A TUESDAY DOWN THE WHITE HART...
FRIDAY NIGHT TOSSIN' OUT TIME, FOLLOWED BY A GOOD PUNCH-UP ON THE TOP DECK OF THE 64 BUS.
MILKY TEA, WITH A DOORSTOP OF WHITE BREAD, THICK WITH BUTTER AND JAM ON A SATURDAY, WHILE YOU CHECK OFF THE LOSING FOOTY POOLS FOR ANOTHER WEEK.
LIKE YOU, IT'S ALL A FUCKIN' RELIC NOW INNIT?...

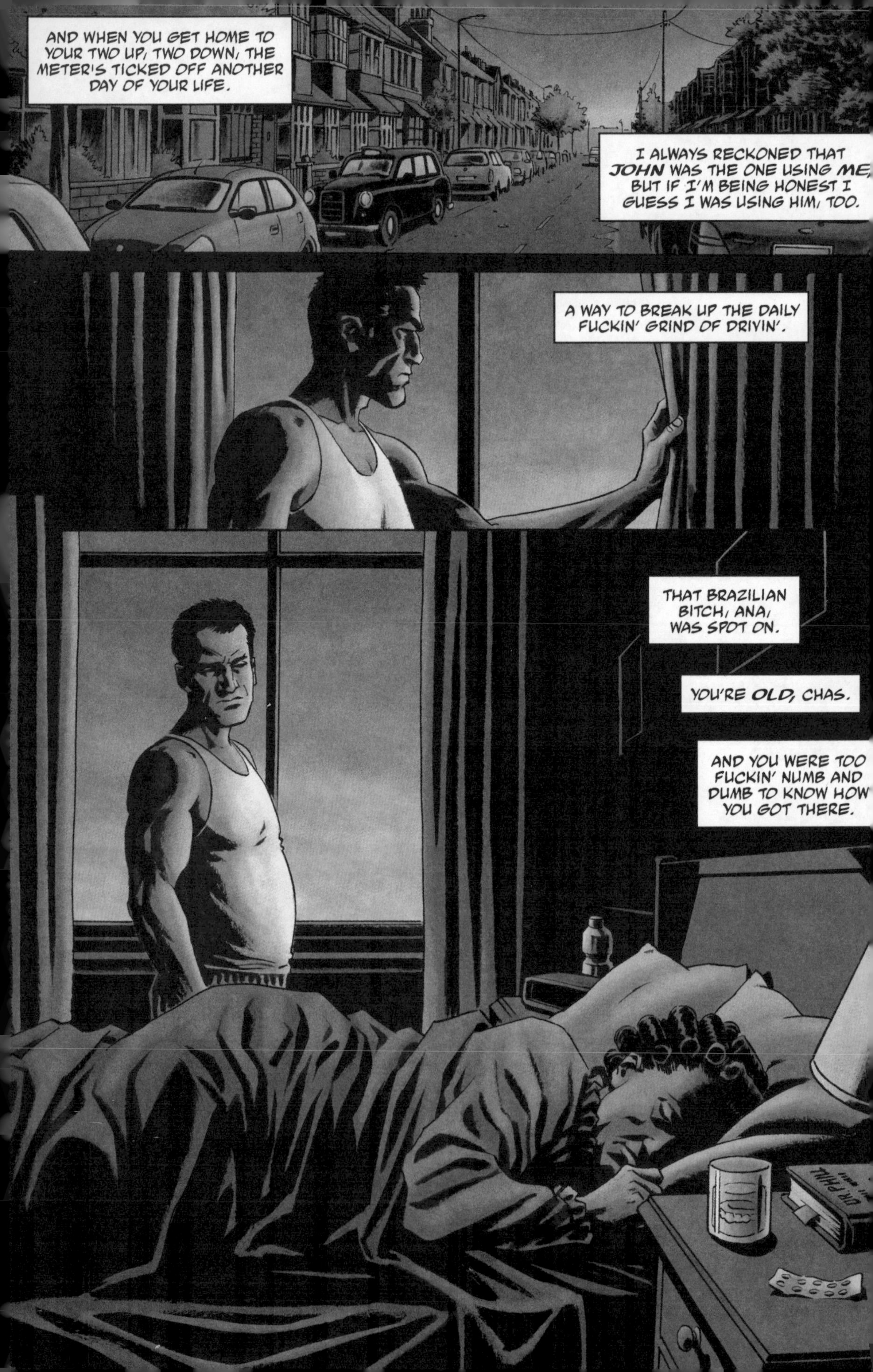
AND WHEN YOU GET HOME TO YOUR TWO UP, TWO DOWN, THE METER'S TICKED OFF ANOTHER DAY OF YOUR LIFE.
I ALWAYS RECKONED THAT JOHN WAS THE ONE USING ME, BUT IF I'M BEING HONEST I GUESS I WAS USING HIM, TOO.
A WAY TO BREAK UP THE DAILY FUCKIN' GRIND OF DRIVIN'.
THAT BRAZILIAN BITCH, ANA, WAS SPOT ON.
YOU'RE OLD, CHAS.
AND YOU WERE TOO FUCKIN' NUMB AND DUMB TO KNOW HOW YOU GOT THERE.
DR PHIL

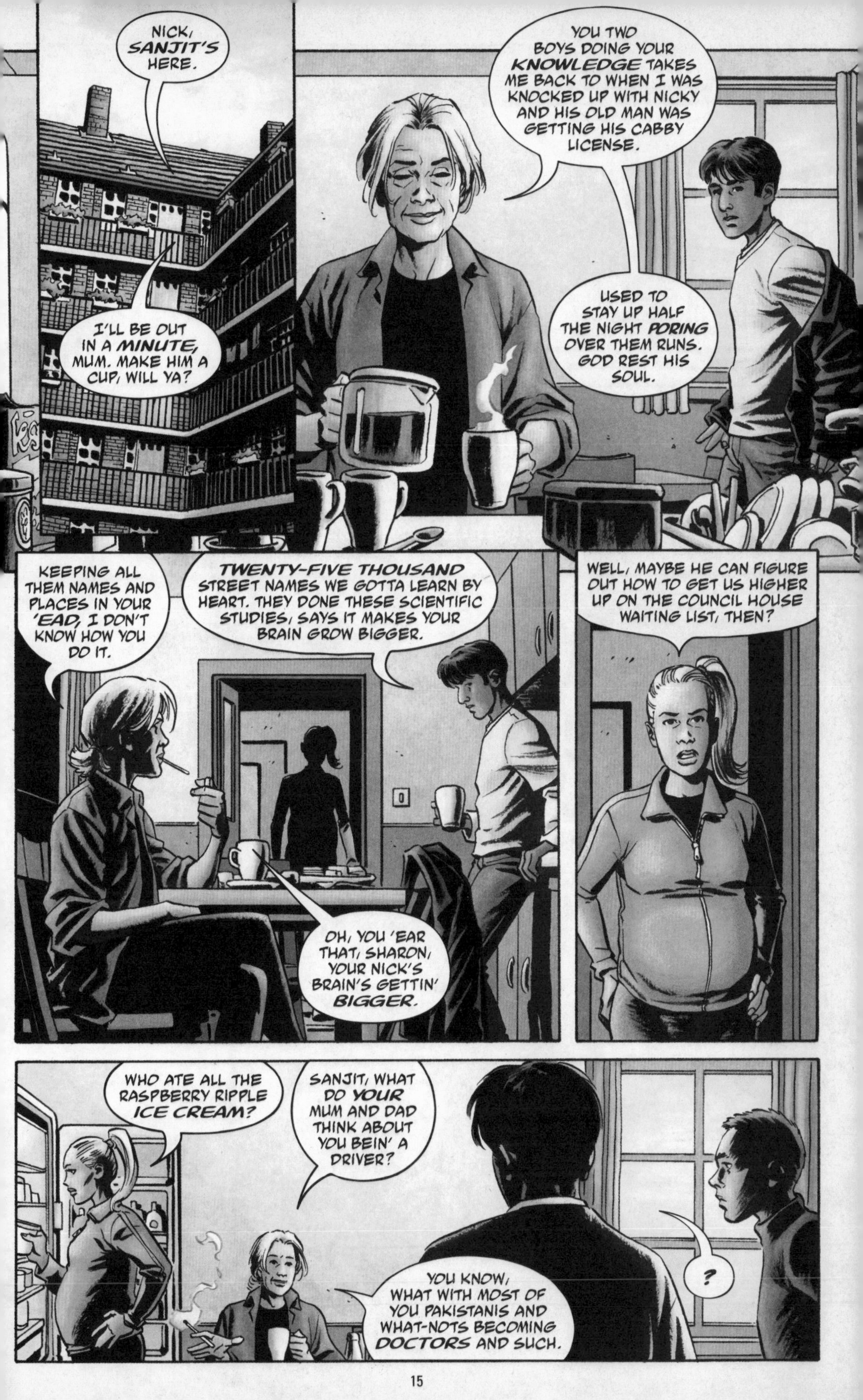
NICK, SANJIT'S HERE.
I'LL BE OUT IN A MINUTE, MUM. MAKE HIM A CUP, WILL YA?
YOU TWO BOYS DOING YOUR KNOWLEDGE TAKES ME BACK TO WHEN I WAS KNOCKED UP WITH NICKY AND HIS OLD MAN WAS GETTING HIS CABBY LICENSE.
USED TO STAY UP HALF THE NIGHT PORING OVER THEM RUNS. GOD REST HIS SOUL.
KEEPING ALL THEM NAMES AND PLACES IN YOUR 'EAD, I DON'T KNOW HOW YOU DO IT.
TWENTY-FIVE THOUSAND STREET NAMES WE GOTTA LEARN BY HEART. THEY DONE THESE SCIENTIFIC STUDIES, SAYS IT MAKES YOUR BRAIN GROW BIGGER.
OH, YOU 'EAR THAT, SHARON, YOUR NICK'S BRAIN'S GETTIN' BIGGER.
WELL, MAYBE HE CAN FIGURE OUT HOW TO GET US HIGHER UP ON THE COUNCIL HOUSE WAITING LIST, THEN?
WHO ATE ALL THE RASPBERRY RIPPLE ICE CREAM?
SANJIT, WHAT DO YOUR MUM AND DAD THINK ABOUT YOU BEIN' A DRIVER?
YOU KNOW, WHAT WITH MOST OF YOU PAKISTANIS AND WHAT-NOTS BECOMING DOCTORS AND SUCH.
?

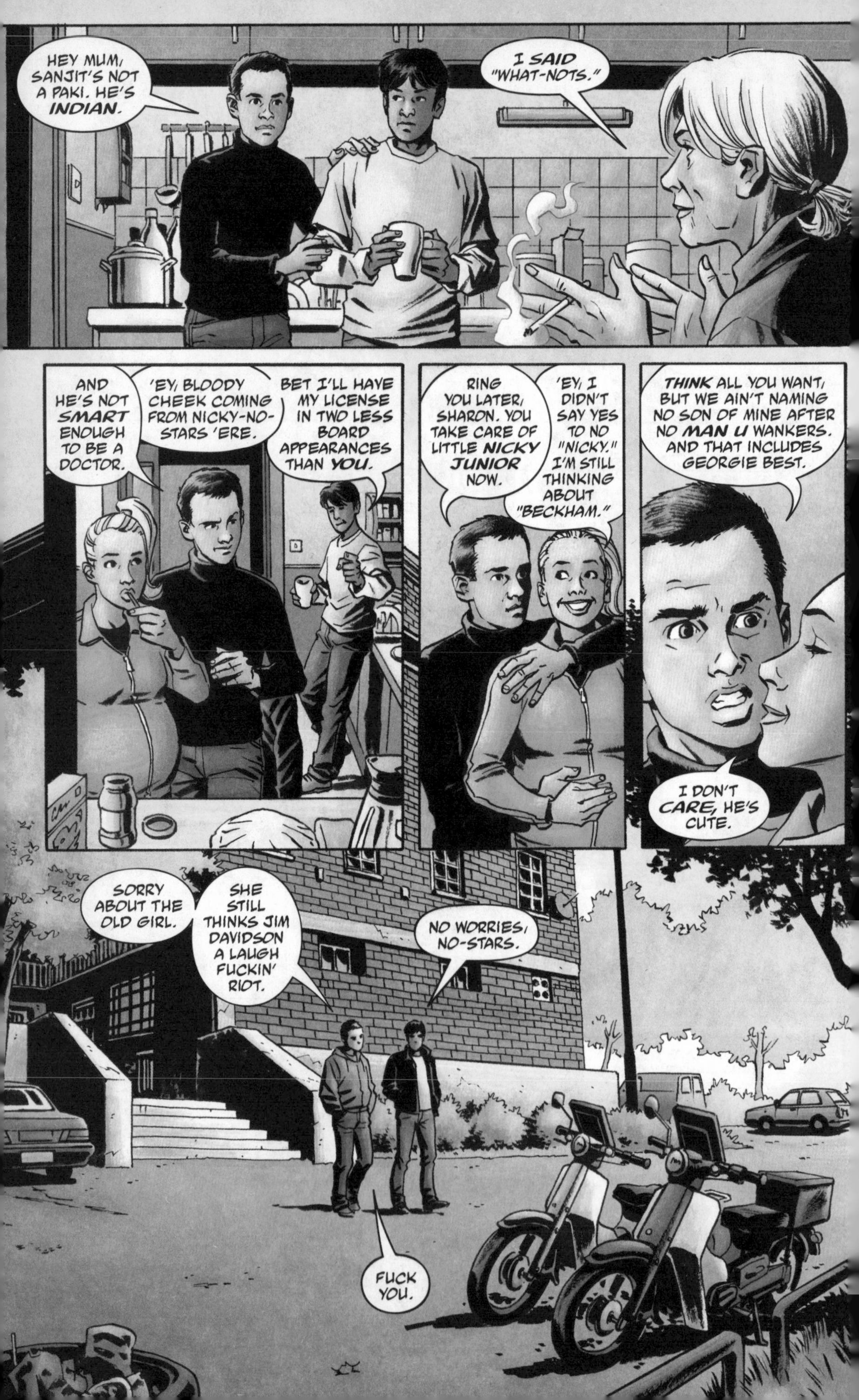
HEY MUM, SANJIT'S NOT A PAKI. HE'S INDIAN.
I SAID "WHAT-NOTS."
AND HE'S NOT SMART ENOUGH TO BE A DOCTOR.
'EY, BLOODY CHEEK COMING FROM NICKY-NO-STARS 'ERE.
BET I'LL HAVE MY LICENSE IN TWO LESS BOARD APPEARANCES THAN YOU.
RING YOU LATER, SHARON. YOU TAKE CARE OF LITTLE NICKY JUNIOR NOW.
'EY, I DIDN'T SAY YES TO NO "NICKY." I'M STILL THINKING ABOUT "BECKHAM."
THINK ALL YOU WANT, BUT WE AIN'T NAMING NO SON OF MINE AFTER NO MAN U WANKERS. AND THAT INCLUDES GEORGIE BEST.
I DON'T CARE, HE'S CUTE.
SORRY ABOUT THE OLD GIRL.
SHE STILL THINKS JIM DAVIDSON A LAUGH FUCKIN' RIOT.
NO WORRIES, NO-STARS.
FUCK YOU.

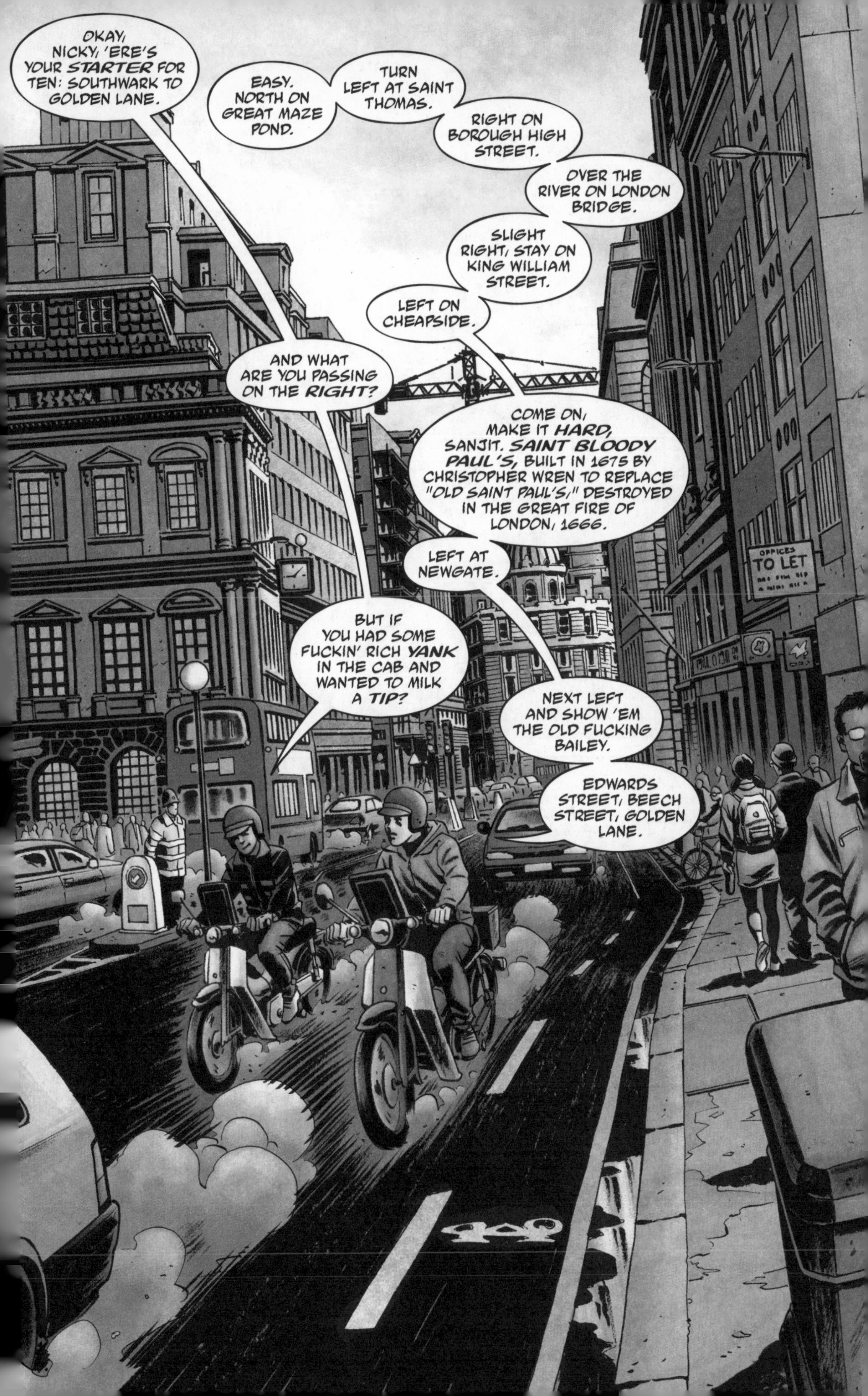
OKAY, NICKY, 'ERE'S YOUR STARTER FOR TEN: SOUTHWARK TO GOLDEN LANE.
EASY. NORTH ON GREAT MAZE POND.
TURN LEFT AT SAINT THOMAS.
RIGHT ON BOROUGH HIGH STREET.
OVER THE RIVER ON LONDON BRIDGE.
SLIGHT RIGHT, STAY ON KING WILLIAM STREET.
LEFT ON CHEAPSIDE.
AND WHAT ARE YOU PASSING ON THE RIGHT?
COME ON, MAKE IT HARD, SANJIT. SAINT BLOODY PAUL'S, BUILT IN 1675 BY CHRISTOPHER WREN TO REPLACE "OLD SAINT PAUL'S," DESTROYED IN THE GREAT FIRE OF LONDON, 1666.
LEFT AT NEWGATE.
BUT IF YOU HAD SOME FUCKIN' RICH YANK IN THE CAB AND WANTED TO MILK A TIP?
NEXT LEFT AND SHOW 'EM THE OLD FUCKING BAILEY.
EDWARDS STREET, BEECH STREET, GOLDEN LANE.
OFFICES TO LET

AND, IN *ORDER*, WHAT *UNDERGROUND* STATIONS YOU PASSING ON THE WAY?

LONDON BRIDGE, BANK, SAINT PAUL'S, THE BARBICAN.

OH NO. AND NICKY-NO-STARS *FALLS* AT THE FINAL HURDLE. FUCKING *MONUMENT*, YOU NONCE.

FUCK.

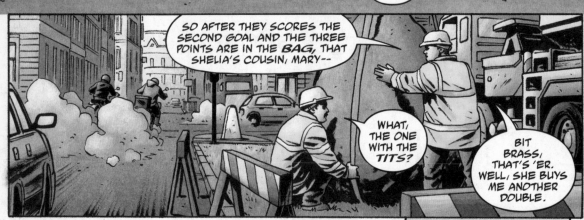

SO AFTER THEY SCORES THE SECOND GOAL AND THE THREE POINTS ARE IN THE *BAG*, THAT SHELIA'S COUSIN, MARY--

WHAT, THE ONE WITH THE *TITS*?

BIT BRASS, THAT'S 'ER. WELL, SHE BUYS ME ANOTHER DOUBLE.

YOU *READY*?

YEAH WELL, FUCKIN' TAKE HER UP LOFTY, SOONER WE GET THIS OLD *ROCK* DOWN THE *MUSEUM*, SOONER WE GET TO PUNCH OUT.

SO WHAT 'APPENED THEN, WITH THAT MARY?

WELL, BIT OF A MUSH ON 'ER...

...BUT THEN YOU DON'T LOOK AT THE *MANTEL-PIECE* WHEN YOU'RE STOKING THE *FIRE*, NOW DO YA?

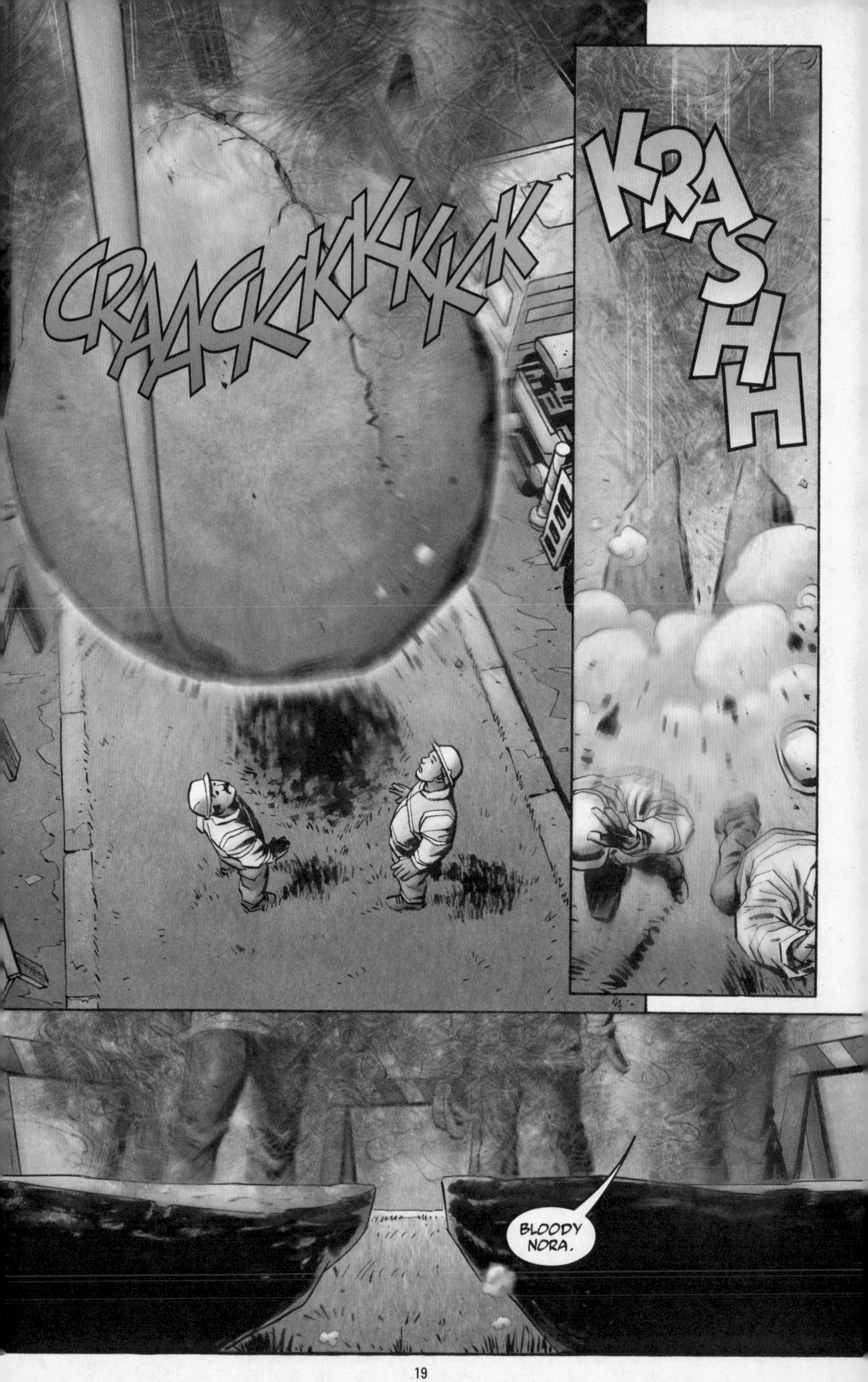
CRAACKKKKKK
KRASHH
BLOODY NORA.

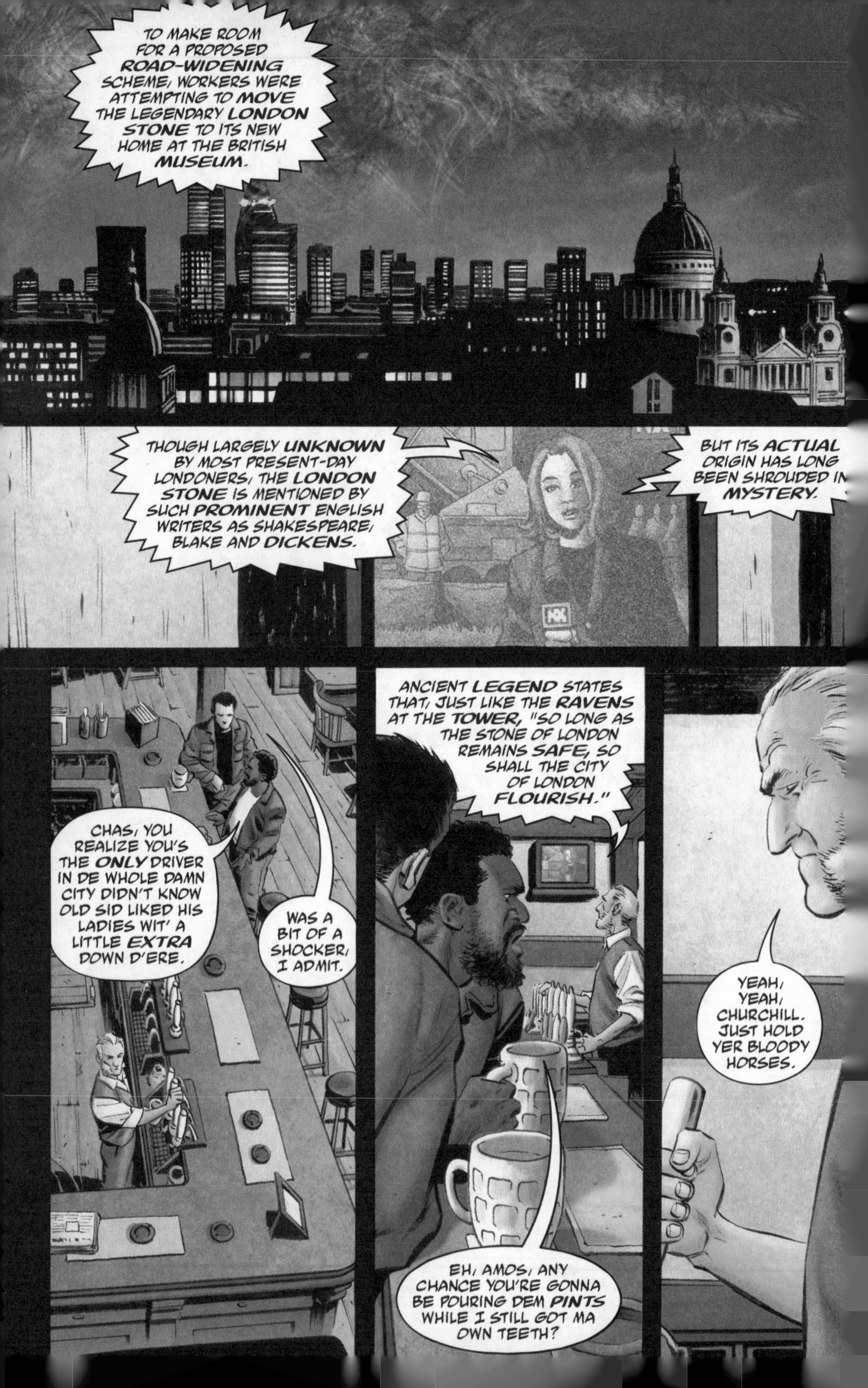
TO MAKE ROOM FOR A PROPOSED ROAD-WIDENING SCHEME, WORKERS WERE ATTEMPTING TO MOVE THE LEGENDARY LONDON STONE TO ITS NEW HOME AT THE BRITISH MUSEUM.
THOUGH LARGELY UNKNOWN BY MOST PRESENT-DAY LONDONERS, THE LONDON STONE IS MENTIONED BY SUCH PROMINENT ENGLISH WRITERS AS SHAKESPEARE, BLAKE AND DICKENS.
BUT ITS ACTUAL ORIGIN HAS LONG BEEN SHROUDED IN MYSTERY.
CHAS, YOU REALIZE YOU'S THE ONLY DRIVER IN DE WHOLE DAMN CITY DIDN'T KNOW OLD SID LIKED HIS LADIES WIT' A LITTLE EXTRA DOWN D'ERE.
WAS A BIT OF A SHOCKER, I ADMIT.
ANCIENT LEGEND STATES THAT, JUST LIKE THE RAVENS AT THE TOWER, "SO LONG AS THE STONE OF LONDON REMAINS SAFE, SO SHALL THE CITY OF LONDON FLOURISH."
EH, AMOS, ANY CHANCE YOU'RE GONNA BE POURING DEM PINTS WHILE I STILL GOT MA OWN TEETH?
YEAH, YEAH, CHURCHILL. JUST HOLD YER BLOODY HORSES.

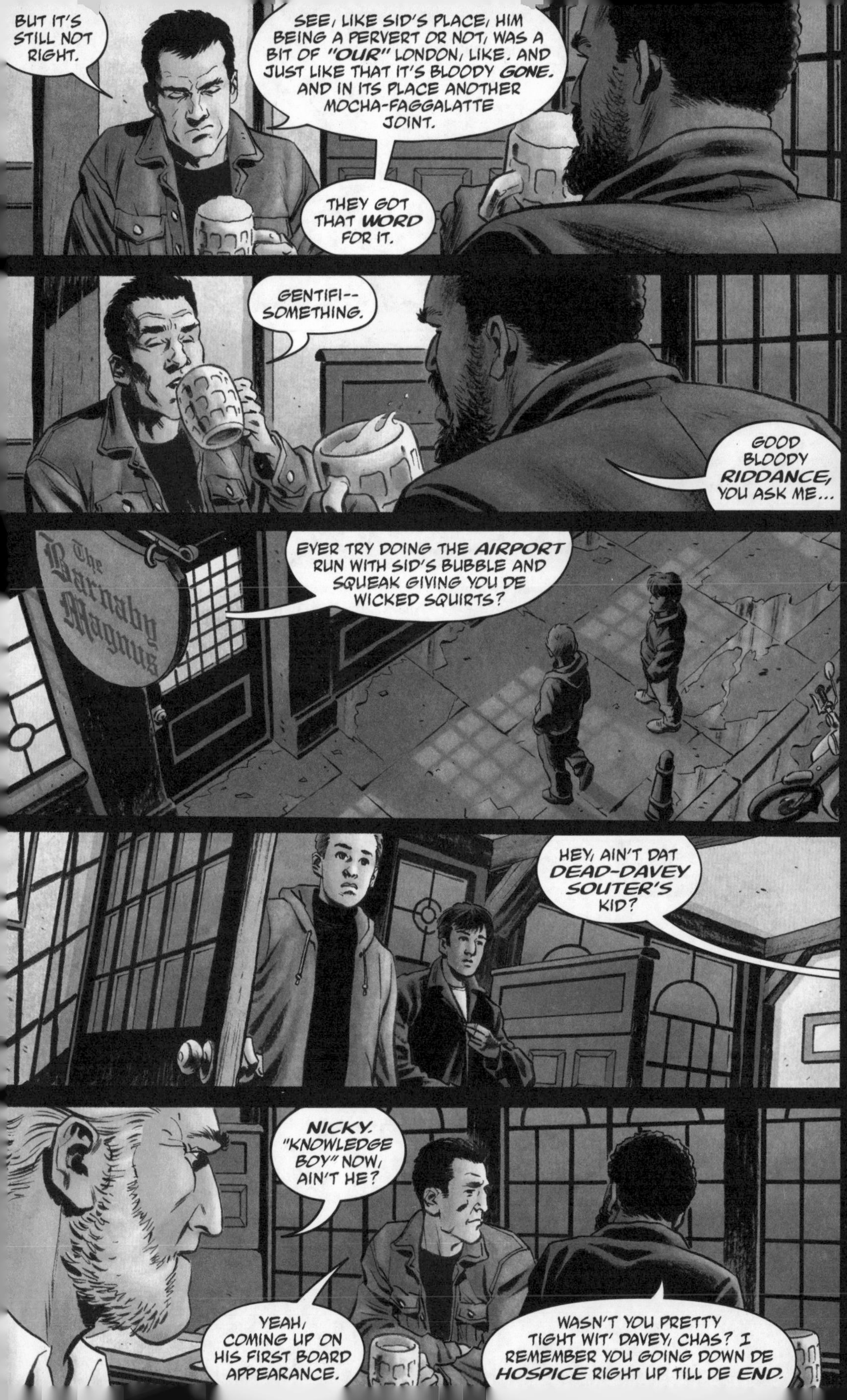

BUT IT'S STILL NOT RIGHT.
SEE, LIKE SID'S PLACE, HIM BEING A PERVERT OR NOT, WAS A BIT OF "OUR" LONDON, LIKE. AND JUST LIKE THAT IT'S BLOODY GONE. AND IN ITS PLACE ANOTHER MOCHA-FAGGALATTE JOINT.
THEY GOT THAT WORD FOR IT.
GENTIFI-- SOMETHING.
GOOD BLOODY RIDDANCE, YOU ASK ME...
The Barnaby Magnus
EVER TRY DOING THE AIRPORT RUN WITH SID'S BUBBLE AND SQUEAK GIVING YOU DE WICKED SQUIRTS?
HEY, AIN'T DAT DEAD-DAVEY SOUTER'S KID?
NICKY. "KNOWLEDGE BOY" NOW, AIN'T HE?
YEAH, COMING UP ON HIS FIRST BOARD APPEARANCE.
WASN'T YOU PRETTY TIGHT WIT' DAVEY, CHAS? I REMEMBER YOU GOING DOWN DE HOSPICE RIGHT UP TILL DE END.

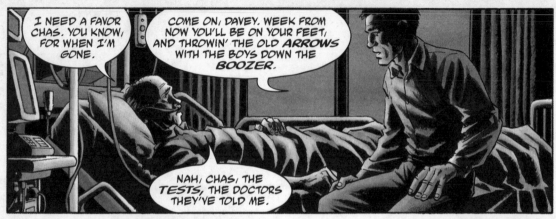

I NEED A FAVOR CHAS. YOU KNOW, FOR WHEN I'M GONE.

COME ON, DAVEY. WEEK FROM NOW YOU'LL BE ON YOUR FEET, AND THROWIN' THE OLD *ARROWS* WITH THE BOYS DOWN THE *BOOZER.*

NAH, CHAS, THE *TESTS*, THE DOCTORS THEY'VE TOLD ME.

SEE, I NEED SOME-ONE, A MATE I KNOW I CAN *RELY* ON TO KEEP AN EYE ON MY *NICKY*. KEEP HIM ON THE STRAIGHT AND NARROW, LIKE.

DAVEY, YOU'VE MY *WORD*, CROSS MY HEART. I'LL TREAT HIM LIKE ONE OF MY *OWN.*

NICHOLAS SOUTER, DESPITE BEING *FULLY* AWARE OF THE TRAGIC LOSS OF YOUR FATHER, AND EVEN TAKING THAT INTO ACCOUNT--

--YOUR BLATANTLY *ANTISOCIAL* BEHAVIOR LEAVES ME NO OTHER OPTION THAN YOUR *IMMEDIATE* EXPULSION FROM THIS SCHOOL.

AS THE SENTENCING JUDGE, I CAN ONLY HOPE THAT A PERIOD OF *JUVENILE* DETENTION--

"--CAN GIVE YOU THE *GUIDANCE* YOU SO SORELY *NEED.*"

"ERH, YEAH, ONE OF THE *BOYS*, DAVEY WAS."

22

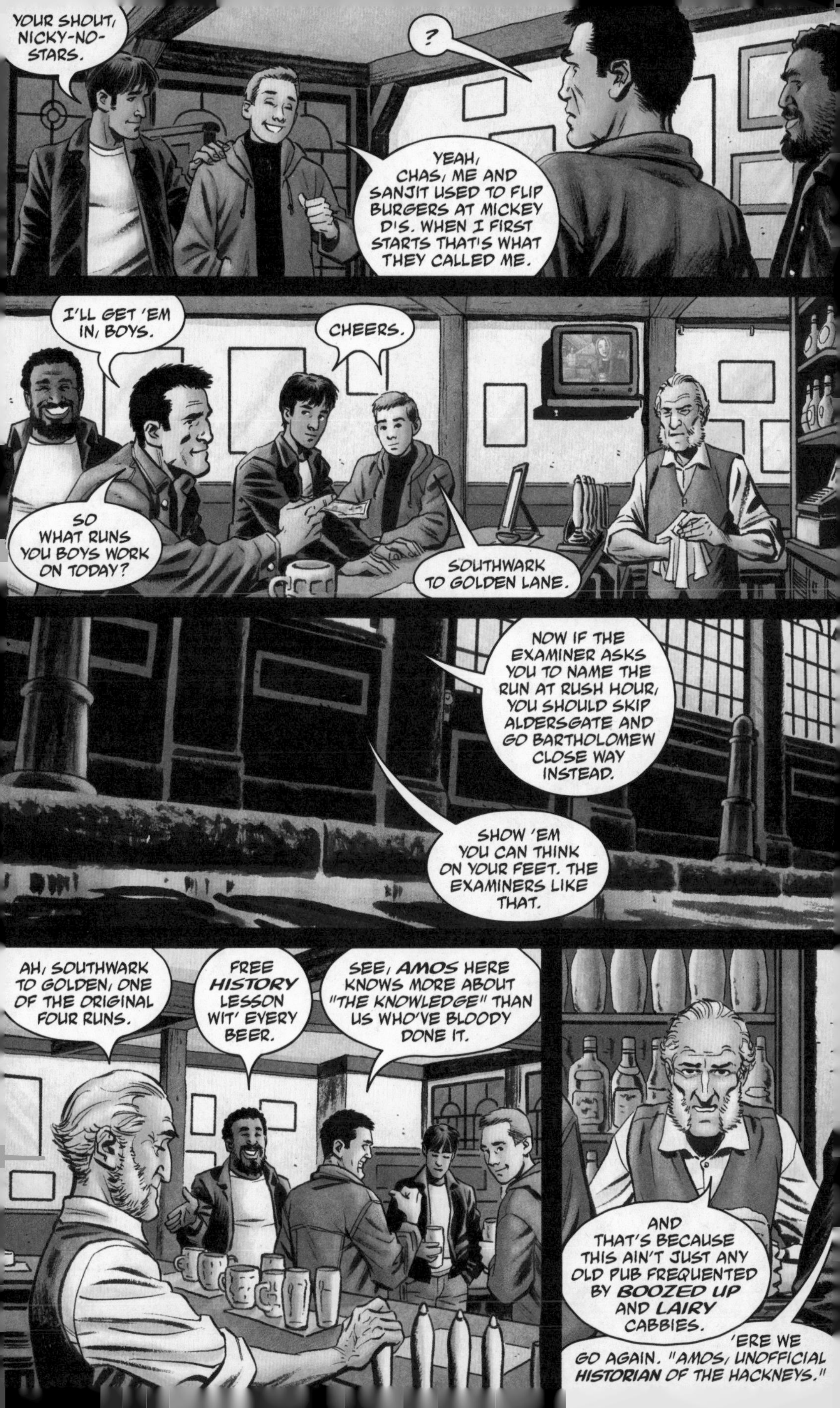
YOUR SHOUT, NICKY-NO-STARS.
?
YEAH, CHAS, ME AND SANJIT USED TO FLIP BURGERS AT MICKEY D'S. WHEN I FIRST STARTS THAT'S WHAT THEY CALLED ME.
I'LL GET 'EM IN, BOYS.
CHEERS.
SO WHAT RUNS YOU BOYS WORK ON TODAY?
SOUTHWARK TO GOLDEN LANE.
NOW IF THE EXAMINER ASKS YOU TO NAME THE RUN AT RUSH HOUR, YOU SHOULD SKIP ALDERSGATE AND GO BARTHOLOMEW CLOSE WAY INSTEAD.
SHOW 'EM YOU CAN THINK ON YOUR FEET. THE EXAMINERS LIKE THAT.
AH, SOUTHWARK TO GOLDEN, ONE OF THE ORIGINAL FOUR RUNS.
FREE HISTORY LESSON WIT' EVERY BEER.
SEE, AMOS HERE KNOWS MORE ABOUT "THE KNOWLEDGE" THAN US WHO'VE BLOODY DONE IT.
AND THAT'S BECAUSE THIS AIN'T JUST ANY OLD PUB FREQUENTED BY BOOZED UP AND LAIRY CABBIES.
'ERE WE GO AGAIN. "AMOS, UNOFFICIAL HISTORIAN OF THE HACKNEYS."

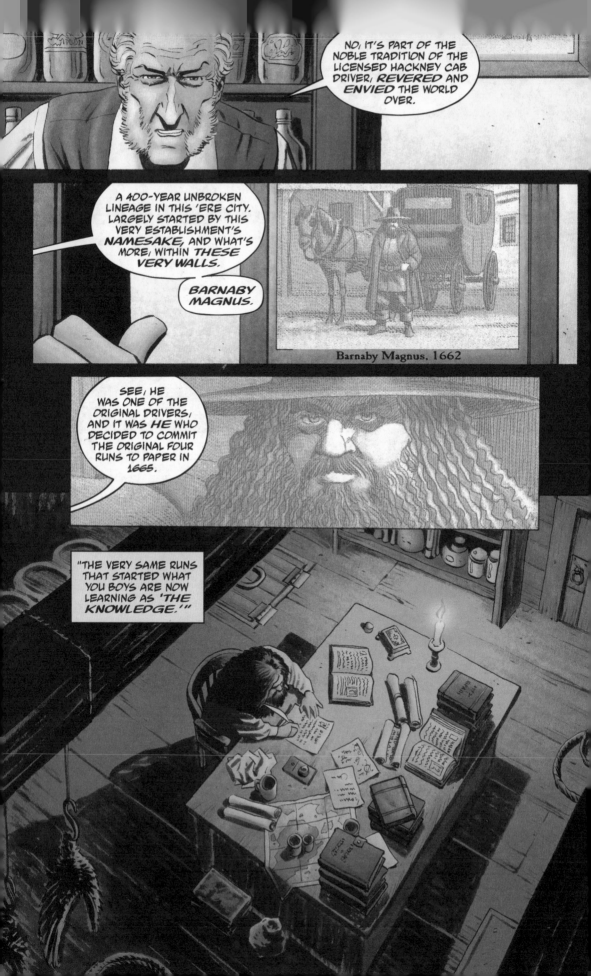

NO, IT'S PART OF THE NOBLE TRADITION OF THE LICENSED HACKNEY CAB DRIVER, *REVERED* AND *ENVIED* THE WORLD OVER.

A *400*-YEAR UNBROKEN LINEAGE IN THIS 'ERE CITY. LARGELY STARTED BY THIS VERY ESTABLISHMENT'S *NAMESAKE*, AND WHAT'S MORE, WITHIN *THESE VERY WALLS*.

BARNABY MAGNUS.

Barnaby Magnus, 1662

SEE, HE WAS ONE OF THE *ORIGINAL* DRIVERS, AND IT WAS *HE* WHO DECIDED TO COMMIT THE ORIGINAL FOUR RUNS TO PAPER IN 1665.

"THE VERY SAME RUNS THAT STARTED WHAT YOU BOYS ARE NOW LEARNING AS *'THE KNOWLEDGE.'*"

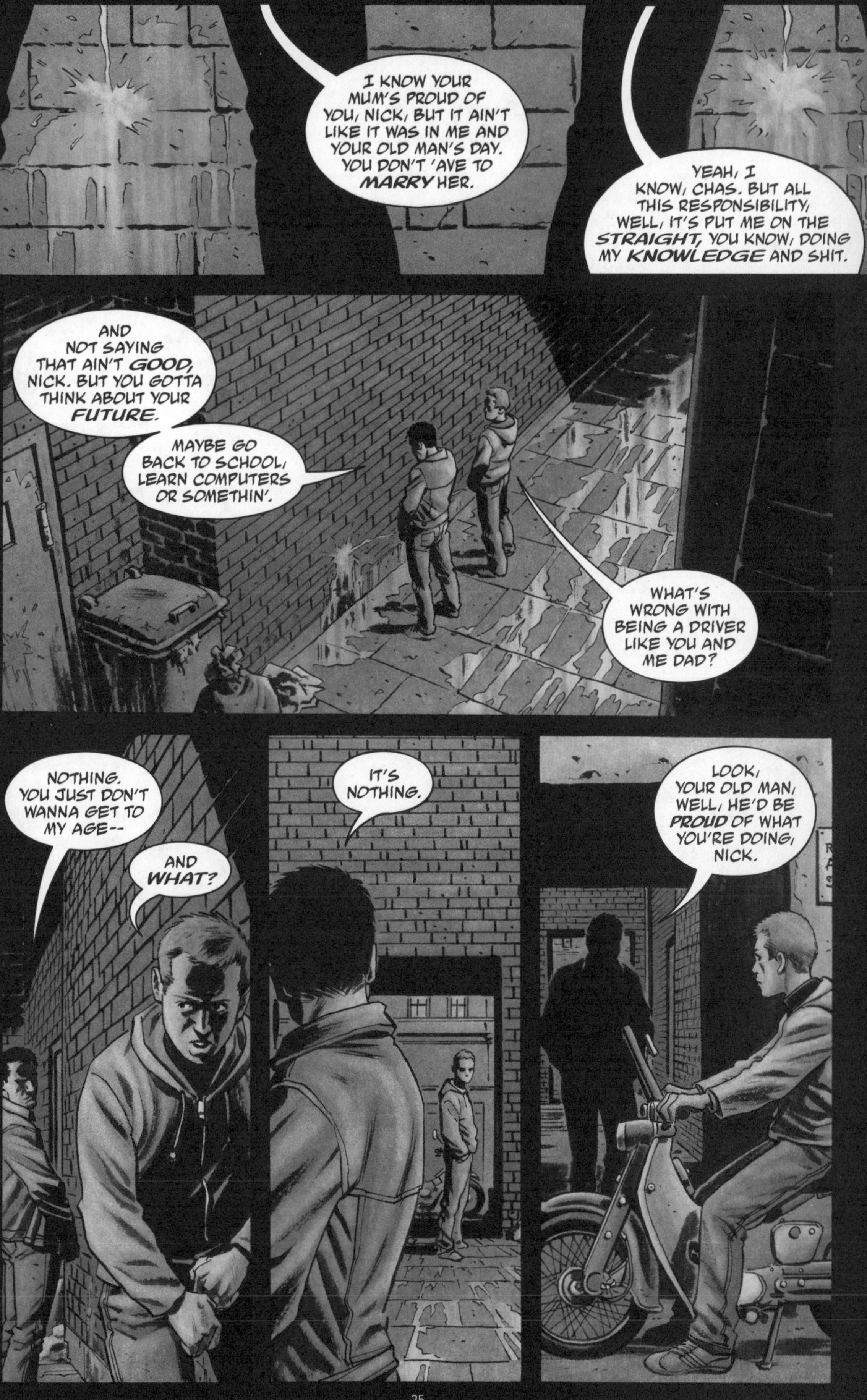

I KNOW YOUR MUM'S PROUD OF YOU, NICK, BUT IT AIN'T LIKE IT WAS IN ME AND YOUR OLD MAN'S DAY. YOU DON'T 'AVE TO *MARRY* HER.
YEAH, I KNOW, CHAS. BUT ALL THIS RESPONSIBILITY, WELL, IT'S PUT ME ON THE *STRAIGHT,* YOU KNOW, DOING MY *KNOWLEDGE* AND SHIT.
AND NOT SAYING THAT AIN'T *GOOD,* NICK. BUT YOU GOTTA THINK ABOUT YOUR *FUTURE.*
MAYBE GO BACK TO SCHOOL, LEARN COMPUTERS OR SOMETHIN'.
WHAT'S WRONG WITH BEING A DRIVER LIKE YOU AND ME DAD?
NOTHING. YOU JUST DON'T WANNA GET TO MY AGE--
AND *WHAT?*
IT'S NOTHING.
LOOK, YOUR OLD MAN, WELL, HE'D BE *PROUD* OF WHAT YOU'RE DOING, NICK.

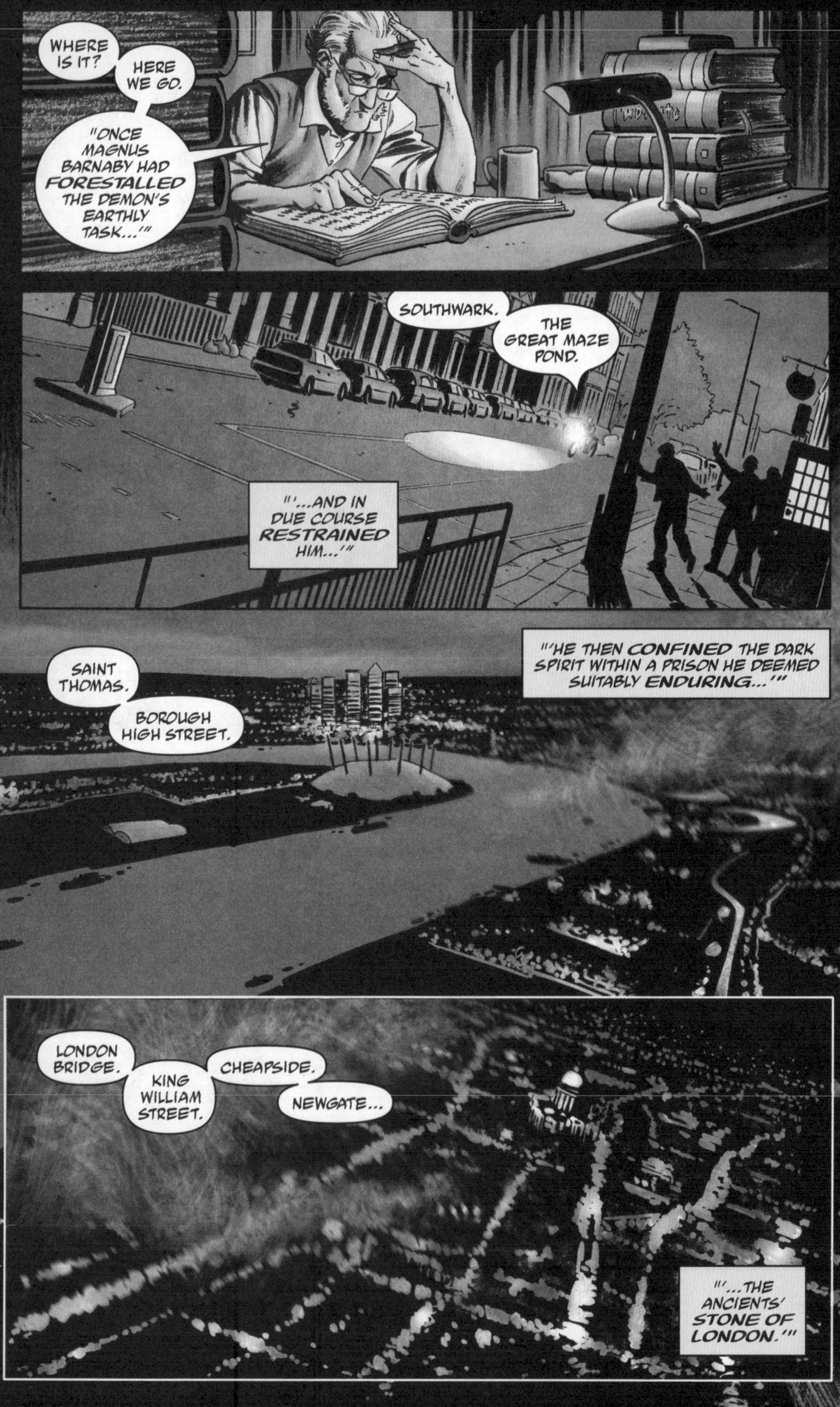
WHERE IS IT?
HERE WE GO.
"ONCE MAGNUS BARNABY HAD FORESTALLED THE DEMON'S EARTHLY TASK...'"
SOUTHWARK.
THE GREAT MAZE POND.
"'...AND IN DUE COURSE RESTRAINED HIM...'"
SAINT THOMAS.
BOROUGH HIGH STREET.
"'HE THEN CONFINED THE DARK SPIRIT WITHIN A PRISON HE DEEMED SUITABLY ENDURING...'"
LONDON BRIDGE.
KING WILLIAM STREET.
CHEAPSIDE.
NEWGATE...
"'...THE ANCIENTS' STONE OF LONDON.'"

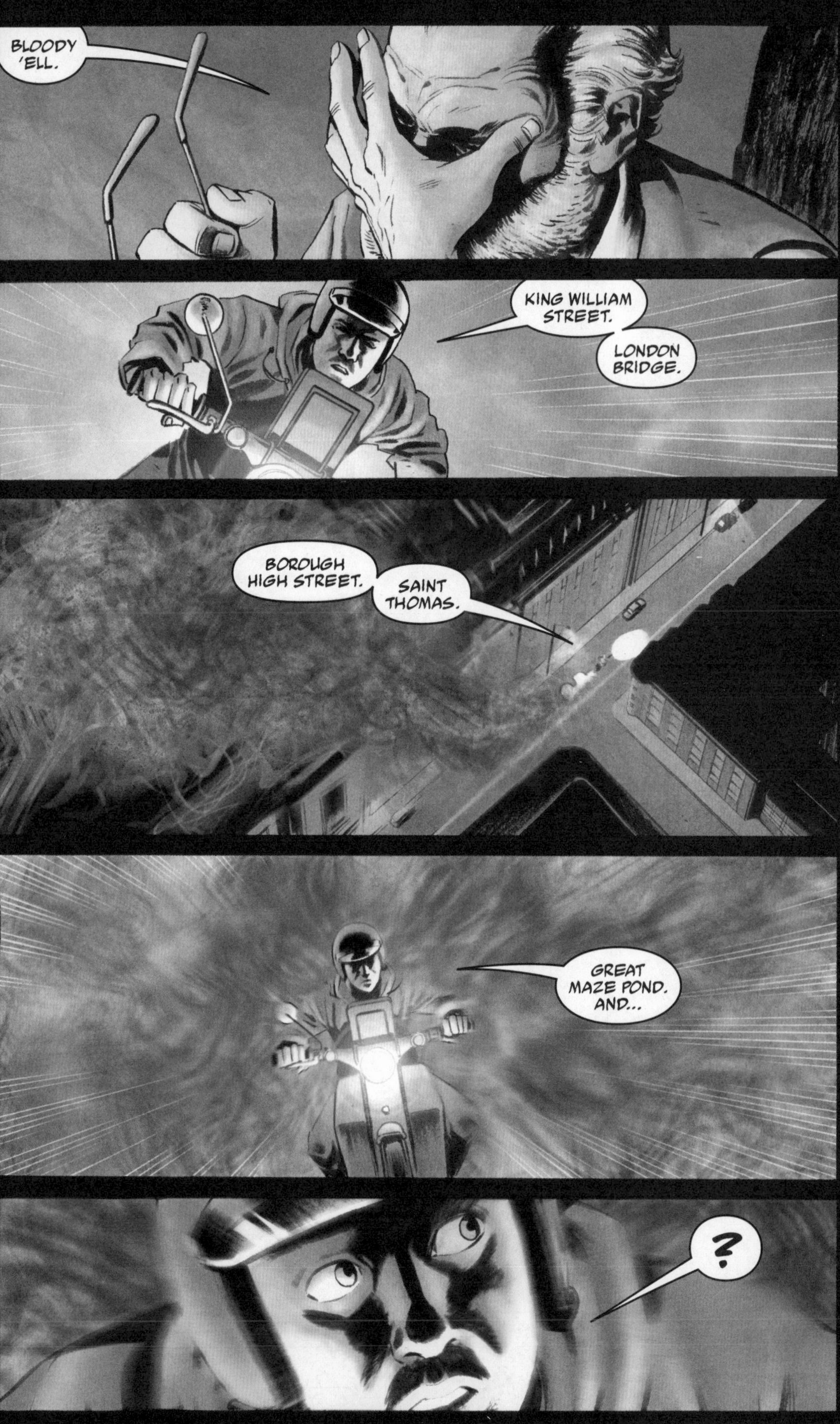
BLOODY 'ELL.
KING WILLIAM STREET.
LONDON BRIDGE.
BOROUGH HIGH STREET.
SAINT THOMAS.
GREAT MAZE POND. AND...
?

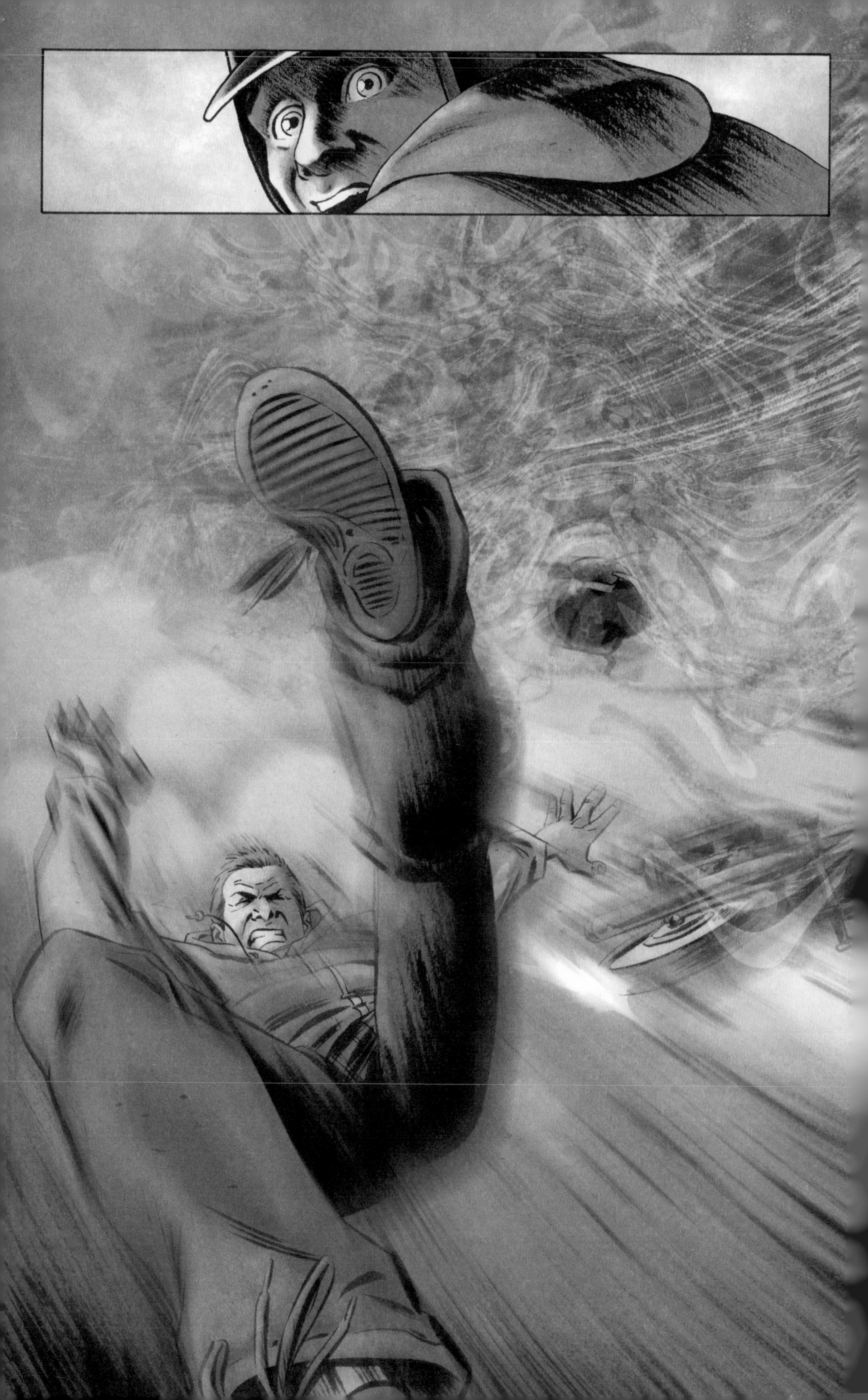

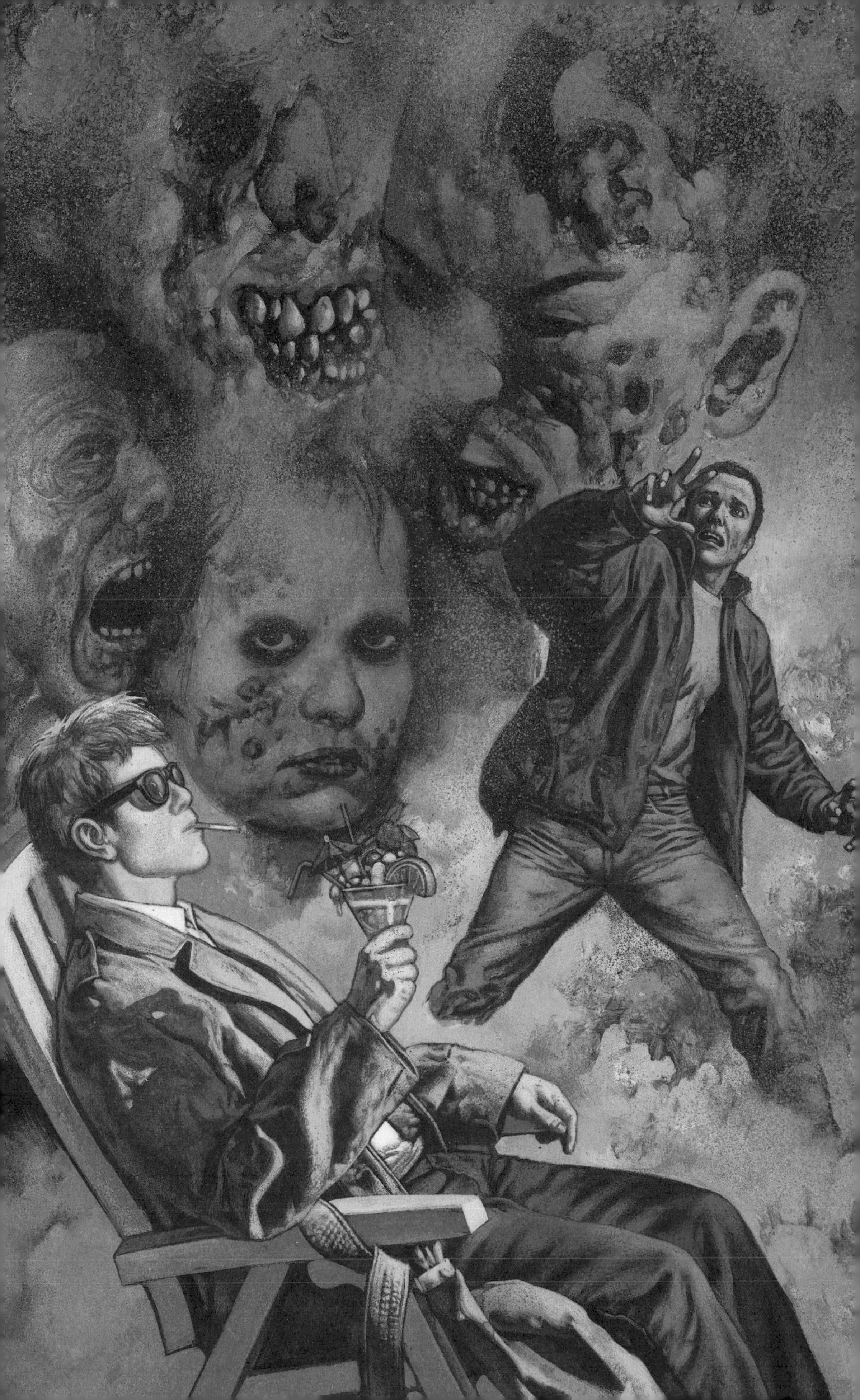

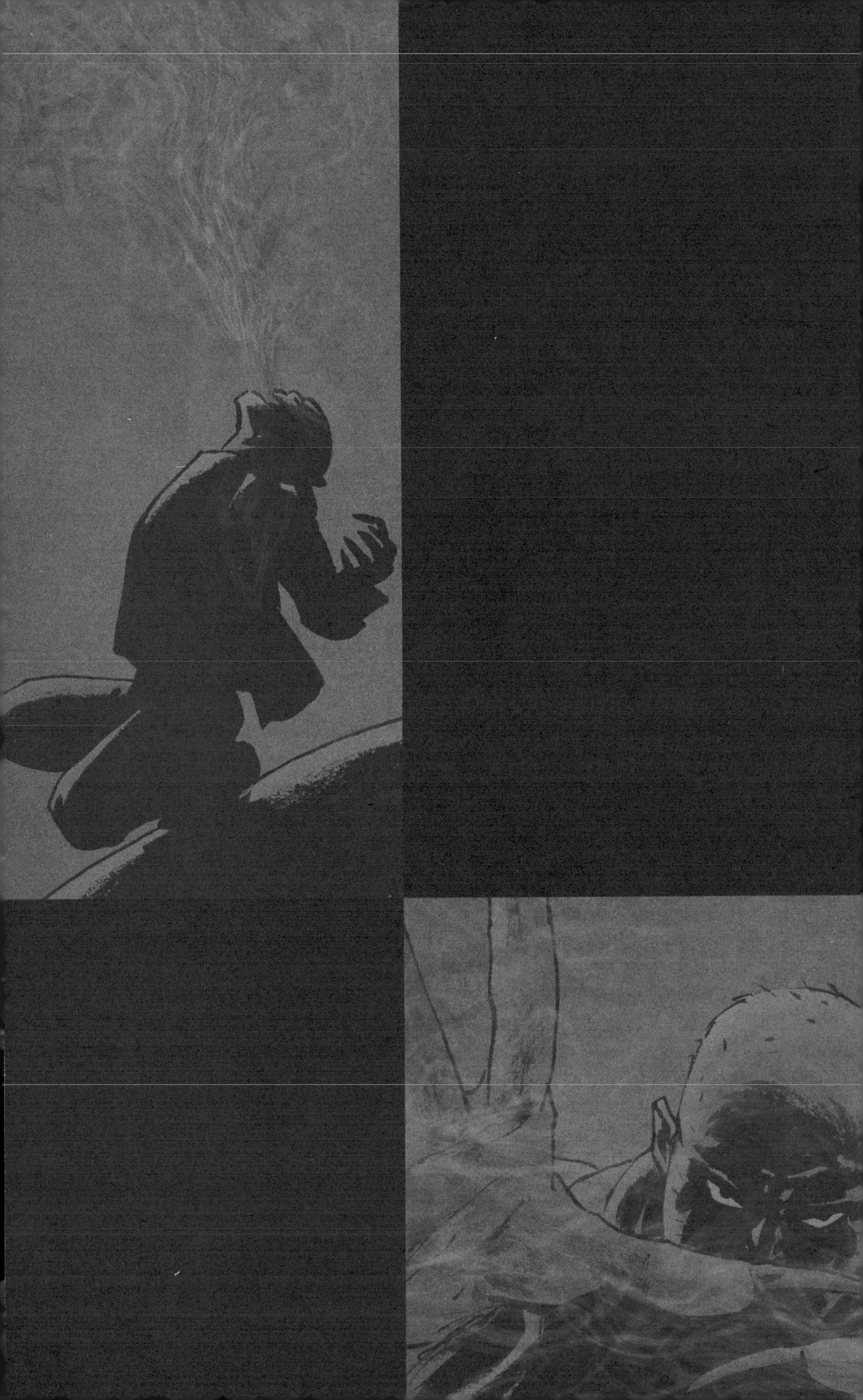

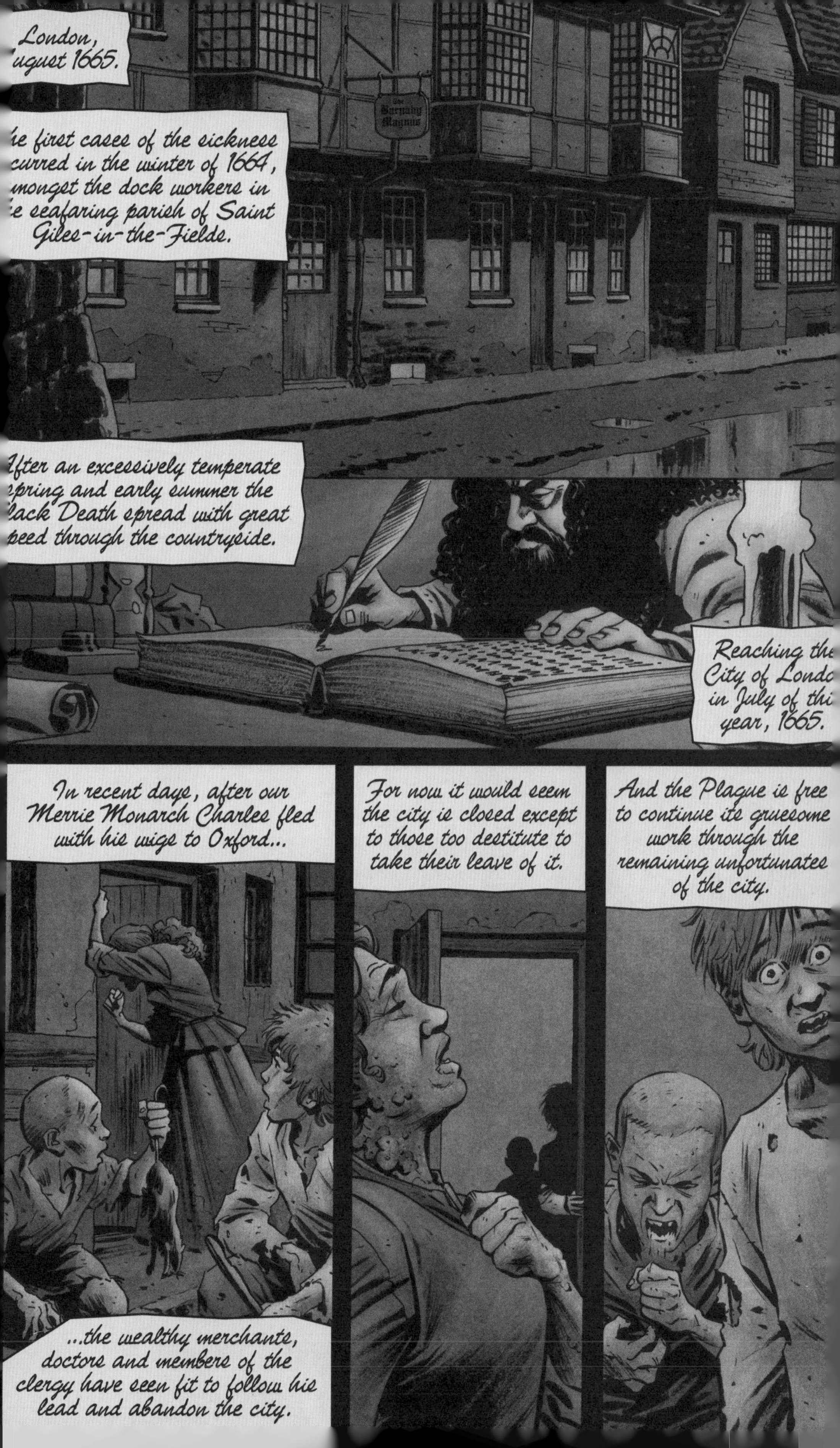

London, ugust 1665.
he first cases of the sickness ccurred in the winter of 1664, mongst the dock workers in e seafaring parish of Saint Giles-in-the-Fields.
fter an excessively temperate pring and early summer the lack Death spread with great peed through the countryside.
Reaching the City of Londo in July of thi year, 1665.
In recent days, after our Merrie Monarch Charles fled with his wigs to Oxford...
...the wealthy merchants, doctors and members of the clergy have seen fit to follow his lead and abandon the city.
For now it would seem the city is closed except to those too destitute to take their leave of it.
And the Plague is free to continue its gruesome work through the remaining unfortunates of the city.

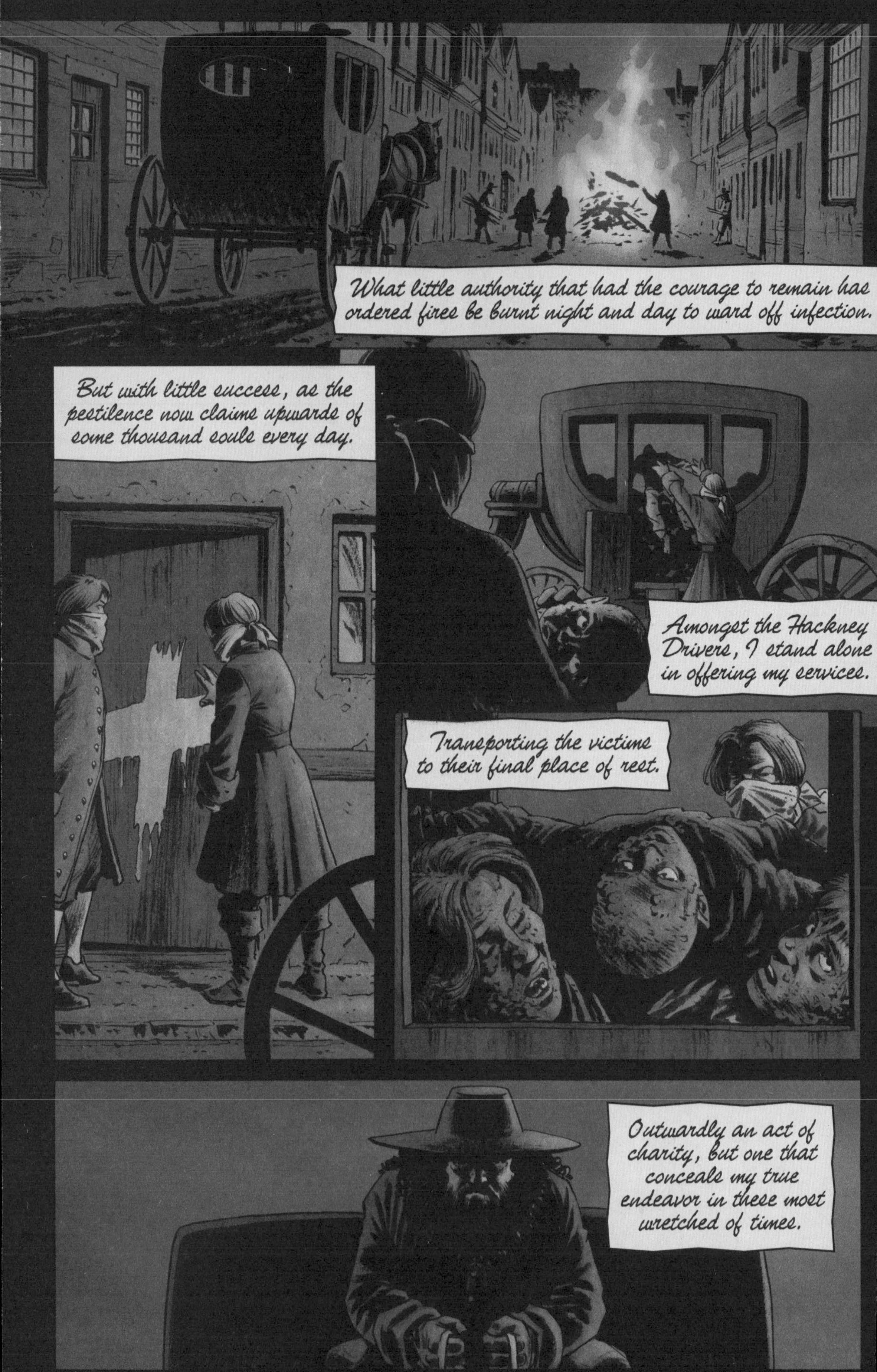
What little authority that had the courage to remain has ordered fires be burnt night and day to ward off infection.
But with little success, as the pestilence now claims upwards of some thousand souls every day.
Amongst the Hackney Drivers, I stand alone in offering my services.
Transporting the victims to their final place of rest.
Outwardly an act of charity, but one that conceals my true endeavor in these most wretched of times.

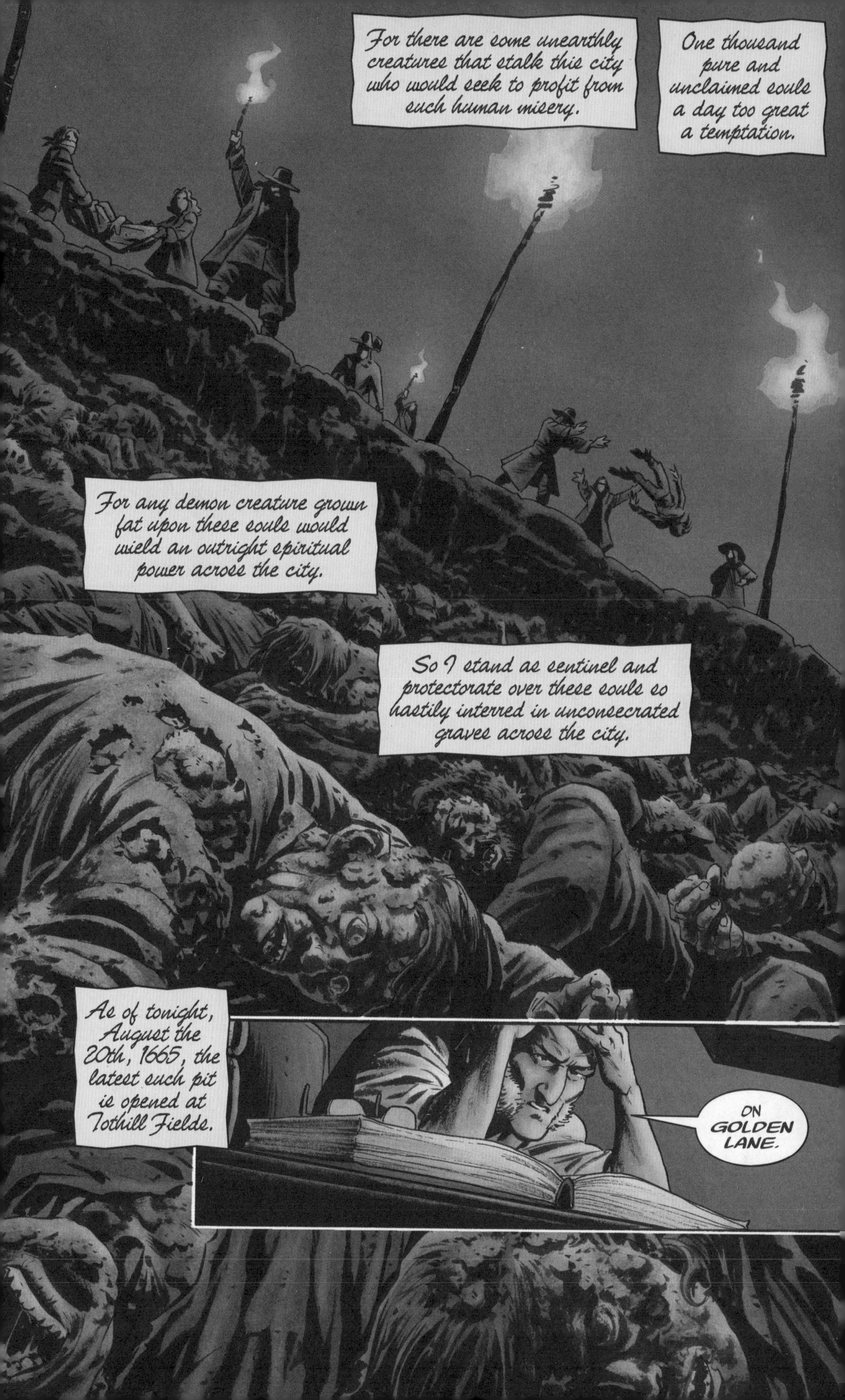
For there are some unearthly creatures that stalk this city who would seek to profit from such human misery.
One thousand pure and unclaimed souls a day too great a temptation.
For any demon creature grown fat upon these souls would wield an outright spiritual power across the city.
So I stand as sentinel and protectorate over these souls so hastily interred in unconsecrated graves across the city.
As of tonight, August the 20th, 1665, the latest such pit is opened at Tothill Fields.
ON GOLDEN LANE.

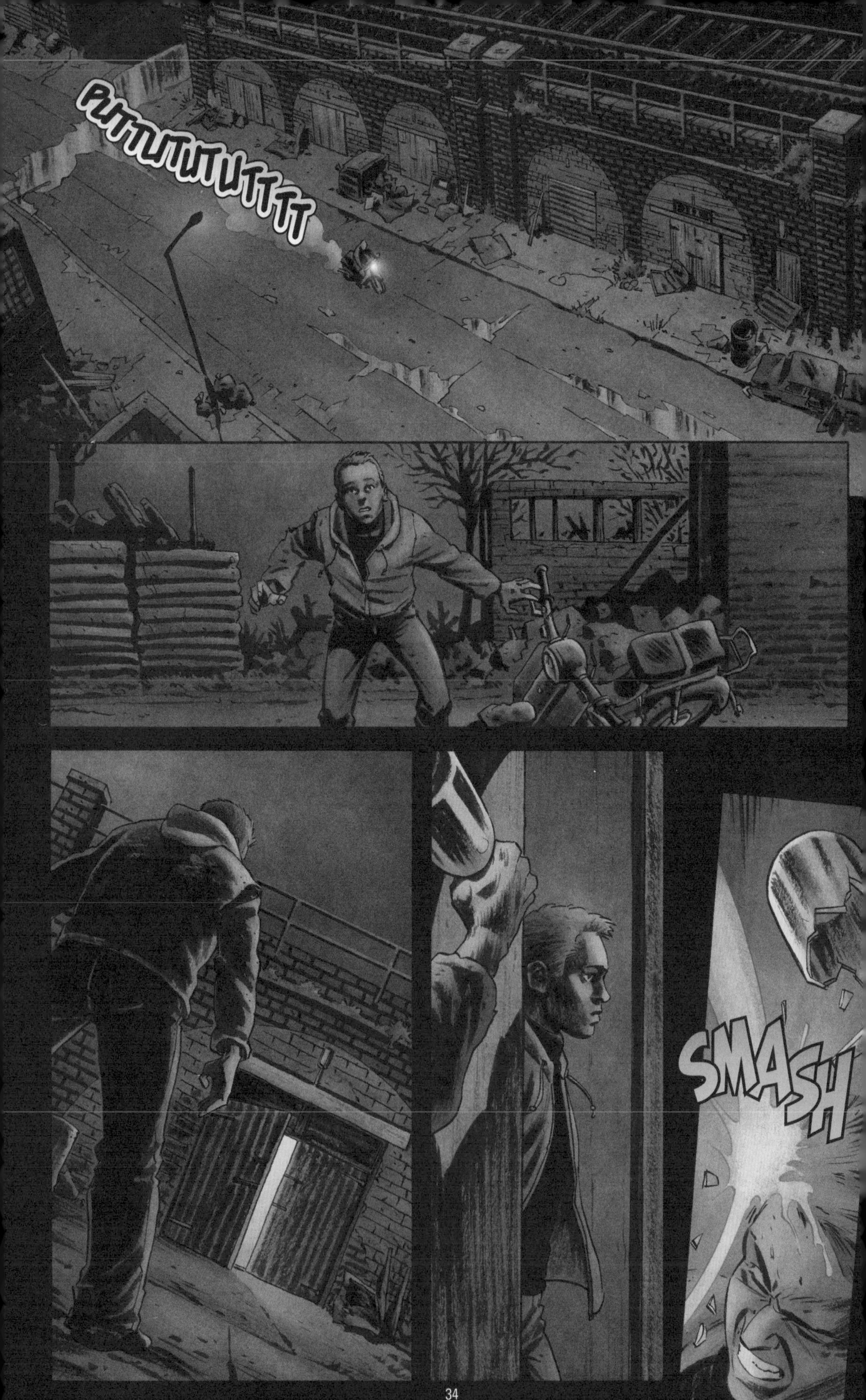
PUTTUTUTUTTTTT
SMASH

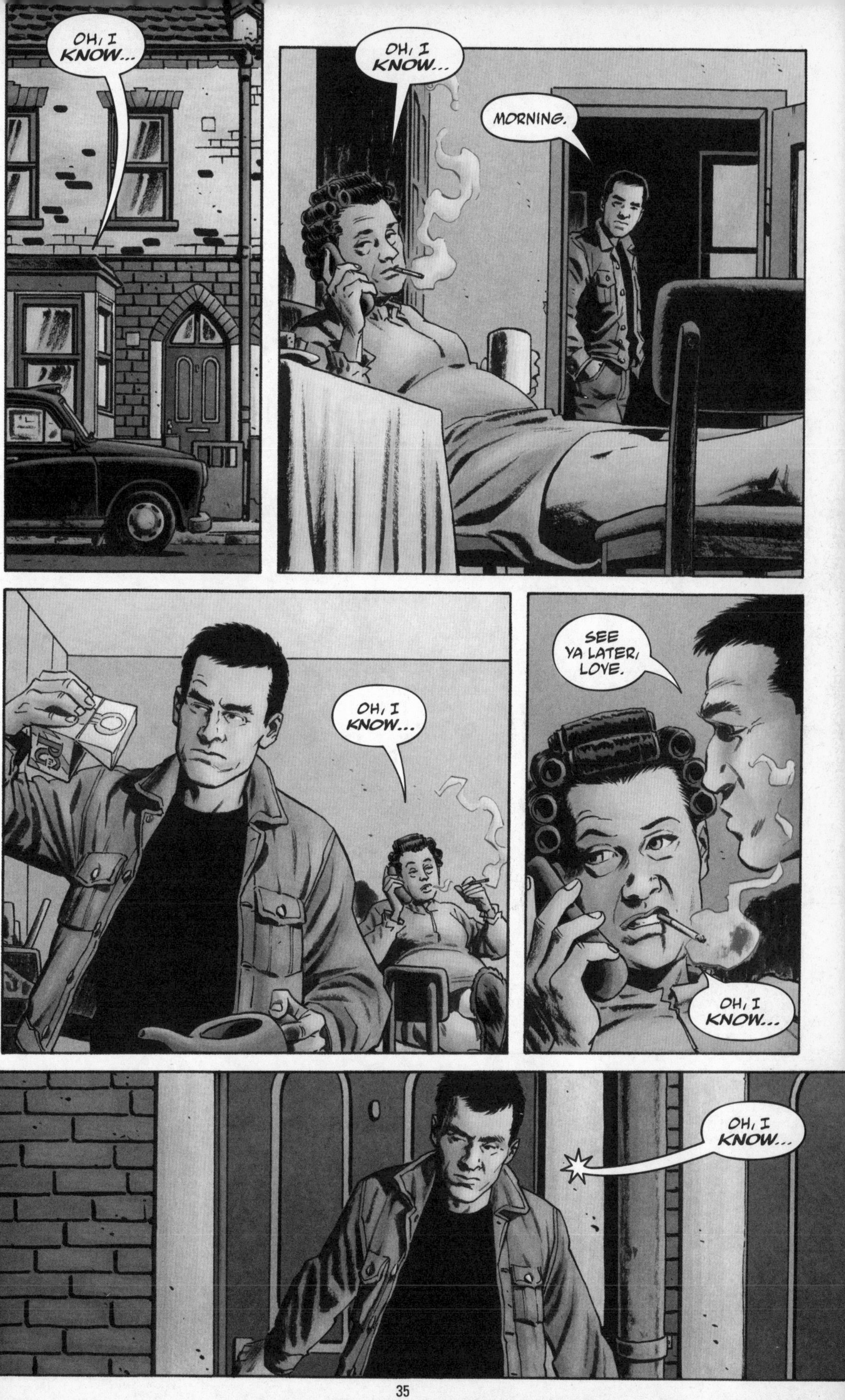
OH, I KNOW...
OH, I KNOW...
MORNING.
OH, I KNOW...
SEE YA LATER, LOVE.
OH, I KNOW...
OH, I KNOW...

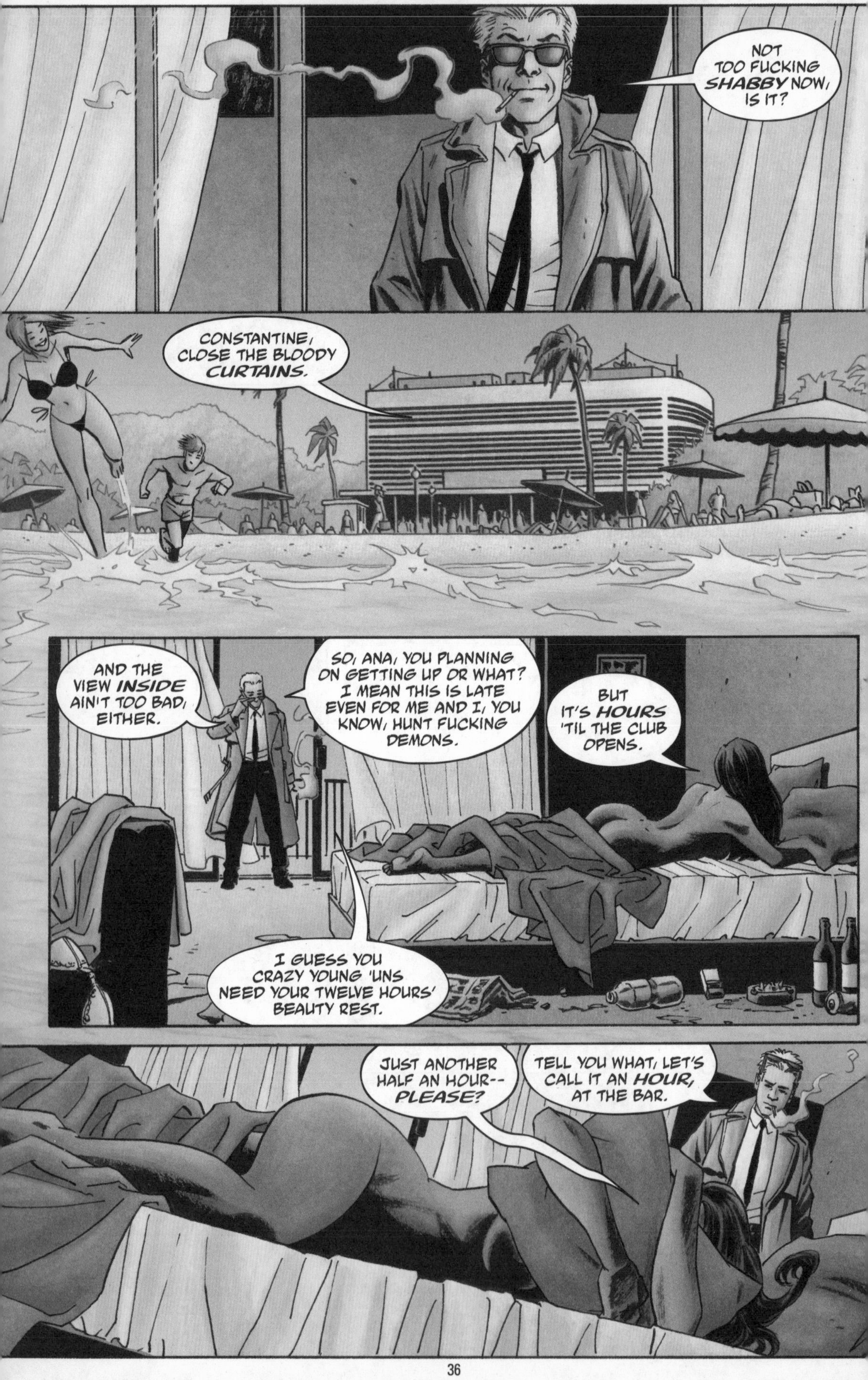
NOT TOO FUCKING SHABBY NOW, IS IT?
CONSTANTINE, CLOSE THE BLOODY CURTAINS.
AND THE VIEW INSIDE AIN'T TOO BAD, EITHER.
SO, ANA, YOU PLANNING ON GETTING UP OR WHAT? I MEAN THIS IS LATE EVEN FOR ME AND I, YOU KNOW, HUNT FUCKING DEMONS.
BUT IT'S HOURS 'TIL THE CLUB OPENS.
I GUESS YOU CRAZY YOUNG 'UNS NEED YOUR TWELVE HOURS' BEAUTY REST.
JUST ANOTHER HALF AN HOUR-- PLEASE?
TELL YOU WHAT, LET'S CALL IT AN HOUR, AT THE BAR.

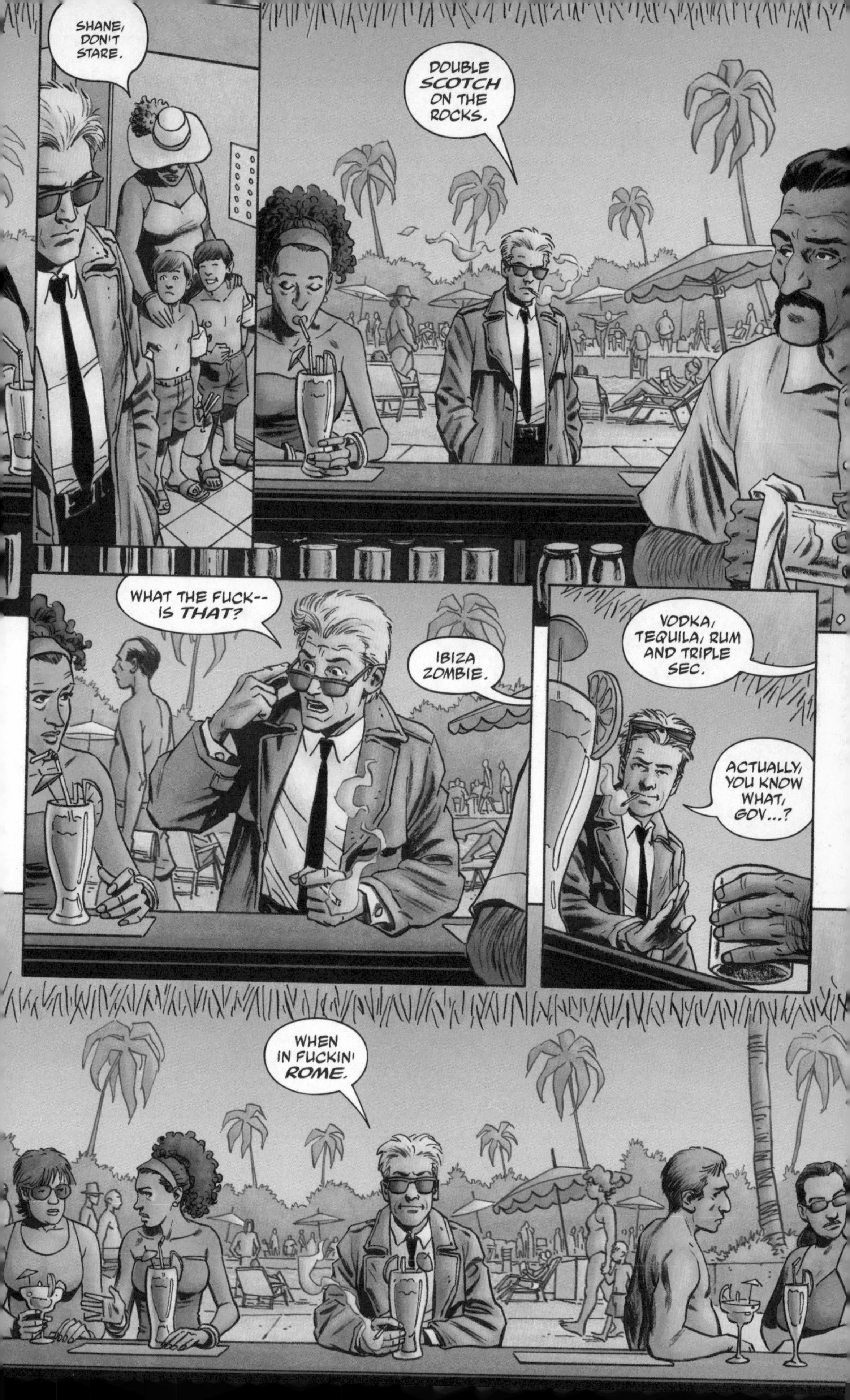
SHANE, DON'T STARE.
DOUBLE SCOTCH ON THE ROCKS.
WHAT THE FUCK-- IS THAT?
IBIZA ZOMBIE.
VODKA, TEQUILA, RUM AND TRIPLE SEC.
ACTUALLY, YOU KNOW WHAT, GOV...?
WHEN IN FUCKIN' ROME.

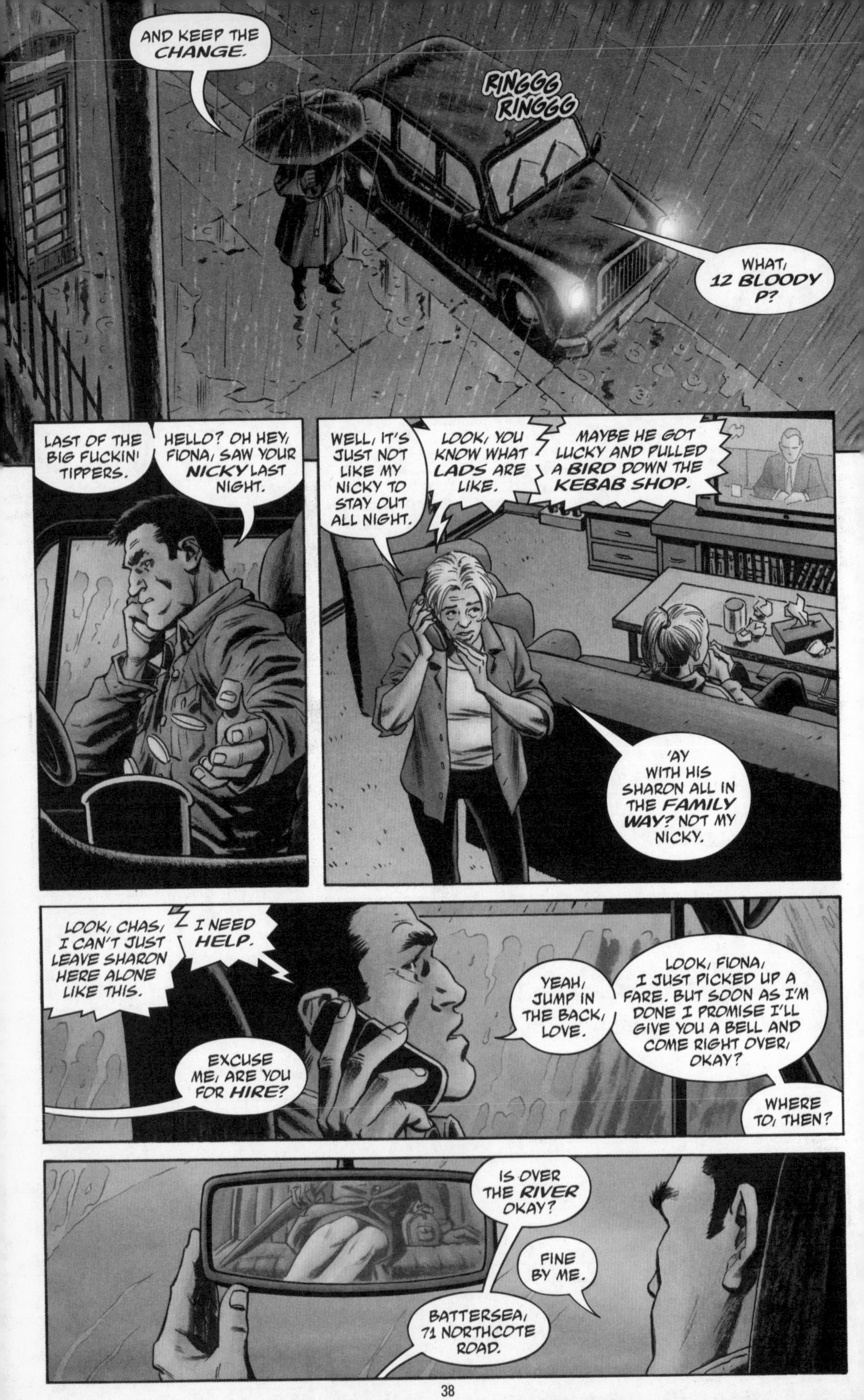
AND KEEP THE CHANGE.
RINGGG RINGGG
WHAT, 12 BLOODY P?
LAST OF THE BIG FUCKIN' TIPPERS.
HELLO? OH HEY, FIONA, SAW YOUR NICKY LAST NIGHT.
WELL, IT'S JUST NOT LIKE MY NICKY TO STAY OUT ALL NIGHT.
LOOK, YOU KNOW WHAT LADS ARE LIKE.
MAYBE HE GOT LUCKY AND PULLED A BIRD DOWN THE KEBAB SHOP.
'AY WITH HIS SHARON ALL IN THE FAMILY WAY? NOT MY NICKY.
LOOK, CHAS, I CAN'T JUST LEAVE SHARON HERE ALONE LIKE THIS.
I NEED HELP.
EXCUSE ME, ARE YOU FOR HIRE?
YEAH, JUMP IN THE BACK, LOVE.
LOOK, FIONA, I JUST PICKED UP A FARE. BUT SOON AS I'M DONE I PROMISE I'LL GIVE YOU A BELL AND COME RIGHT OVER, OKAY?
WHERE TO, THEN?
IS OVER THE RIVER OKAY?
FINE BY ME.
BATTERSEA, 71 NORTHCOTE ROAD.

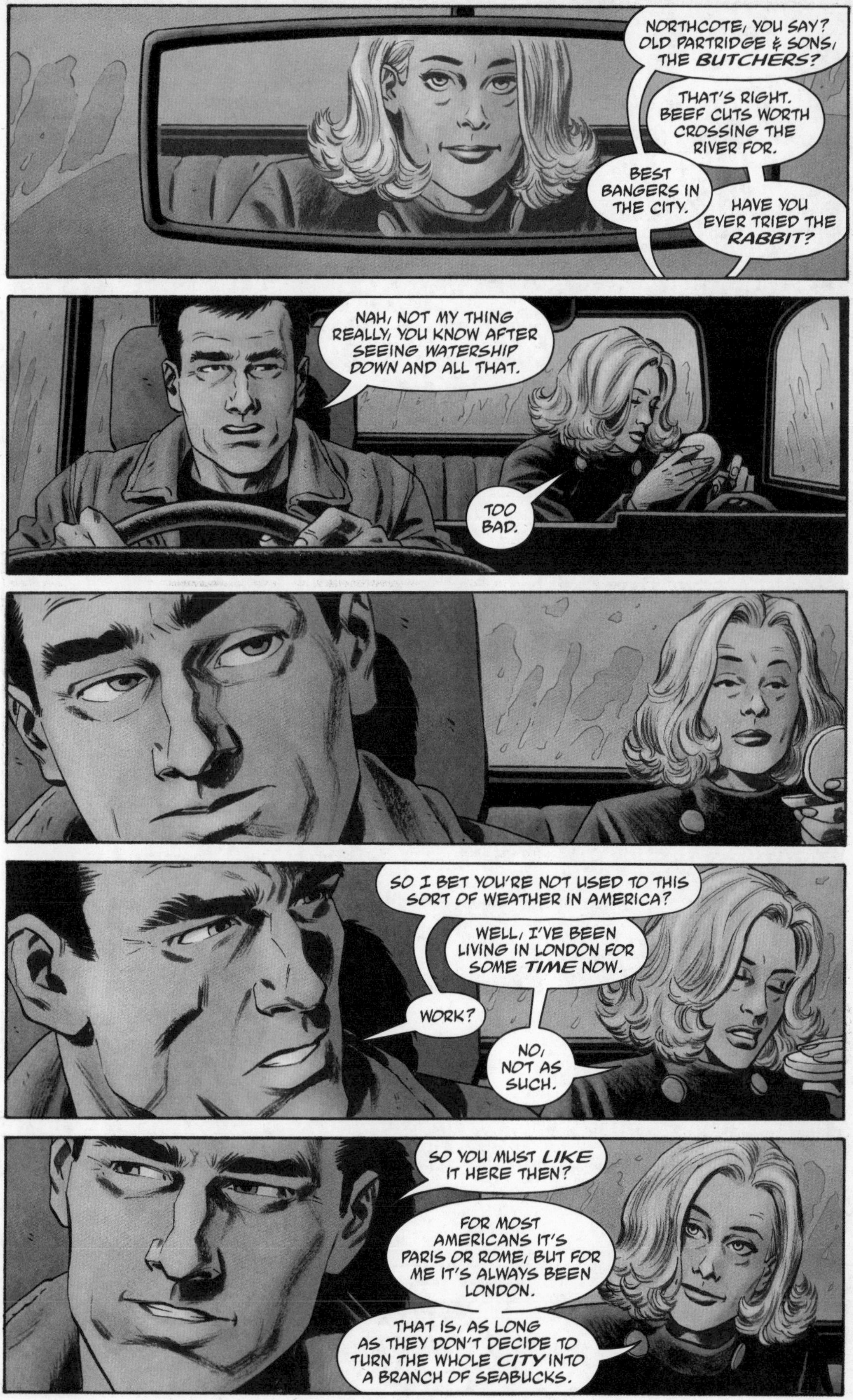
NORTHCOTE, YOU SAY? OLD PARTRIDGE & SONS, THE BUTCHERS?
THAT'S RIGHT. BEEF CUTS WORTH CROSSING THE RIVER FOR.
BEST BANGERS IN THE CITY.
HAVE YOU EVER TRIED THE RABBIT?
NAH, NOT MY THING REALLY, YOU KNOW AFTER SEEING WATERSHIP DOWN AND ALL THAT.
TOO BAD.
SO I BET YOU'RE NOT USED TO THIS SORT OF WEATHER IN AMERICA?
WELL, I'VE BEEN LIVING IN LONDON FOR SOME TIME NOW.
WORK?
NO, NOT AS SUCH.
SO YOU MUST LIKE IT HERE THEN?
FOR MOST AMERICANS IT'S PARIS OR ROME, BUT FOR ME IT'S ALWAYS BEEN LONDON.
THAT IS, AS LONG AS THEY DON'T DECIDE TO TURN THE WHOLE CITY INTO A BRANCH OF SEABUCKS.

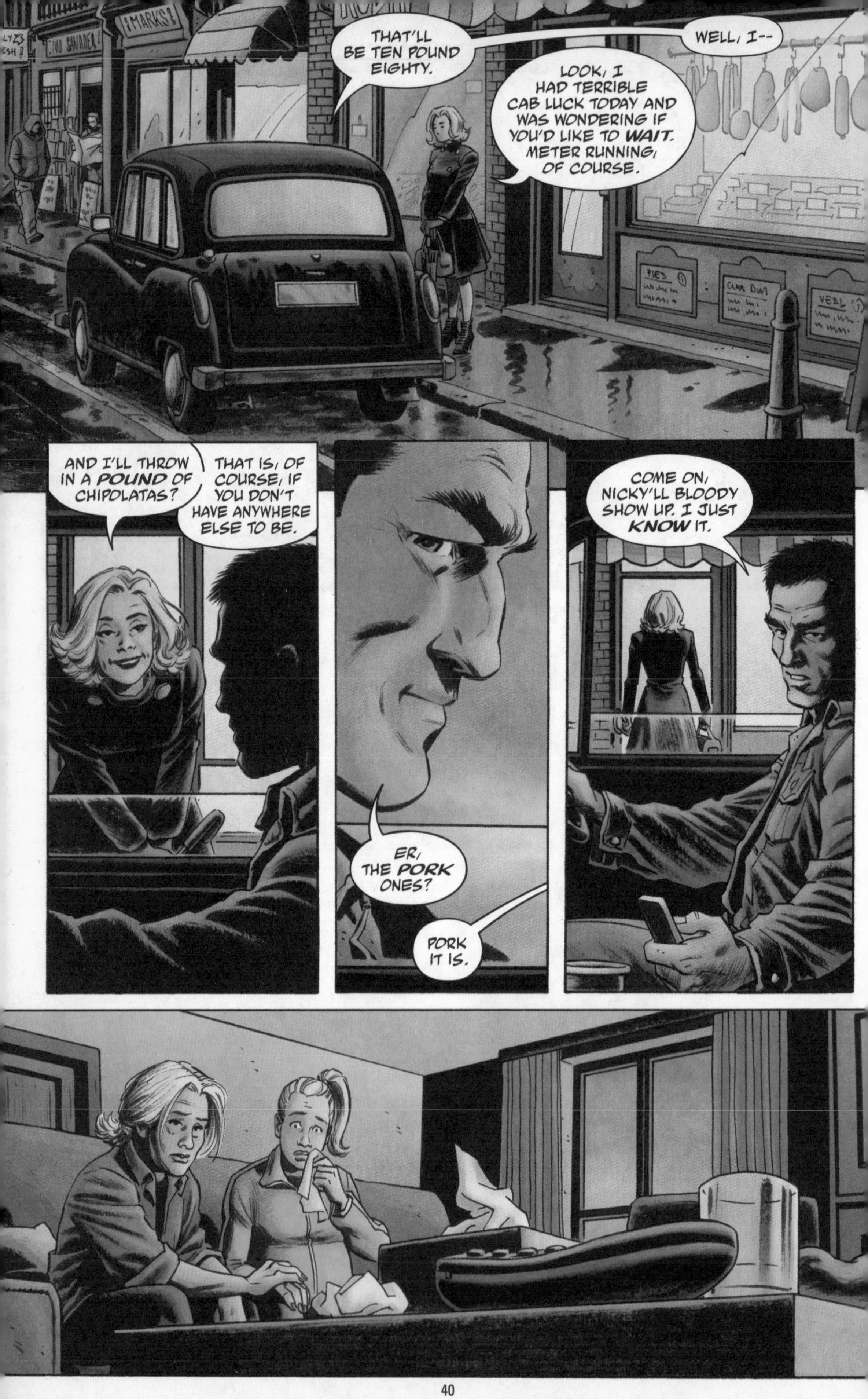
THAT'LL BE TEN POUND EIGHTY.
WELL, I--
LOOK, I HAD TERRIBLE CAB LUCK TODAY AND WAS WONDERING IF YOU'D LIKE TO WAIT. METER RUNNING, OF COURSE.
AND I'LL THROW IN A POUND OF CHIPOLATAS?
THAT IS, OF COURSE, IF YOU DON'T HAVE ANYWHERE ELSE TO BE.
ER, THE PORK ONES?
PORK IT IS.
COME ON, NICKY'LL BLOODY SHOW UP. I JUST KNOW IT.

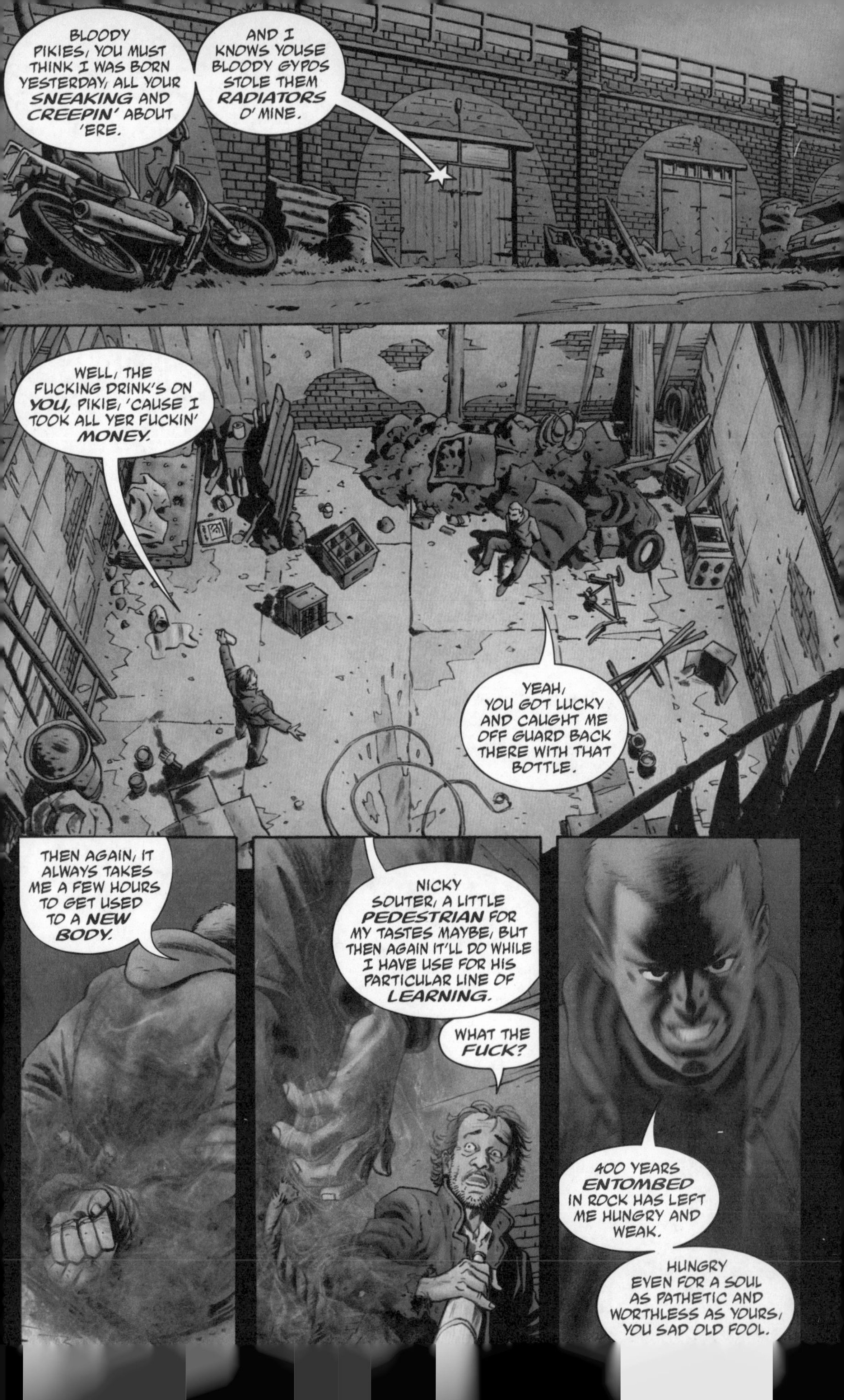
BLOODY PIKIES, YOU MUST THINK I WAS BORN YESTERDAY, ALL YOUR SNEAKING AND CREEPIN' ABOUT 'ERE.
AND I KNOWS YOUSE BLOODY GYPOS STOLE THEM RADIATORS O' MINE.
WELL, THE FUCKING DRINK'S ON YOU, PIKIE, 'CAUSE I TOOK ALL YER FUCKIN' MONEY.
YEAH, YOU GOT LUCKY AND CAUGHT ME OFF GUARD BACK THERE WITH THAT BOTTLE.
THEN AGAIN, IT ALWAYS TAKES ME A FEW HOURS TO GET USED TO A NEW BODY.
NICKY SOUTER, A LITTLE PEDESTRIAN FOR MY TASTES MAYBE, BUT THEN AGAIN IT'LL DO WHILE I HAVE USE FOR HIS PARTICULAR LINE OF LEARNING.
WHAT THE FUCK?
400 YEARS ENTOMBED IN ROCK HAS LEFT ME HUNGRY AND WEAK.
HUNGRY EVEN FOR A SOUL AS PATHETIC AND WORTHLESS AS YOURS, YOU SAD OLD FOOL.

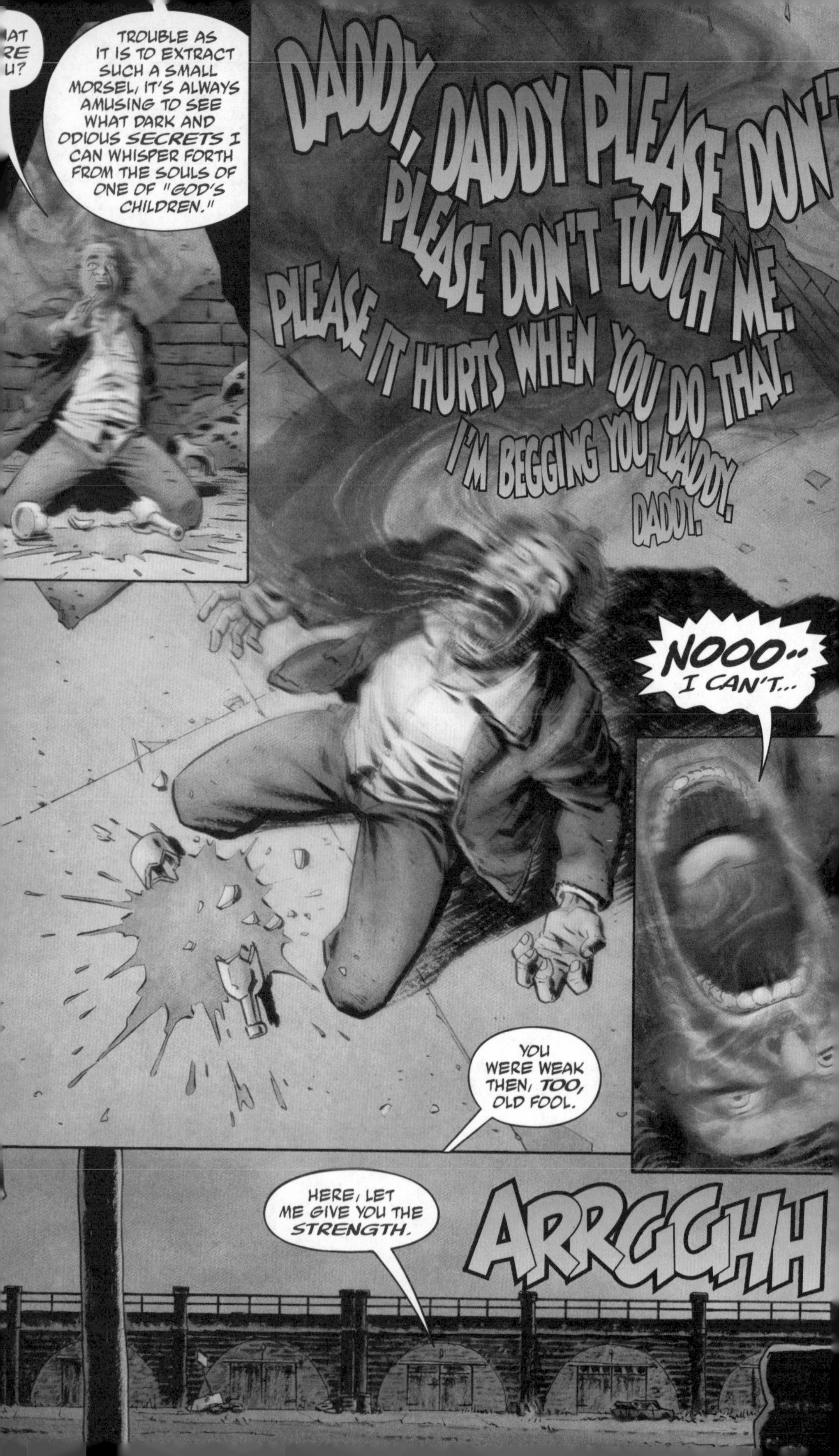

TROUBLE AS IT IS TO EXTRACT SUCH A SMALL MORSEL, IT'S ALWAYS AMUSING TO SEE WHAT DARK AND ODIOUS SECRETS I CAN WHISPER FORTH FROM THE SOULS OF ONE OF "GOD'S CHILDREN."
DADDY, DADDY PLEASE DON'T
PLEASE DON'T TOUCH ME.
PLEASE IT HURTS WHEN YOU DO THAT.
I'M BEGGING YOU, DADDY.
DADDY.
NOOO-- I CAN'T...
YOU WERE WEAK THEN, TOO, OLD FOOL.
HERE, LET ME GIVE YOU THE STRENGTH.
ARRGGHH

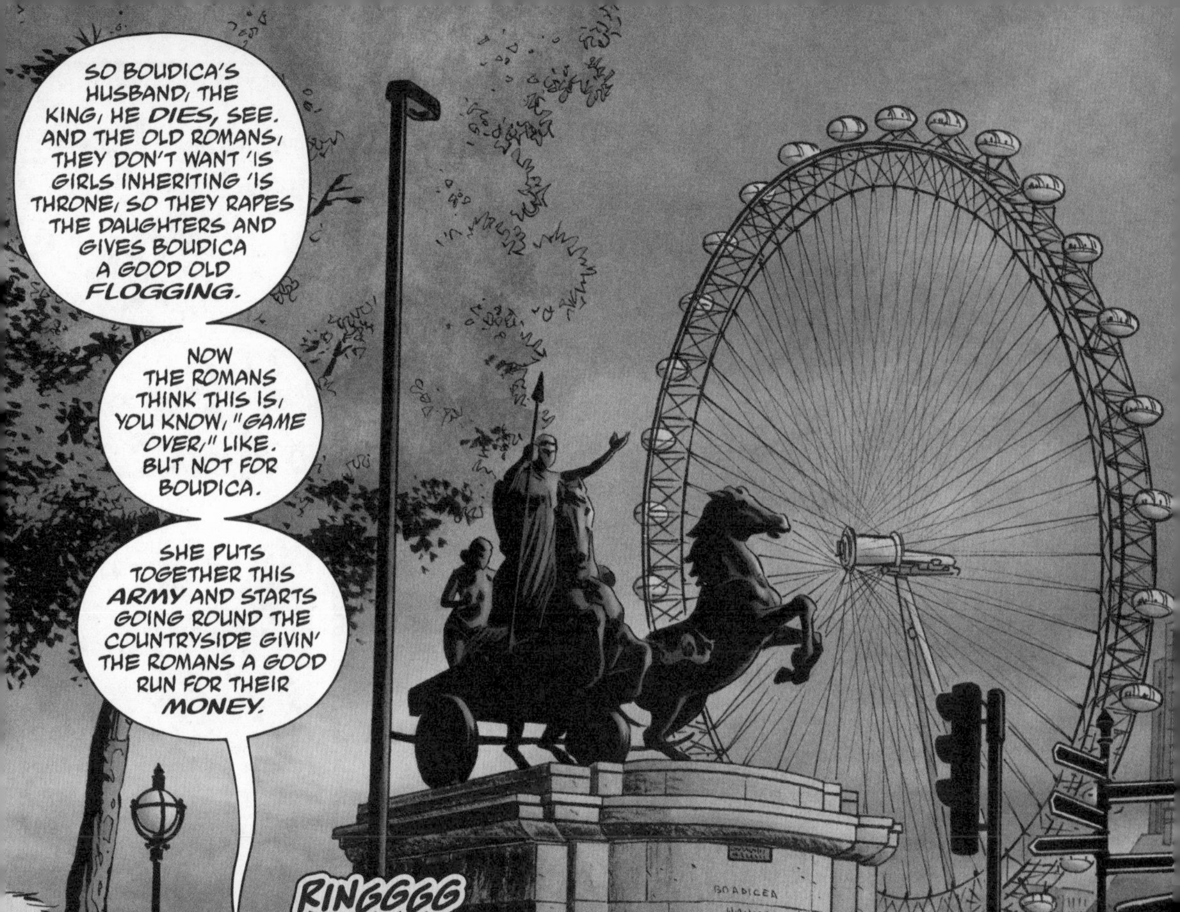
SO BOUDICA'S HUSBAND, THE KING, HE *DIES*, SEE. AND THE OLD ROMANS, THEY DON'T WANT 'IS GIRLS INHERITING 'IS THRONE, SO THEY RAPES THE DAUGHTERS AND GIVES BOUDICA A GOOD OLD *FLOGGING*.
NOW THE ROMANS THINK THIS IS, YOU KNOW, "GAME OVER," LIKE. BUT NOT FOR BOUDICA.
SHE PUTS TOGETHER THIS *ARMY* AND STARTS GOING ROUND THE COUNTRYSIDE GIVIN' THE ROMANS A GOOD RUN FOR THEIR *MONEY*.
RINGGGG RINGGGG
BOADICEA

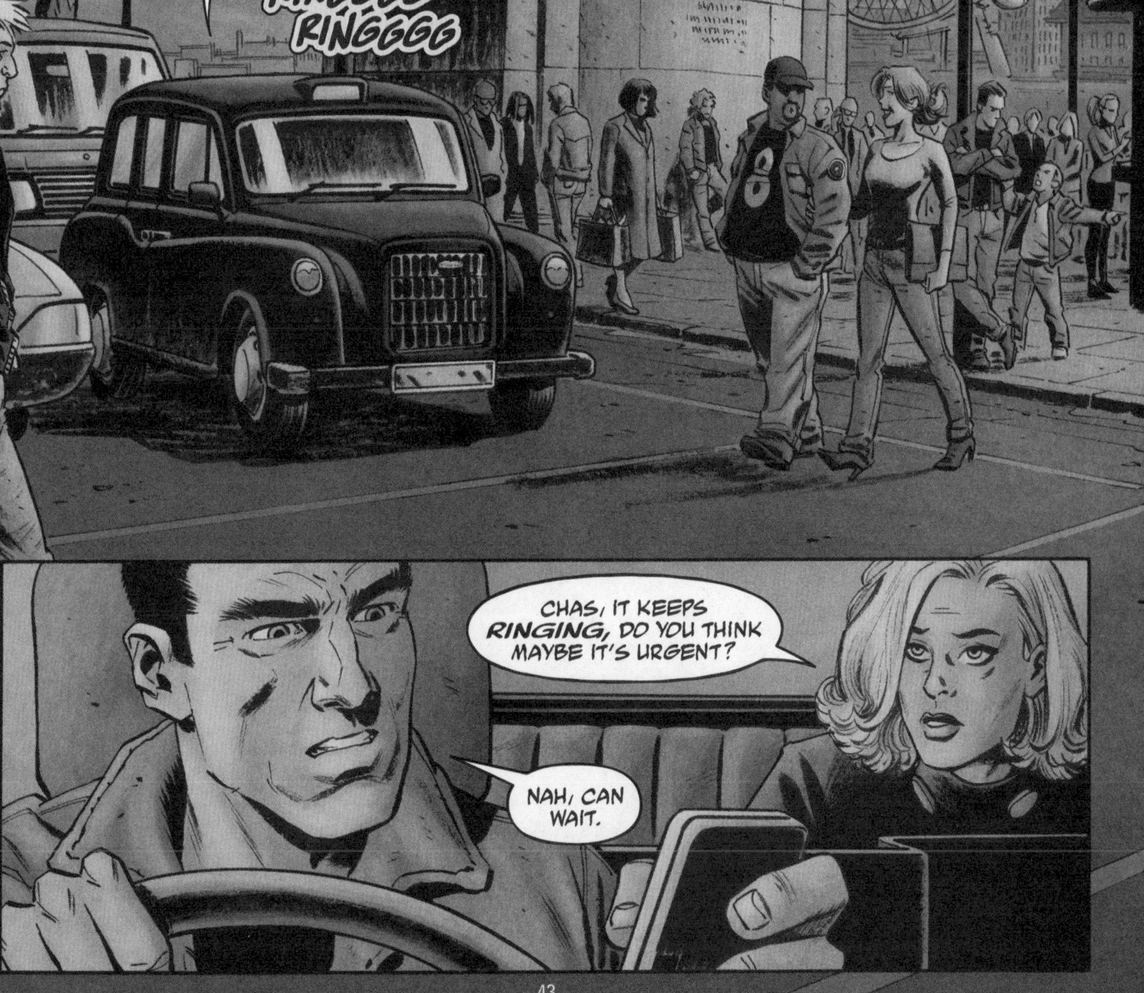
CHAS, IT KEEPS *RINGING*, DO YOU THINK MAYBE IT'S URGENT?
NAH, CAN WAIT.

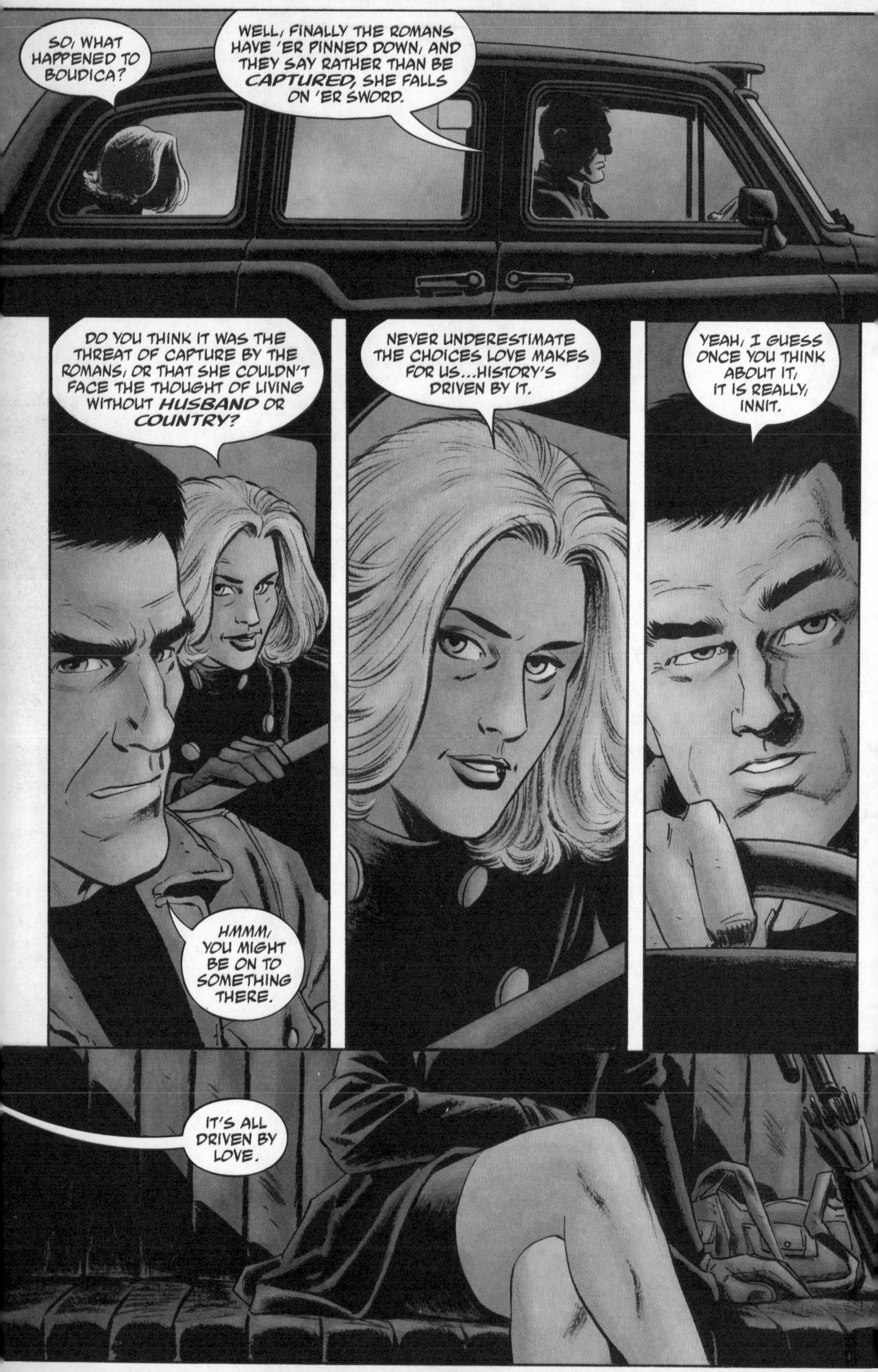
SO, WHAT HAPPENED TO BOUDICA?
WELL, FINALLY THE ROMANS HAVE 'ER PINNED DOWN, AND THEY SAY RATHER THAN BE CAPTURED, SHE FALLS ON 'ER SWORD.
DO YOU THINK IT WAS THE THREAT OF CAPTURE BY THE ROMANS, OR THAT SHE COULDN'T FACE THE THOUGHT OF LIVING WITHOUT HUSBAND OR COUNTRY?
HMMM, YOU MIGHT BE ON TO SOMETHING THERE.
NEVER UNDERESTIMATE THE CHOICES LOVE MAKES FOR US...HISTORY'S DRIVEN BY IT.
YEAH, I GUESS ONCE YOU THINK ABOUT IT, IT IS REALLY, INNIT.
IT'S ALL DRIVEN BY LOVE.

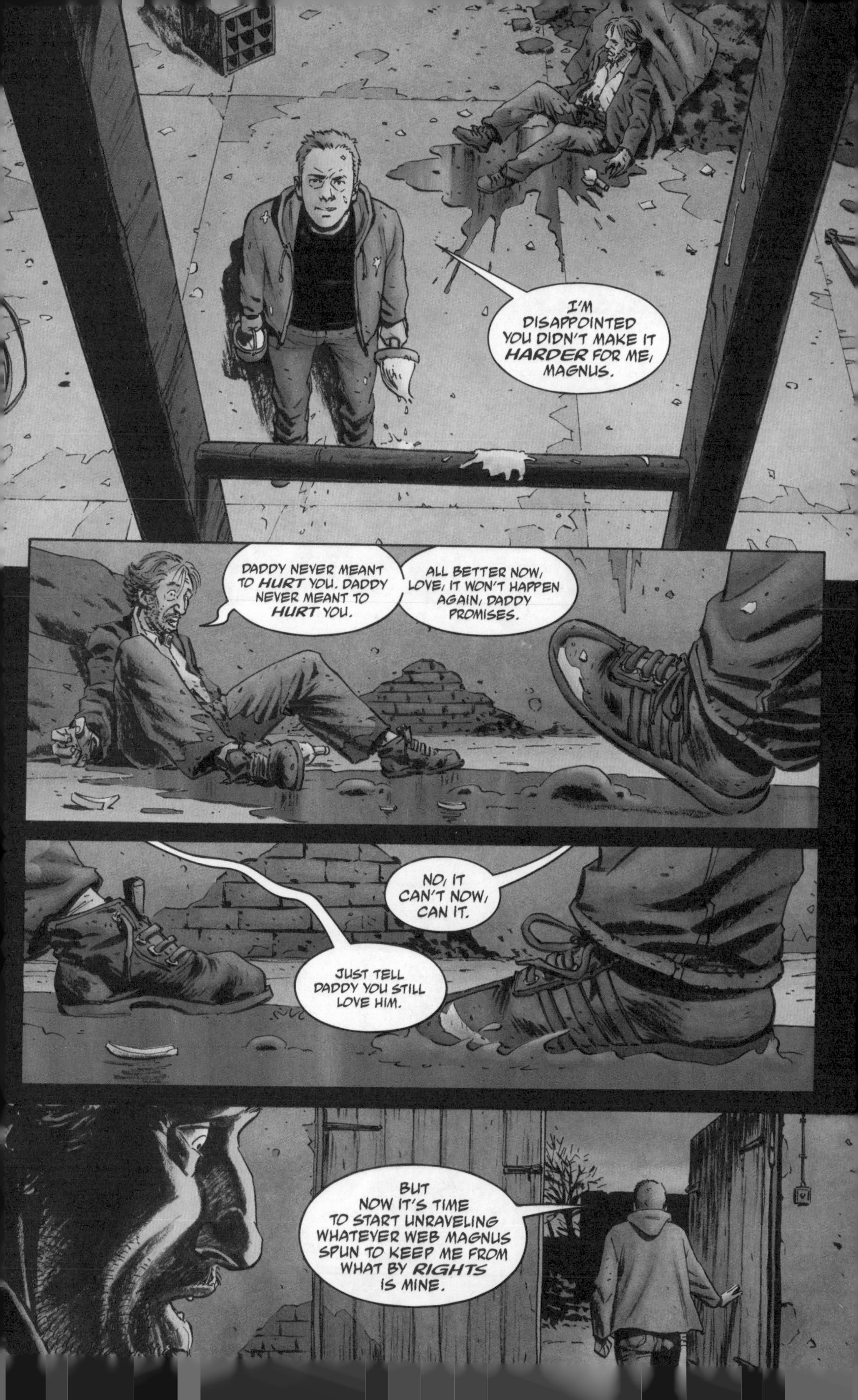
I'M DISAPPOINTED YOU DIDN'T MAKE IT HARDER FOR ME, MAGNUS.
DADDY NEVER MEANT TO HURT YOU. DADDY NEVER MEANT TO HURT YOU.
ALL BETTER NOW, LOVE, IT WON'T HAPPEN AGAIN, DADDY PROMISES.
NO, IT CAN'T NOW, CAN IT.
JUST TELL DADDY YOU STILL LOVE HIM.
BUT NOW IT'S TIME TO START UNRAVELING WHATEVER WEB MAGNUS SPUN TO KEEP ME FROM WHAT BY RIGHTS IS MINE.

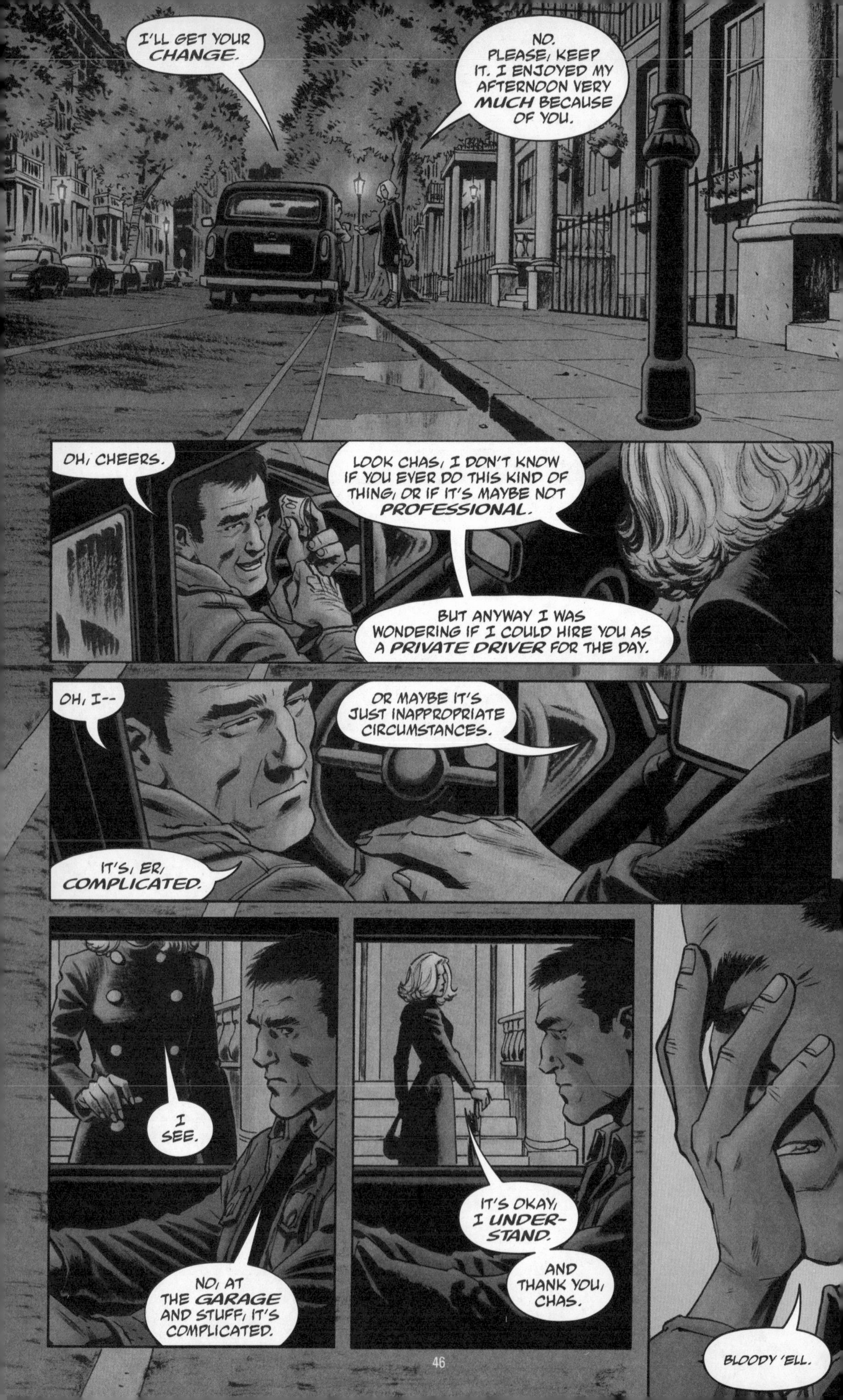
I'LL GET YOUR CHANGE.
NO. PLEASE, KEEP IT. I ENJOYED MY AFTERNOON VERY MUCH BECAUSE OF YOU.
OH, CHEERS.
LOOK CHAS, I DON'T KNOW IF YOU EVER DO THIS KIND OF THING, OR IF IT'S MAYBE NOT PROFESSIONAL.
BUT ANYWAY I WAS WONDERING IF I COULD HIRE YOU AS A PRIVATE DRIVER FOR THE DAY.
OH, I--
OR MAYBE IT'S JUST INAPPROPRIATE CIRCUMSTANCES.
IT'S, ER, COMPLICATED.
I SEE.
NO, AT THE GARAGE AND STUFF, IT'S COMPLICATED.
IT'S OKAY, I UNDER-STAND.
AND THANK YOU, CHAS.
BLOODY 'ELL.

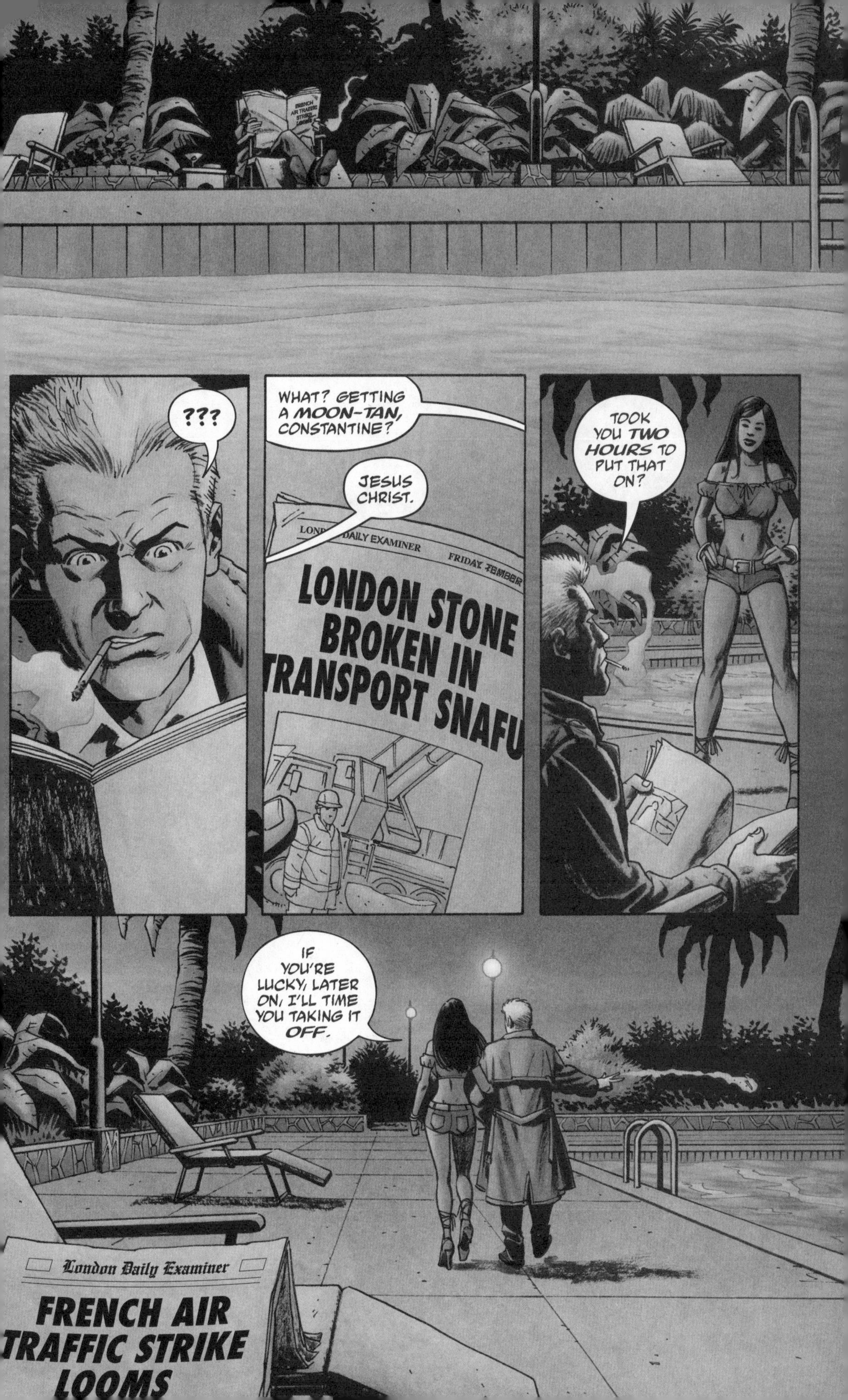
???
WHAT? GETTING A MOON-TAN, CONSTANTINE?
JESUS CHRIST.
DAILY EXAMINER
LONDON STONE BROKEN IN TRANSPORT SNAFU
TOOK YOU TWO HOURS TO PUT THAT ON?
IF YOU'RE LUCKY, LATER ON, I'LL TIME YOU TAKING IT OFF.
London Daily Examiner
FRENCH AIR TRAFFIC STRIKE LOOMS

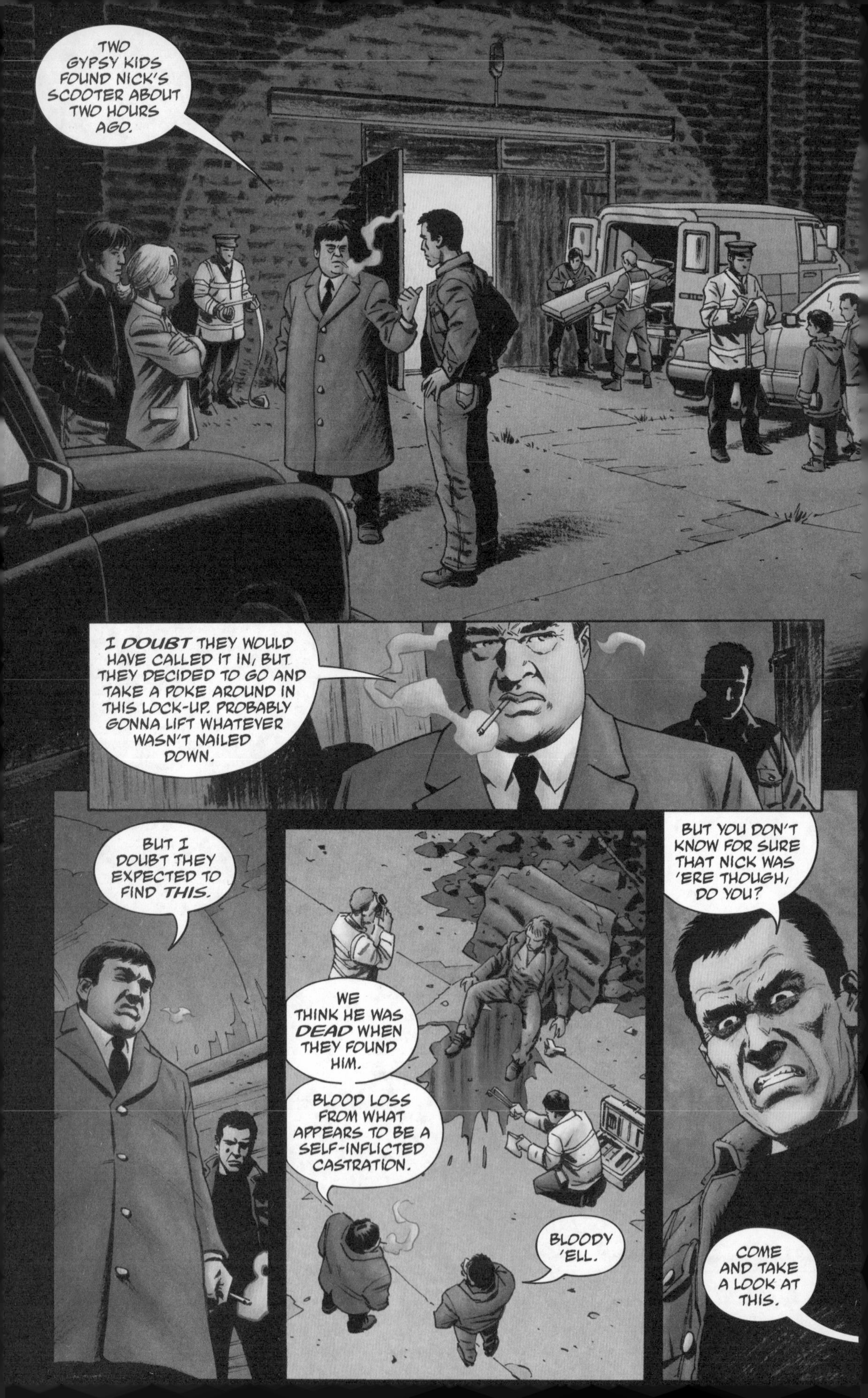
TWO GYPSY KIDS FOUND NICK'S SCOOTER ABOUT TWO HOURS AGO.
I DOUBT THEY WOULD HAVE CALLED IT IN, BUT THEY DECIDED TO GO AND TAKE A POKE AROUND IN THIS LOCK-UP. PROBABLY GONNA LIFT WHATEVER WASN'T NAILED DOWN.
BUT I DOUBT THEY EXPECTED TO FIND THIS.
WE THINK HE WAS DEAD WHEN THEY FOUND HIM.
BLOOD LOSS FROM WHAT APPEARS TO BE A SELF-INFLICTED CASTRATION.
BLOODY 'ELL.
BUT YOU DON'T KNOW FOR SURE THAT NICK WAS 'ERE THOUGH, DO YOU?
COME AND TAKE A LOOK AT THIS.

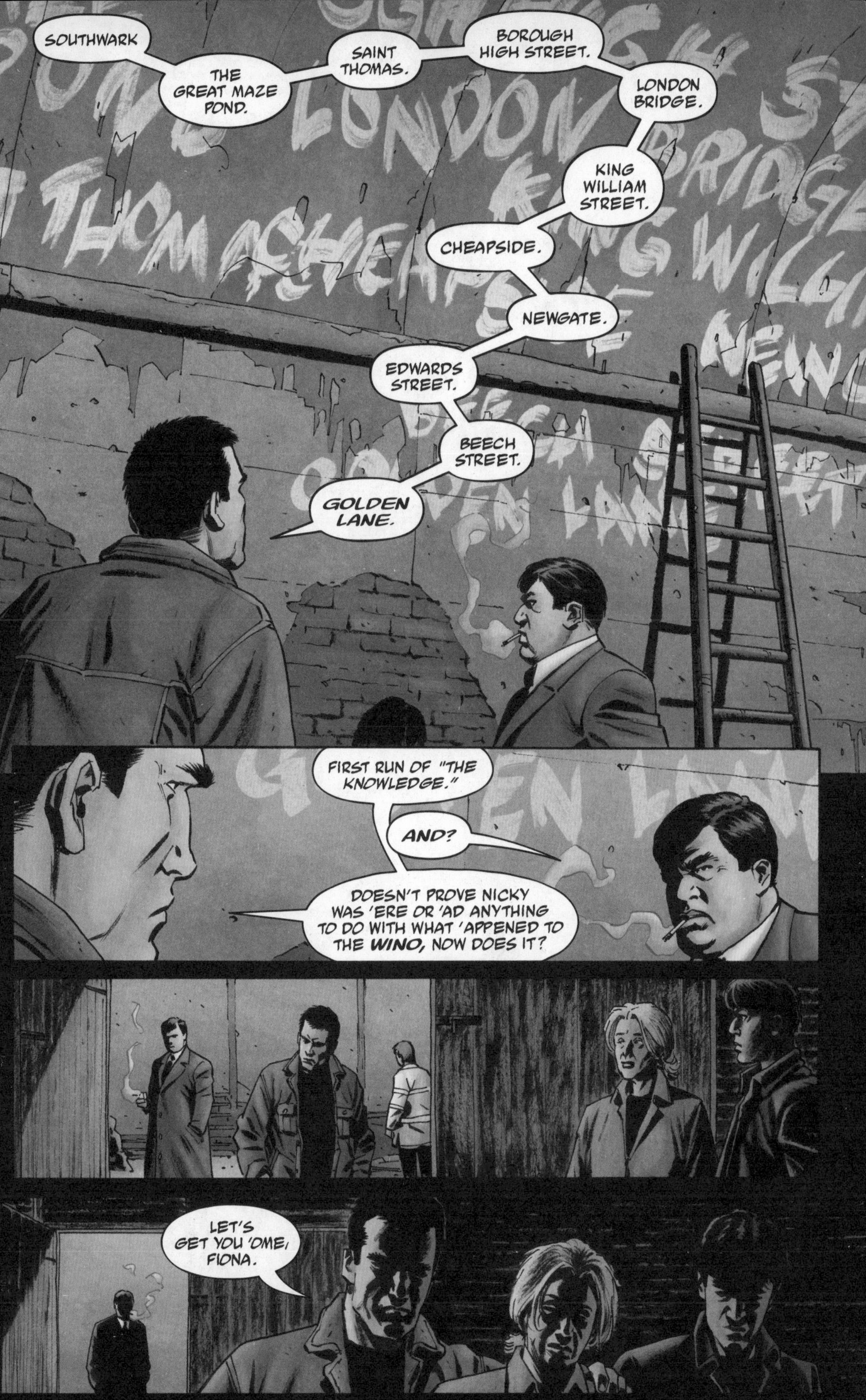
SOUTHWARK
THE GREAT MAZE POND.
SAINT THOMAS.
BOROUGH HIGH STREET.
LONDON BRIDGE.
KING WILLIAM STREET.
CHEAPSIDE.
NEWGATE.
EDWARDS STREET.
BEECH STREET.
GOLDEN LANE.
FIRST RUN OF "THE KNOWLEDGE."
AND?
DOESN'T PROVE NICKY WAS 'ERE OR 'AD ANYTHING TO DO WITH WHAT 'APPENED TO THE WINO, NOW DOES IT?
LET'S GET YOU 'OME, FIONA.

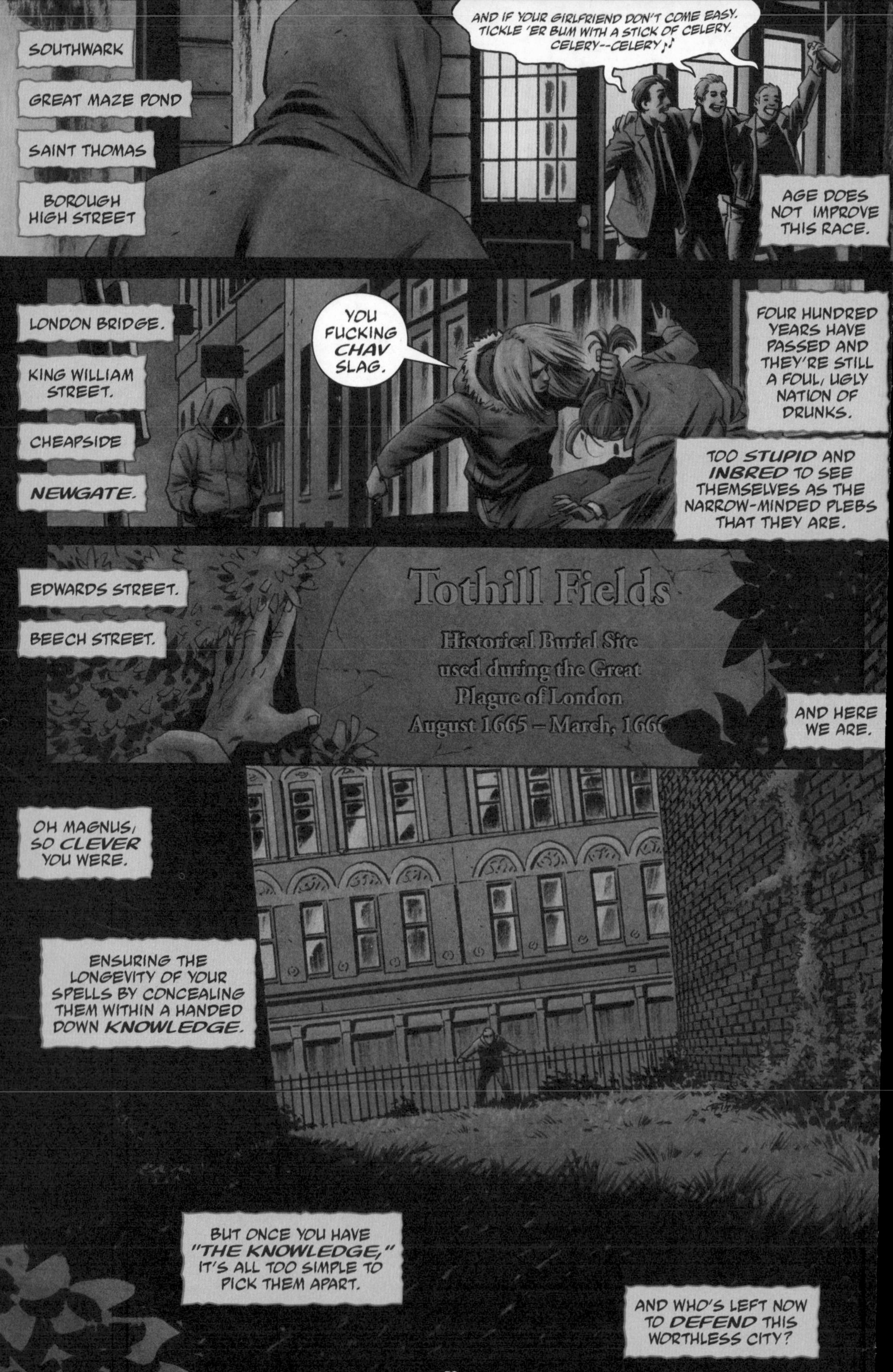
SOUTHWARK
GREAT MAZE POND
SAINT THOMAS
BOROUGH HIGH STREET
AND IF YOUR GIRLFRIEND DON'T COME EASY. TICKLE 'ER BUM WITH A STICK OF CELERY. CELERY--CELERY ♪
AGE DOES NOT IMPROVE THIS RACE.
LONDON BRIDGE.
KING WILLIAM STREET.
CHEAPSIDE
NEWGATE.
YOU FUCKING CHAV SLAG.
FOUR HUNDRED YEARS HAVE PASSED AND THEY'RE STILL A FOUL, UGLY NATION OF DRUNKS.
TOO STUPID AND INBRED TO SEE THEMSELVES AS THE NARROW-MINDED PLEBS THAT THEY ARE.
EDWARDS STREET.
BEECH STREET.
Tothill Fields
Historical Burial Site used during the Great Plague of London August 1665 – March, 166
AND HERE WE ARE.
OH MAGNUS, SO CLEVER YOU WERE.
ENSURING THE LONGEVITY OF YOUR SPELLS BY CONCEALING THEM WITHIN A HANDED DOWN KNOWLEDGE.
BUT ONCE YOU HAVE "THE KNOWLEDGE," IT'S ALL TOO SIMPLE TO PICK THEM APART.
AND WHO'S LEFT NOW TO DEFEND THIS WORTHLESS CITY?

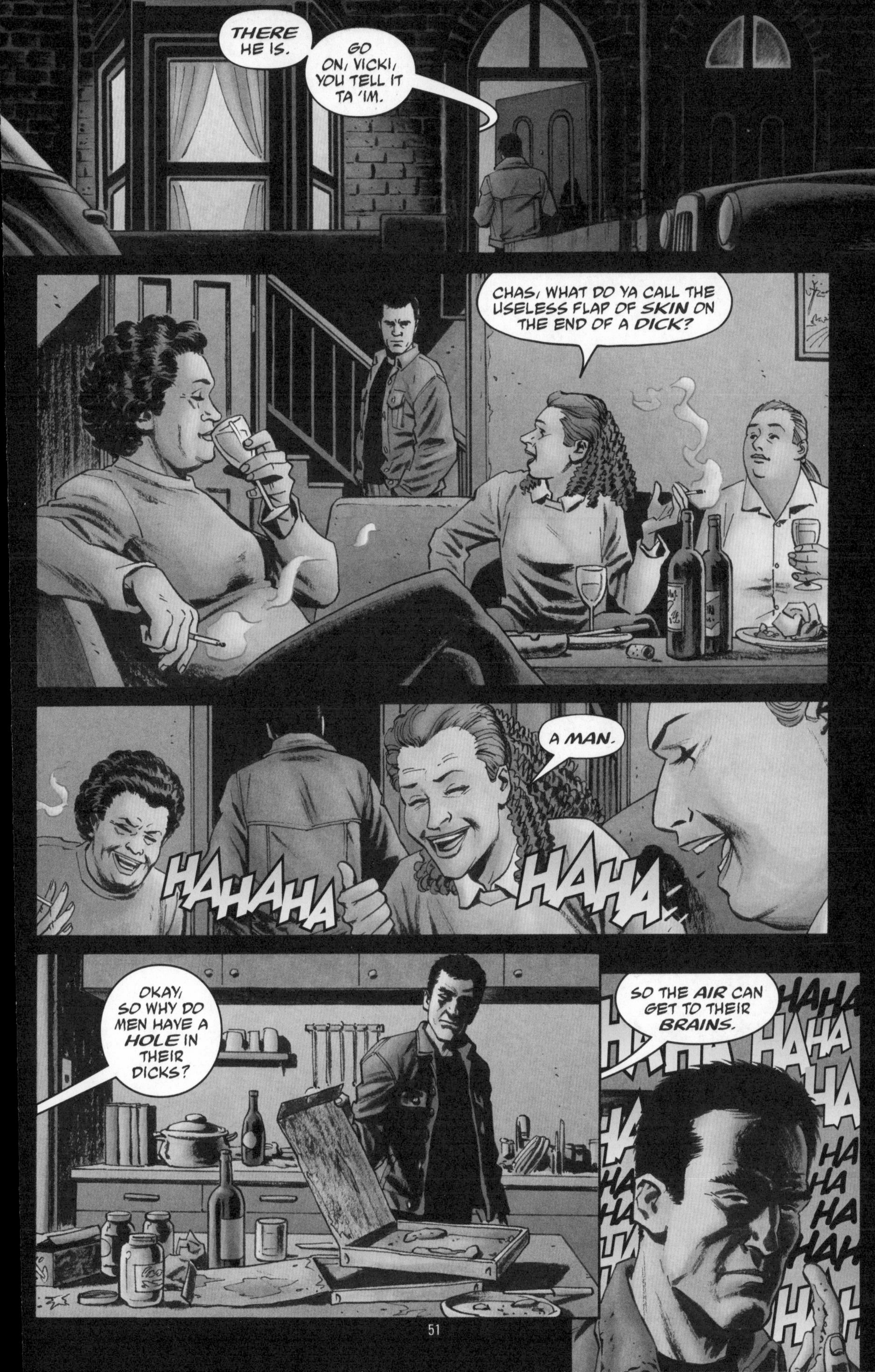

THERE HE IS.
GO ON, VICKI, YOU TELL IT TA 'IM.
CHAS, WHAT DO YA CALL THE USELESS FLAP OF SKIN ON THE END OF A DICK?
A MAN.
HAHAHA
HAHA
OKAY, SO WHY DO MEN HAVE A HOLE IN THEIR DICKS?
SO THE AIR CAN GET TO THEIR BRAINS.

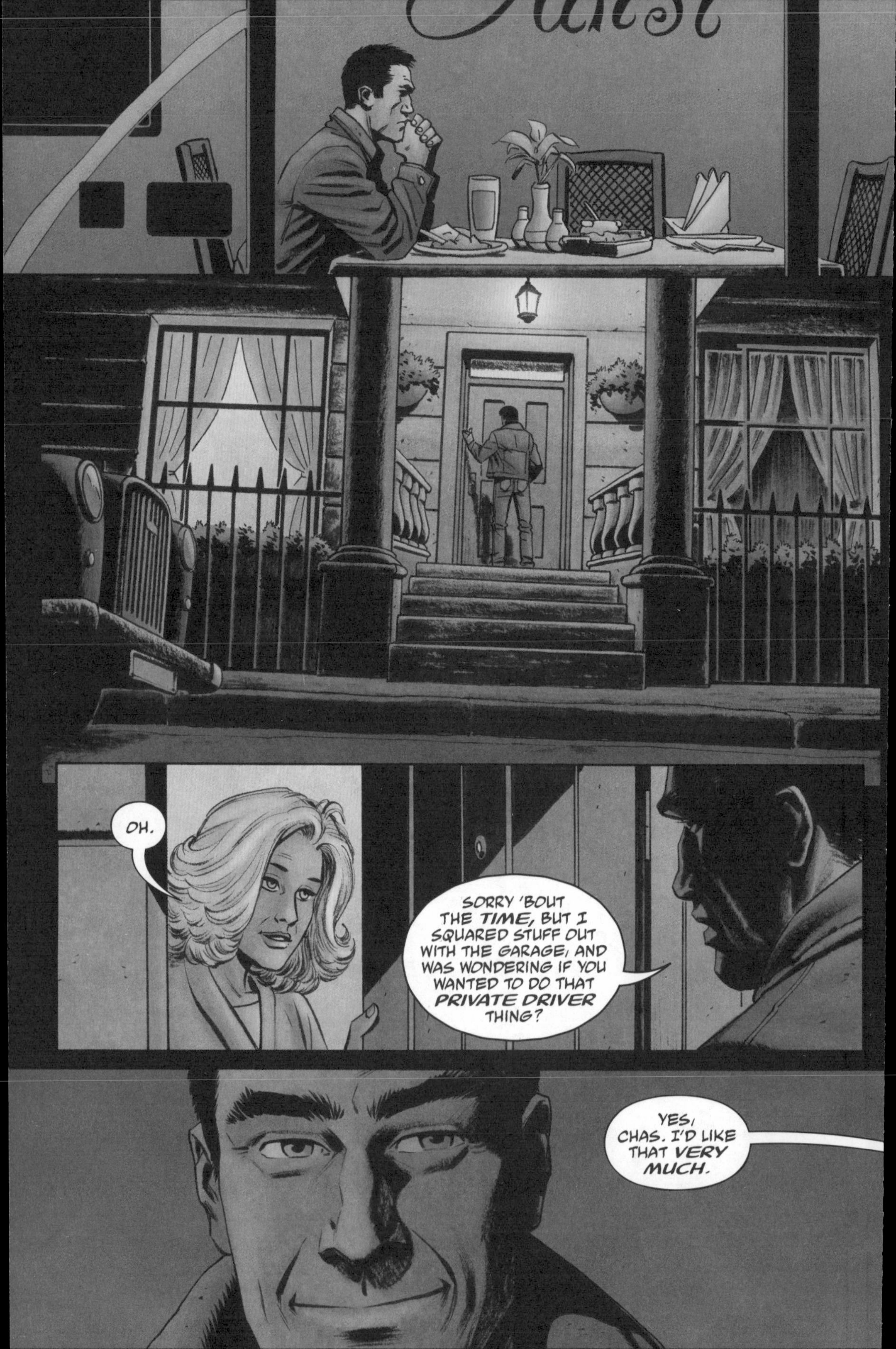
OH.
SORRY 'BOUT THE TIME, BUT I SQUARED STUFF OUT WITH THE GARAGE, AND WAS WONDERING IF YOU WANTED TO DO THAT PRIVATE DRIVER THING?
YES, CHAS. I'D LIKE THAT VERY MUCH.

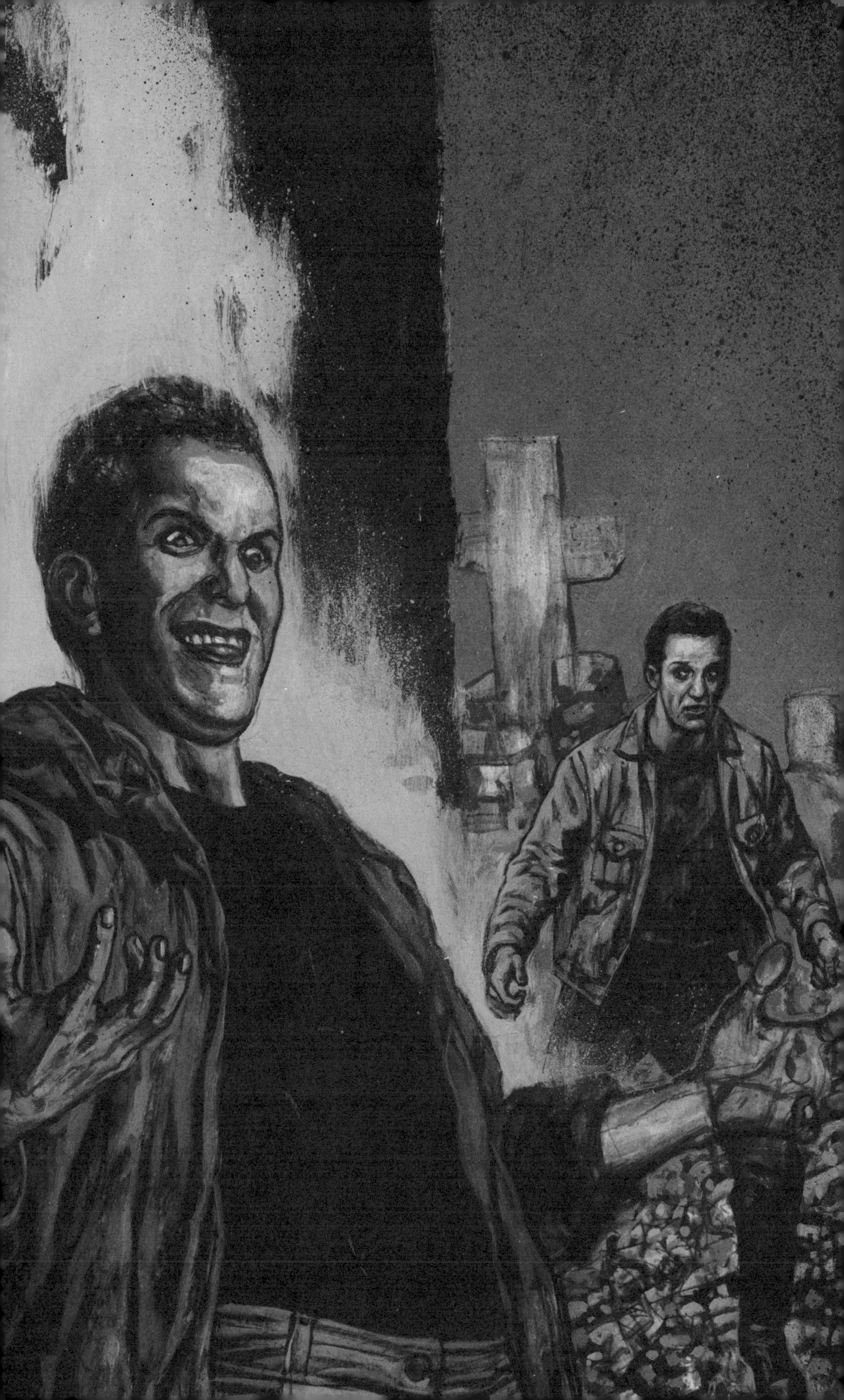

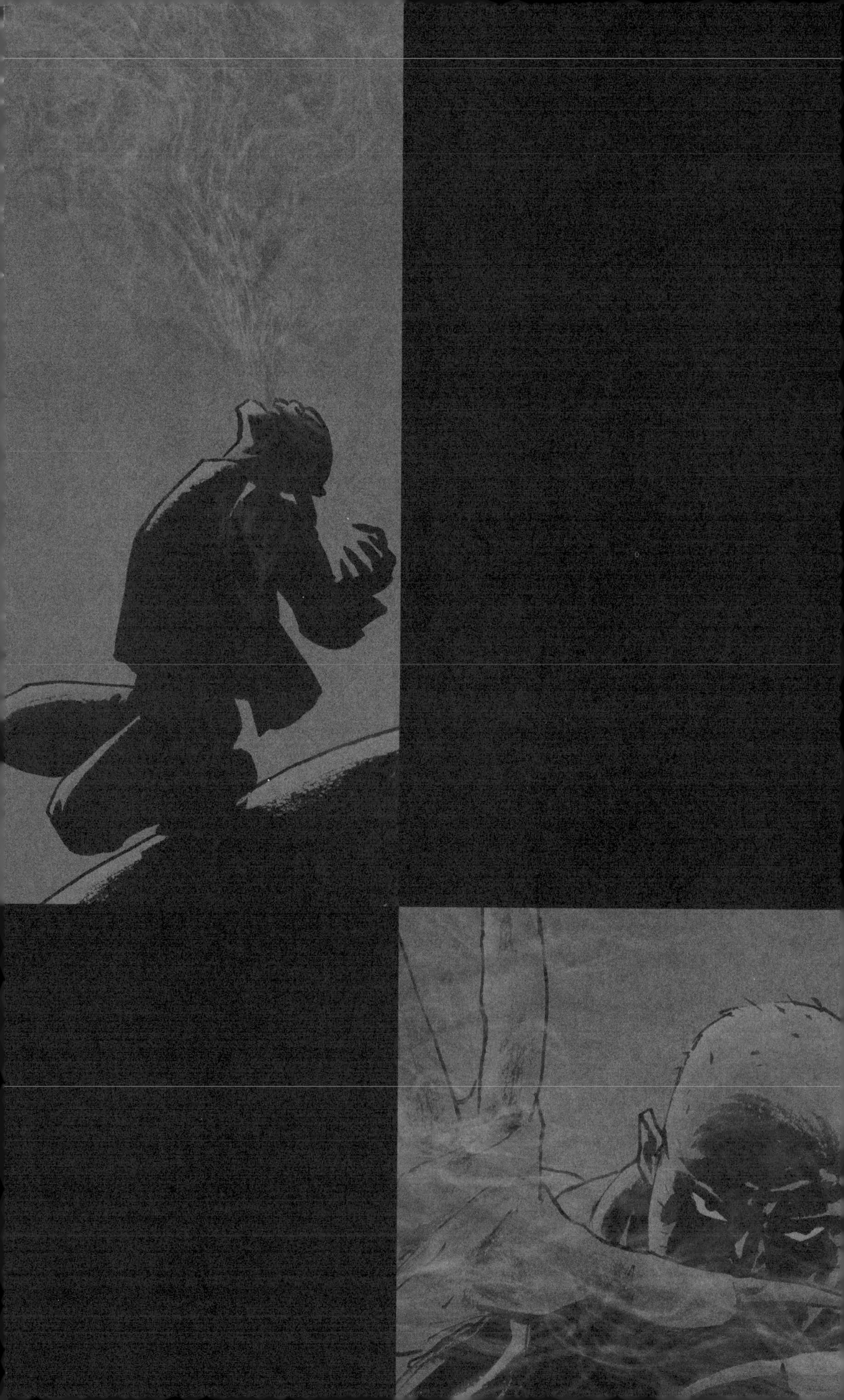

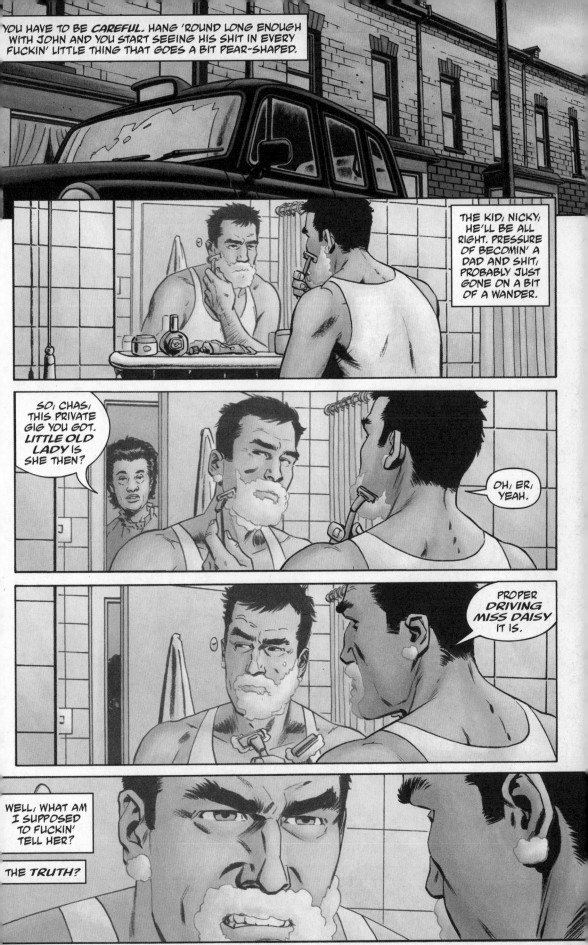

YOU HAVE TO BE *CAREFUL*. HANG 'ROUND LONG ENOUGH WITH JOHN AND YOU START SEEING HIS SHIT IN EVERY FUCKIN' LITTLE THING THAT GOES A BIT PEAR-SHAPED.

THE KID, NICKY, HE'LL BE ALL RIGHT. PRESSURE OF BECOMIN' A DAD AND SHIT, PROBABLY JUST GONE ON A BIT OF A WANDER.

SO, CHAS, THIS PRIVATE GIG YOU GOT. *LITTLE OLD LADY* IS SHE THEN?

OH, ER, YEAH.

PROPER *DRIVING MISS DAISY* IT IS.

WELL, WHAT AM I SUPPOSED TO FUCKIN' TELL HER?

THE *TRUTH?*

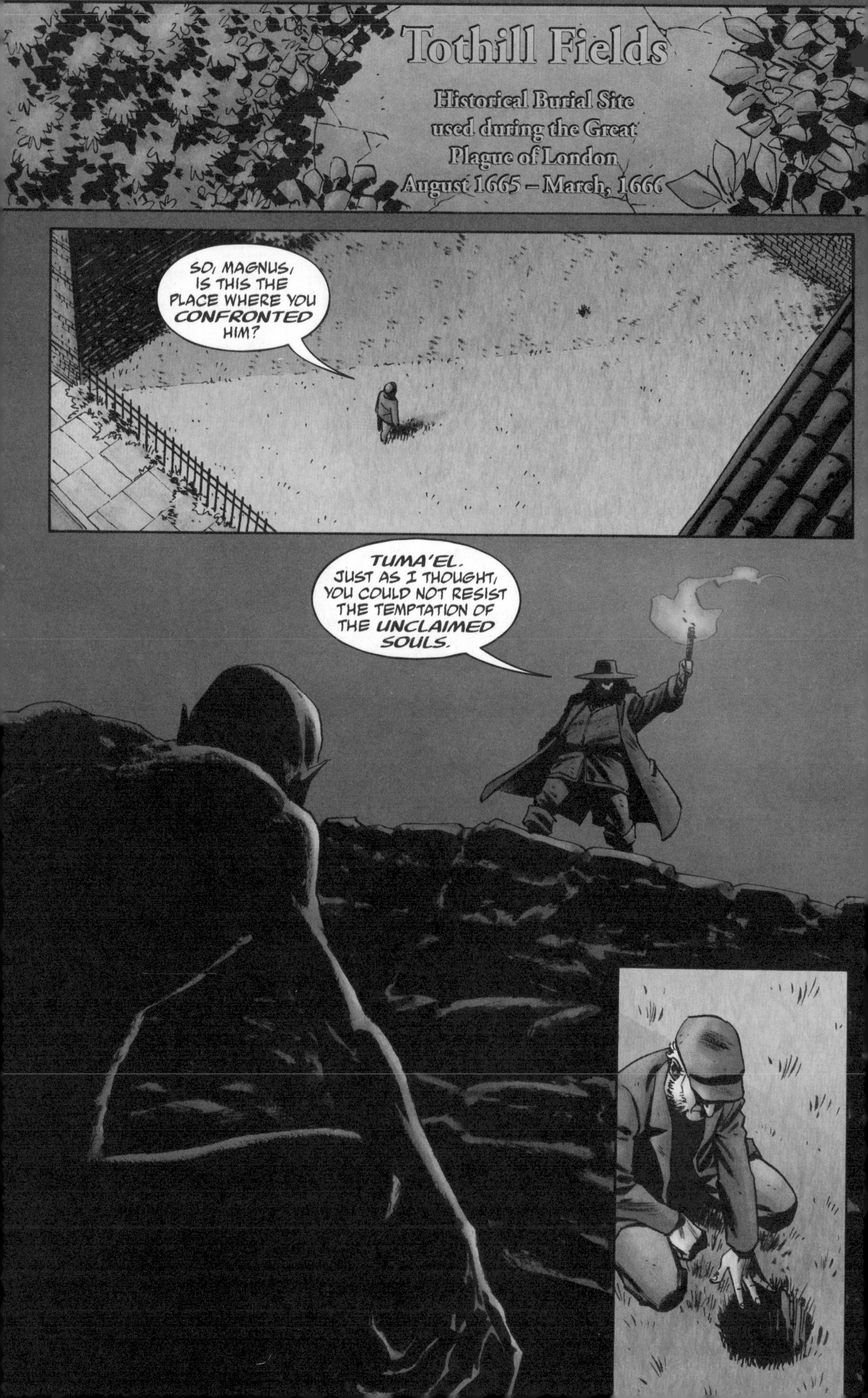
Tothill Fields
Historical Burial Site used during the Great Plague of London August 1665 – March, 1666
SO, MAGNUS, IS THIS THE PLACE WHERE YOU CONFRONTED HIM?
TUMA'EL. JUST AS I THOUGHT, YOU COULD NOT RESIST THE TEMPTATION OF THE UNCLAIMED SOULS.

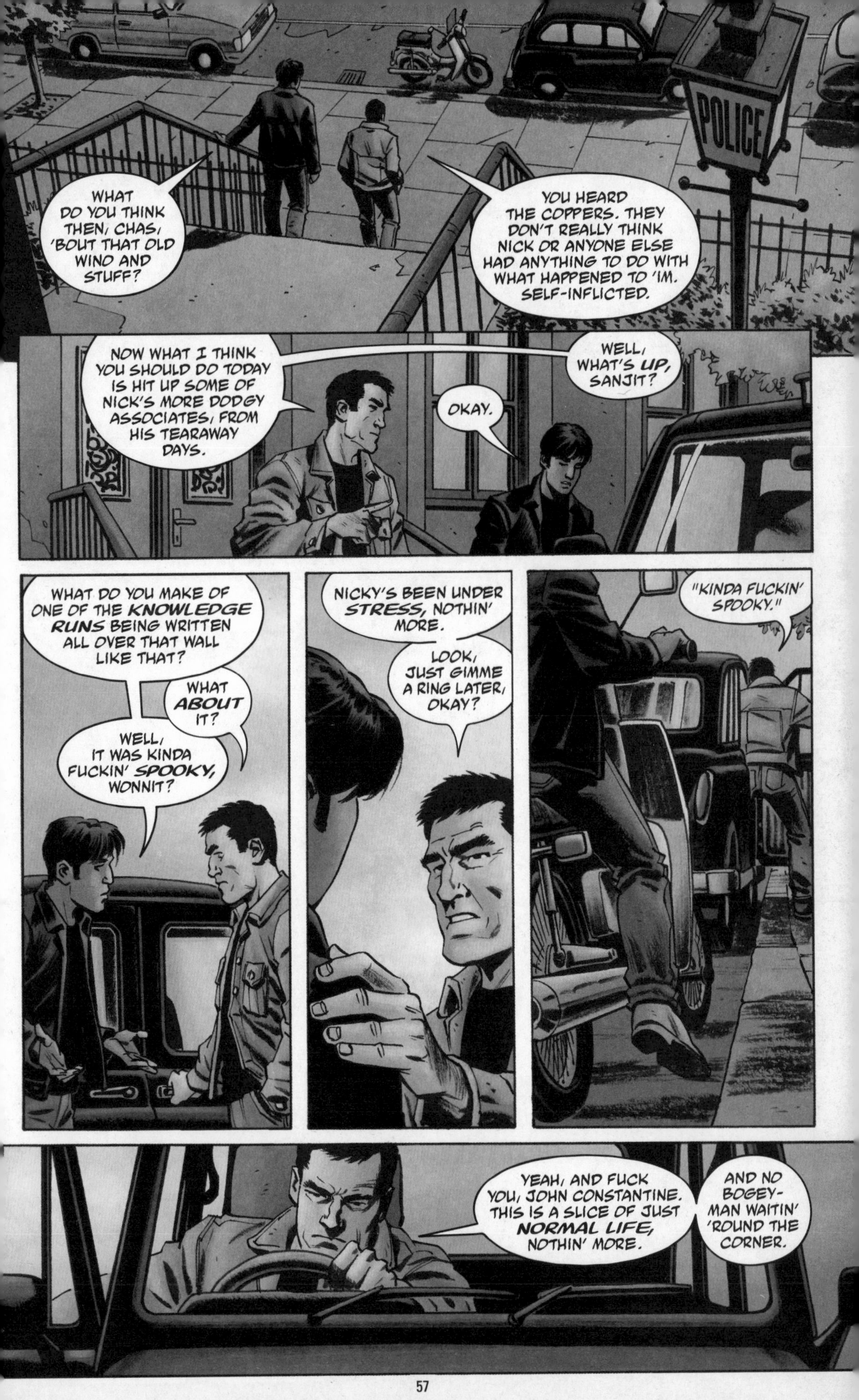

POLICE
WHAT DO YOU THINK THEN, CHAS, 'BOUT THAT OLD WIND AND STUFF?
YOU HEARD THE COPPERS. THEY DON'T REALLY THINK NICK OR ANYONE ELSE HAD ANYTHING TO DO WITH WHAT HAPPENED TO 'IM. SELF-INFLICTED.
NOW WHAT I THINK YOU SHOULD DO TODAY IS HIT UP SOME OF NICK'S MORE DODGY ASSOCIATES, FROM HIS TEARAWAY DAYS.
OKAY.
WELL, WHAT'S UP, SANJIT?
WHAT DO YOU MAKE OF ONE OF THE KNOWLEDGE RUNS BEING WRITTEN ALL OVER THAT WALL LIKE THAT?
WHAT ABOUT IT?
WELL, IT WAS KINDA FUCKIN' SPOOKY, WONNIT?
NICKY'S BEEN UNDER STRESS, NOTHIN' MORE.
LOOK, JUST GIMME A RING LATER, OKAY?
"KINDA FUCKIN' SPOOKY."
YEAH, AND FUCK YOU, JOHN CONSTANTINE. THIS IS A SLICE OF JUST NORMAL LIFE, NOTHIN' MORE.
AND NO BOGEY-MAN WAITIN' 'ROUND THE CORNER.

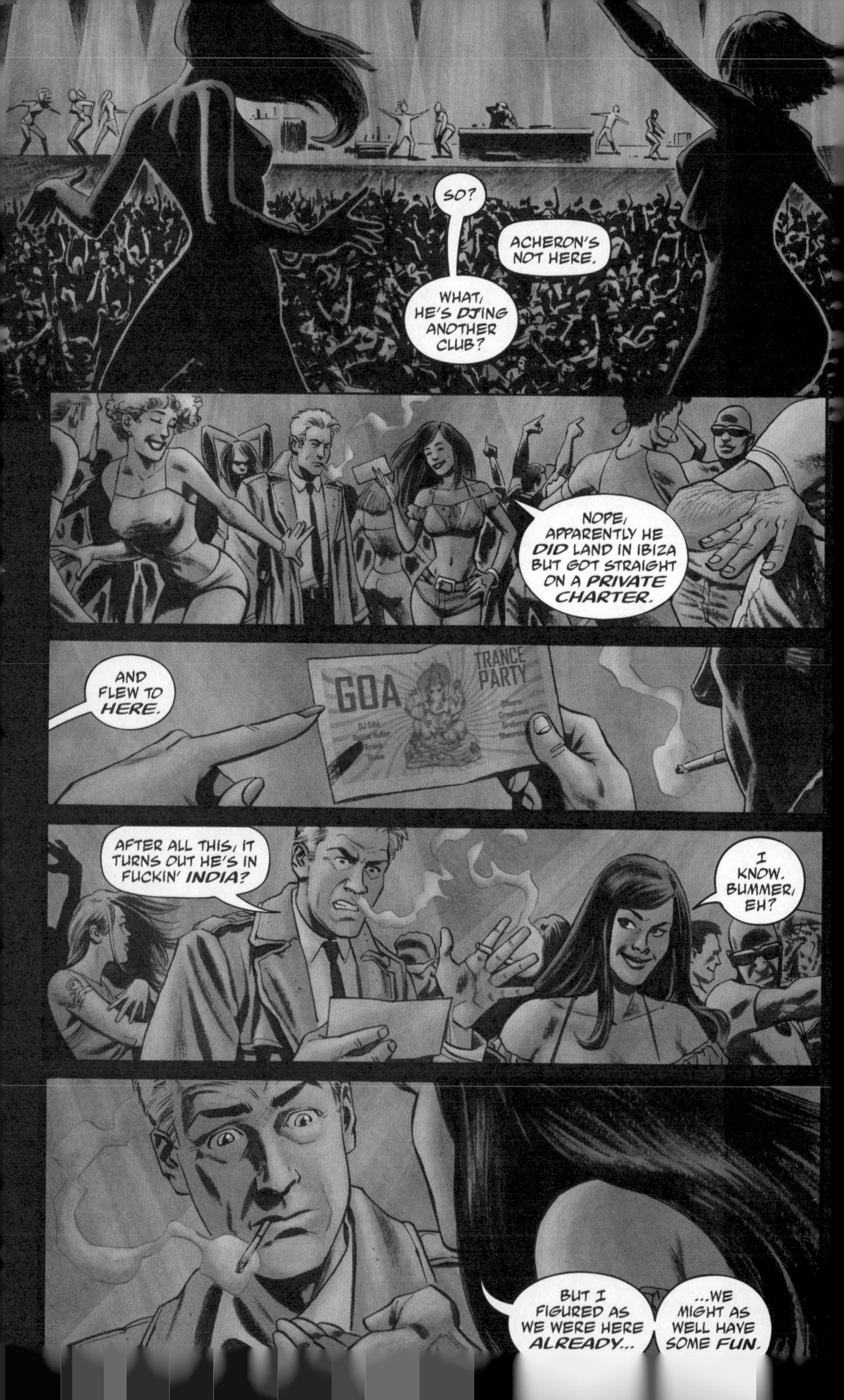
SO?
ACHERON'S NOT HERE.
WHAT, HE'S DJING ANOTHER CLUB?
NOPE, APPARENTLY HE DID LAND IN IBIZA BUT GOT STRAIGHT ON A PRIVATE CHARTER.
AND FLEW TO HERE.
GOA
TRANCE PARTY
AFTER ALL THIS, IT TURNS OUT HE'S IN FUCKIN' INDIA?
I KNOW. BUMMER, EH?
BUT I FIGURED AS WE WERE HERE ALREADY...
...WE MIGHT AS WELL HAVE SOME FUN.

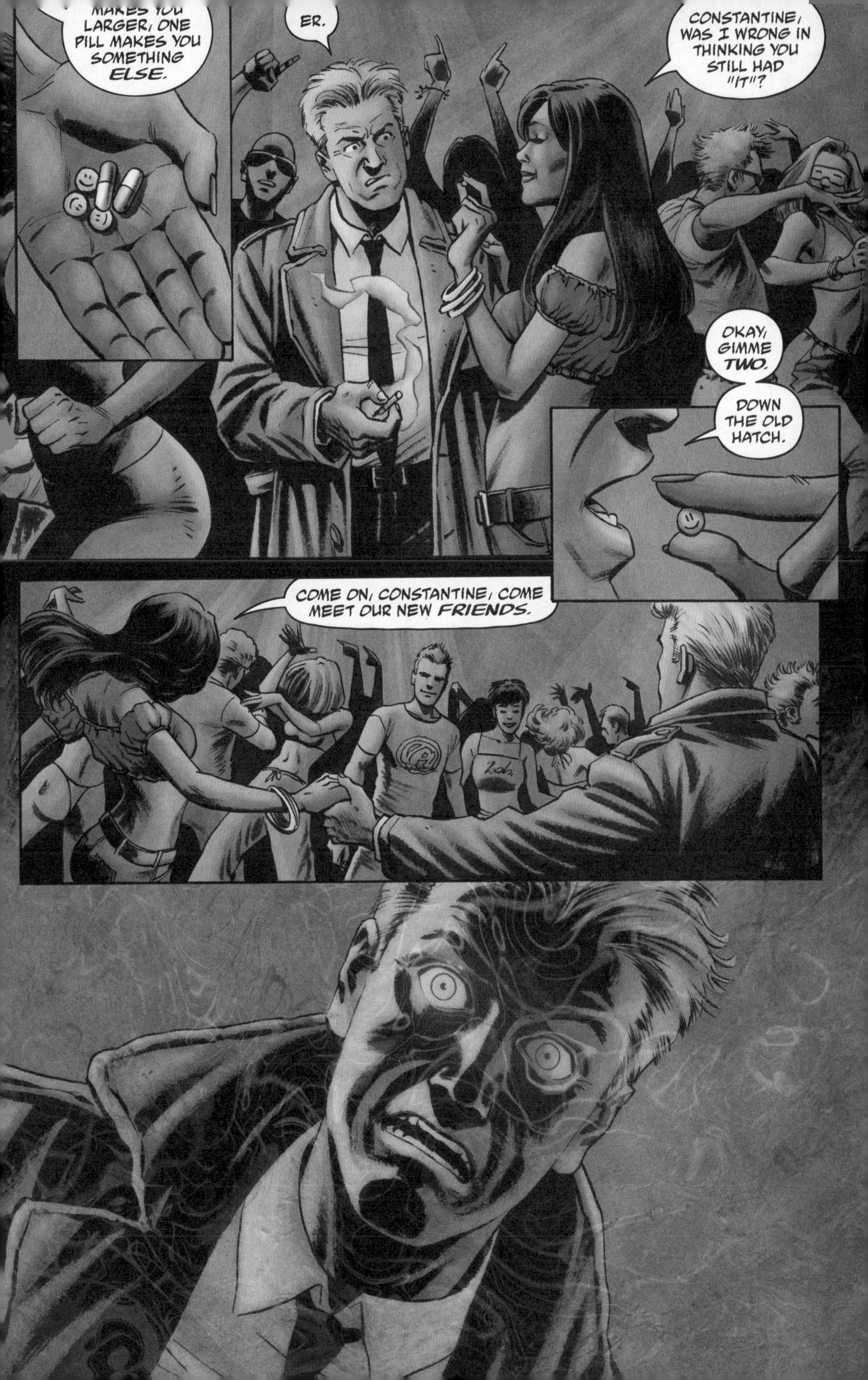

MAKES YOU LARGER, ONE PILL MAKES YOU SOMETHING ELSE.
ER.
CONSTANTINE, WAS I WRONG IN THINKING YOU STILL HAD "IT"?
OKAY, GIMME TWO.
DOWN THE OLD HATCH.
COME ON, CONSTANTINE, COME MEET OUR NEW FRIENDS.

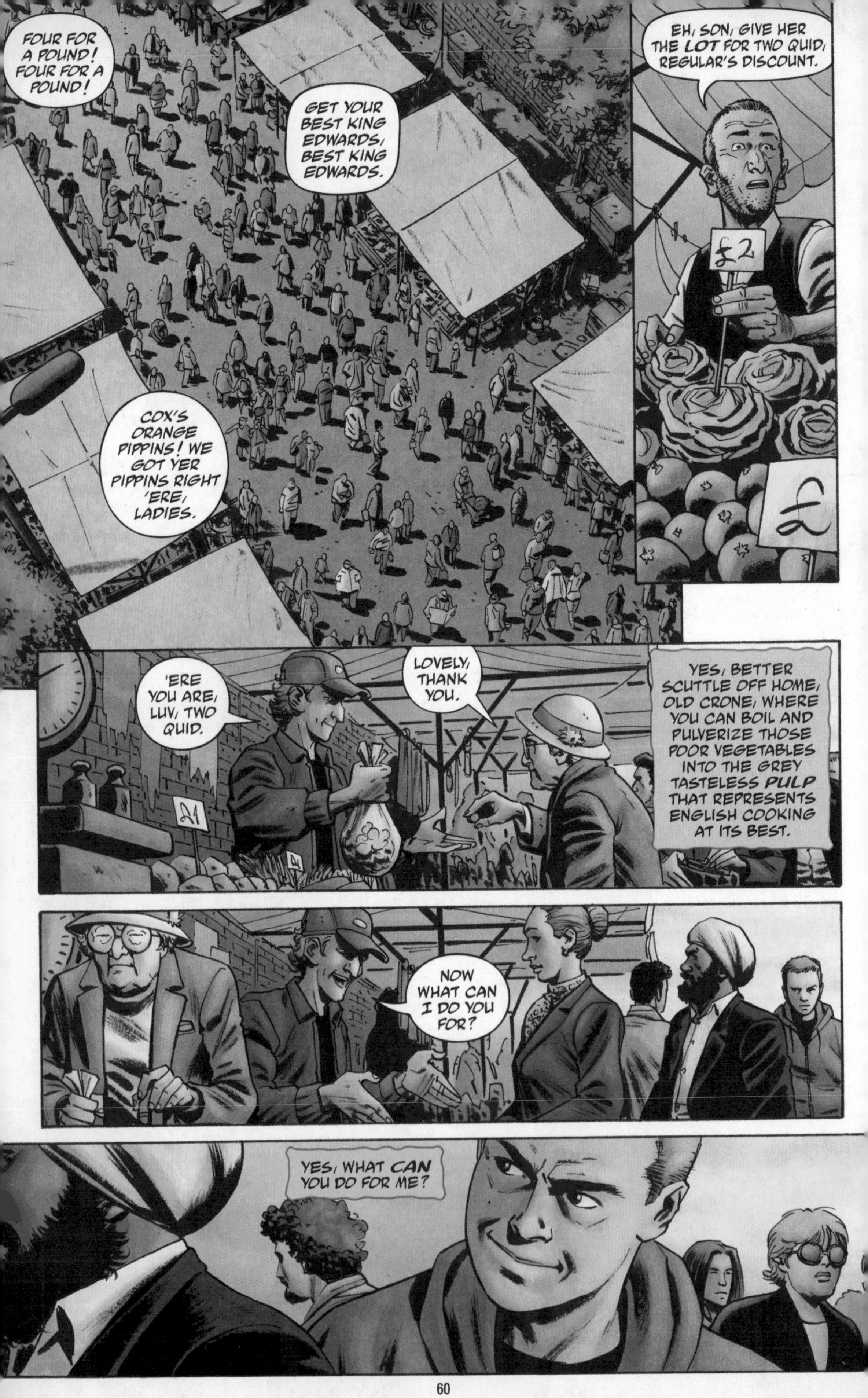
FOUR FOR A POUND! FOUR FOR A POUND!
GET YOUR BEST KING EDWARDS, BEST KING EDWARDS.
COX'S ORANGE PIPPINS! WE GOT YER PIPPINS RIGHT 'ERE, LADIES.
EH, SON, GIVE HER THE LOT FOR TWO QUID, REGULAR'S DISCOUNT.
£2
£
'ERE YOU ARE, LUV, TWO QUID.
LOVELY, THANK YOU.
YES, BETTER SCUTTLE OFF HOME, OLD CRONE, WHERE YOU CAN BOIL AND PULVERIZE THOSE POOR VEGETABLES INTO THE GREY TASTELESS PULP THAT REPRESENTS ENGLISH COOKING AT ITS BEST.
NOW WHAT CAN I DO YOU FOR?
YES, WHAT CAN YOU DO FOR ME?

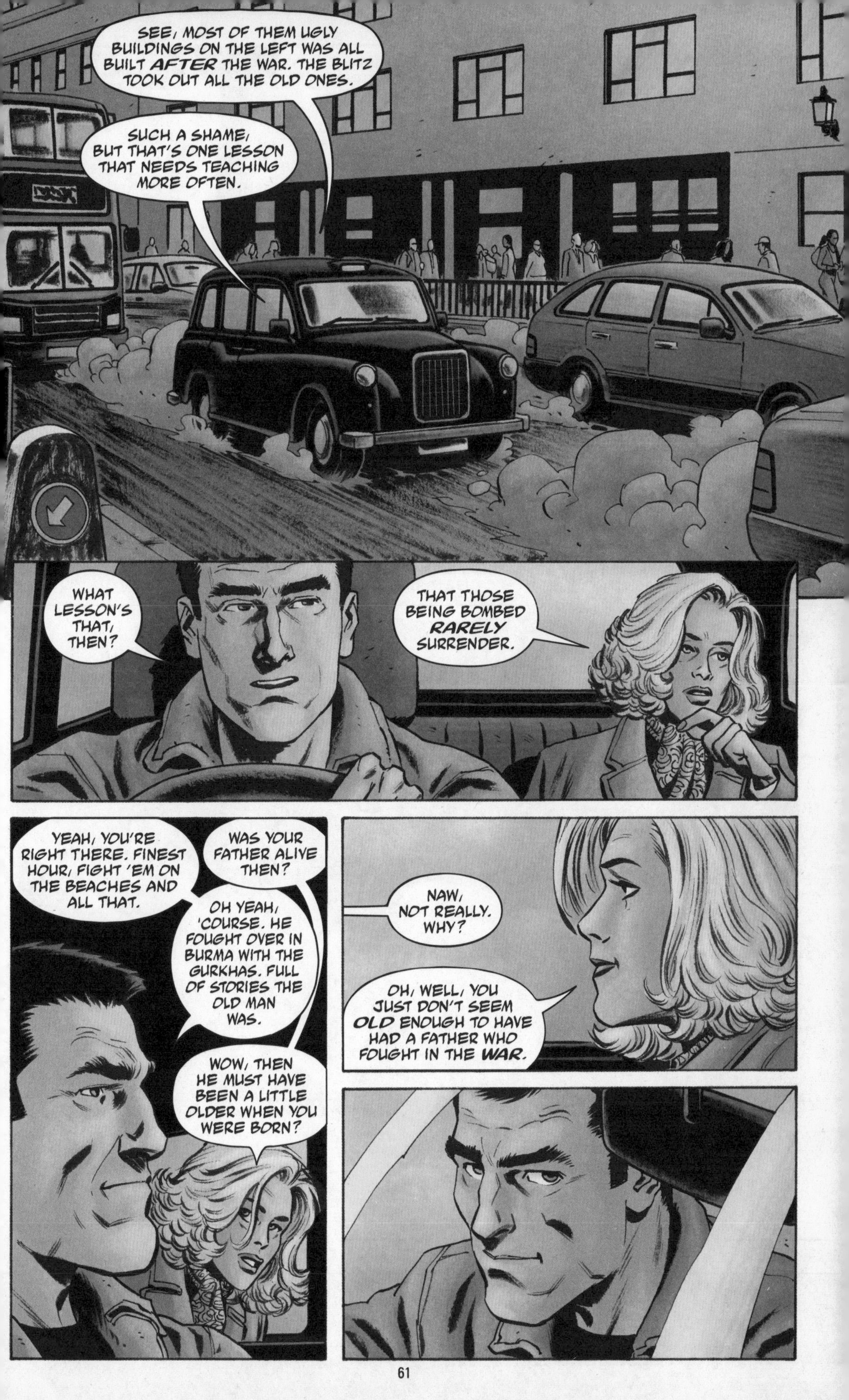

SEE, MOST OF THEM UGLY BUILDINGS ON THE LEFT WAS ALL BUILT AFTER THE WAR. THE BLITZ TOOK OUT ALL THE OLD ONES.
SUCH A SHAME, BUT THAT'S ONE LESSON THAT NEEDS TEACHING MORE OFTEN.
WHAT LESSON'S THAT, THEN?
THAT THOSE BEING BOMBED RARELY SURRENDER.
YEAH, YOU'RE RIGHT THERE. FINEST HOUR, FIGHT 'EM ON THE BEACHES AND ALL THAT.
WAS YOUR FATHER ALIVE THEN?
OH YEAH, 'COURSE. HE FOUGHT OVER IN BURMA WITH THE GURKHAS. FULL OF STORIES THE OLD MAN WAS.
WOW, THEN HE MUST HAVE BEEN A LITTLE OLDER WHEN YOU WERE BORN?
NAW, NOT REALLY. WHY?
OH, WELL, YOU JUST DON'T SEEM OLD ENOUGH TO HAVE HAD A FATHER WHO FOUGHT IN THE WAR.

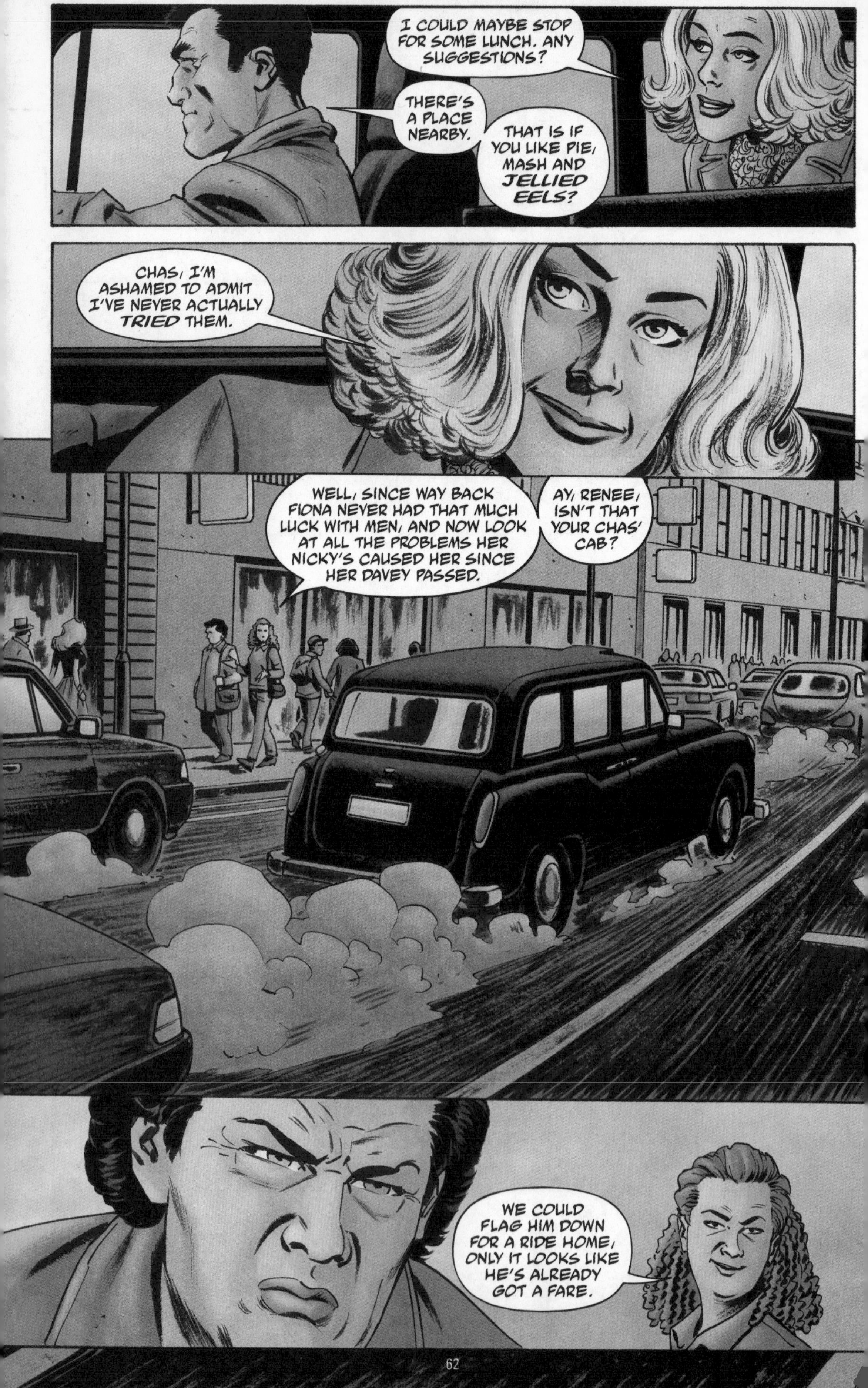
I COULD MAYBE STOP FOR SOME LUNCH. ANY SUGGESTIONS?
THERE'S A PLACE NEARBY.
THAT IS IF YOU LIKE PIE, MASH AND JELLIED EELS?
CHAS, I'M ASHAMED TO ADMIT I'VE NEVER ACTUALLY TRIED THEM.
WELL, SINCE WAY BACK FIONA NEVER HAD THAT MUCH LUCK WITH MEN, AND NOW LOOK AT ALL THE PROBLEMS HER NICKY'S CAUSED HER SINCE HER DAVEY PASSED.
AY, RENEE, ISN'T THAT YOUR CHAS' CAB?
WE COULD FLAG HIM DOWN FOR A RIDE HOME, ONLY IT LOOKS LIKE HE'S ALREADY GOT A FARE.

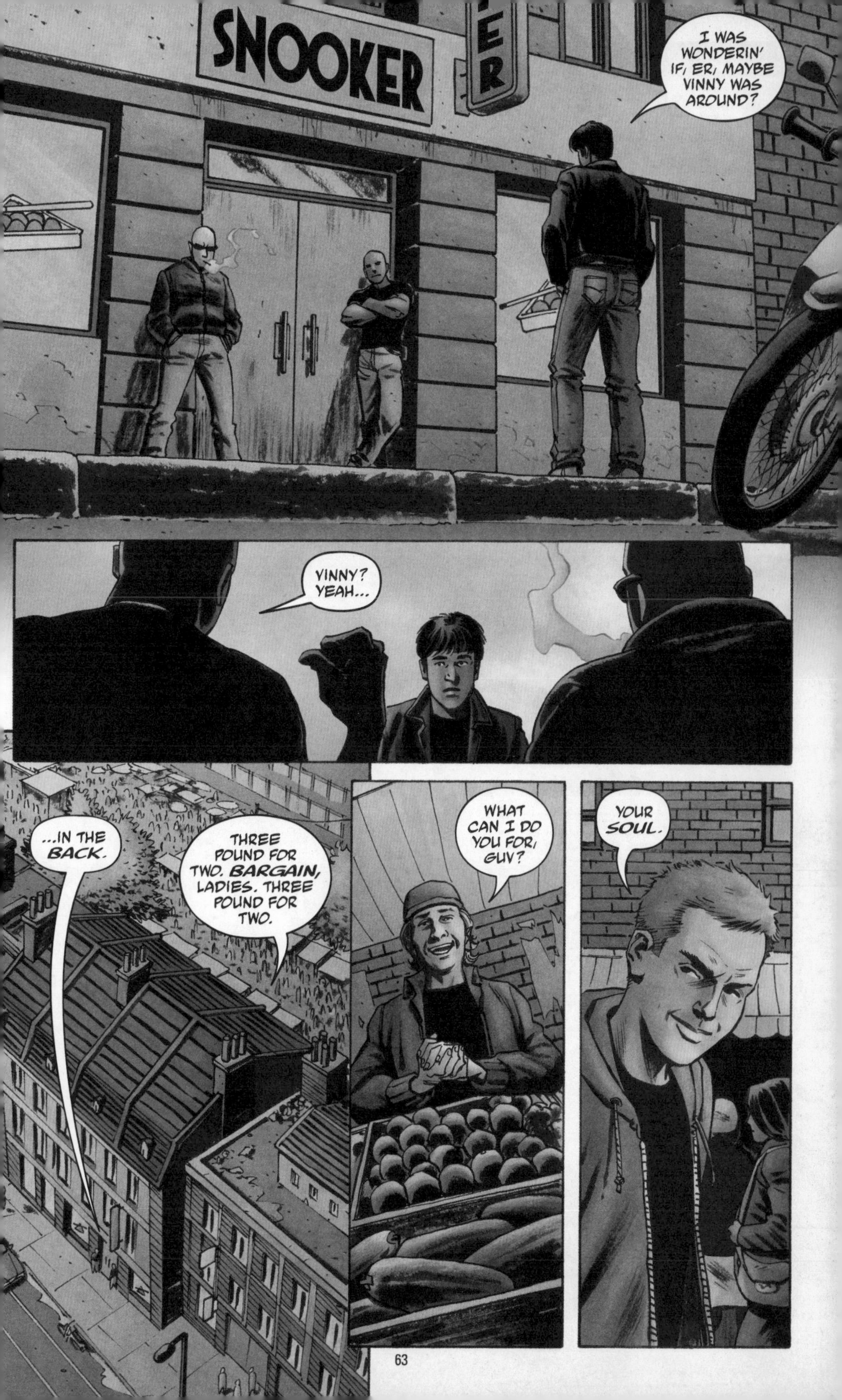
SNOOKER
ER
I WAS WONDERIN' IF, ER, MAYBE VINNY WAS AROUND?
VINNY? YEAH...
...IN THE BACK.
THREE POUND FOR TWO. BARGAIN, LADIES. THREE POUND FOR TWO.
WHAT CAN I DO YOU FOR, GUV?
YOUR SOUL.

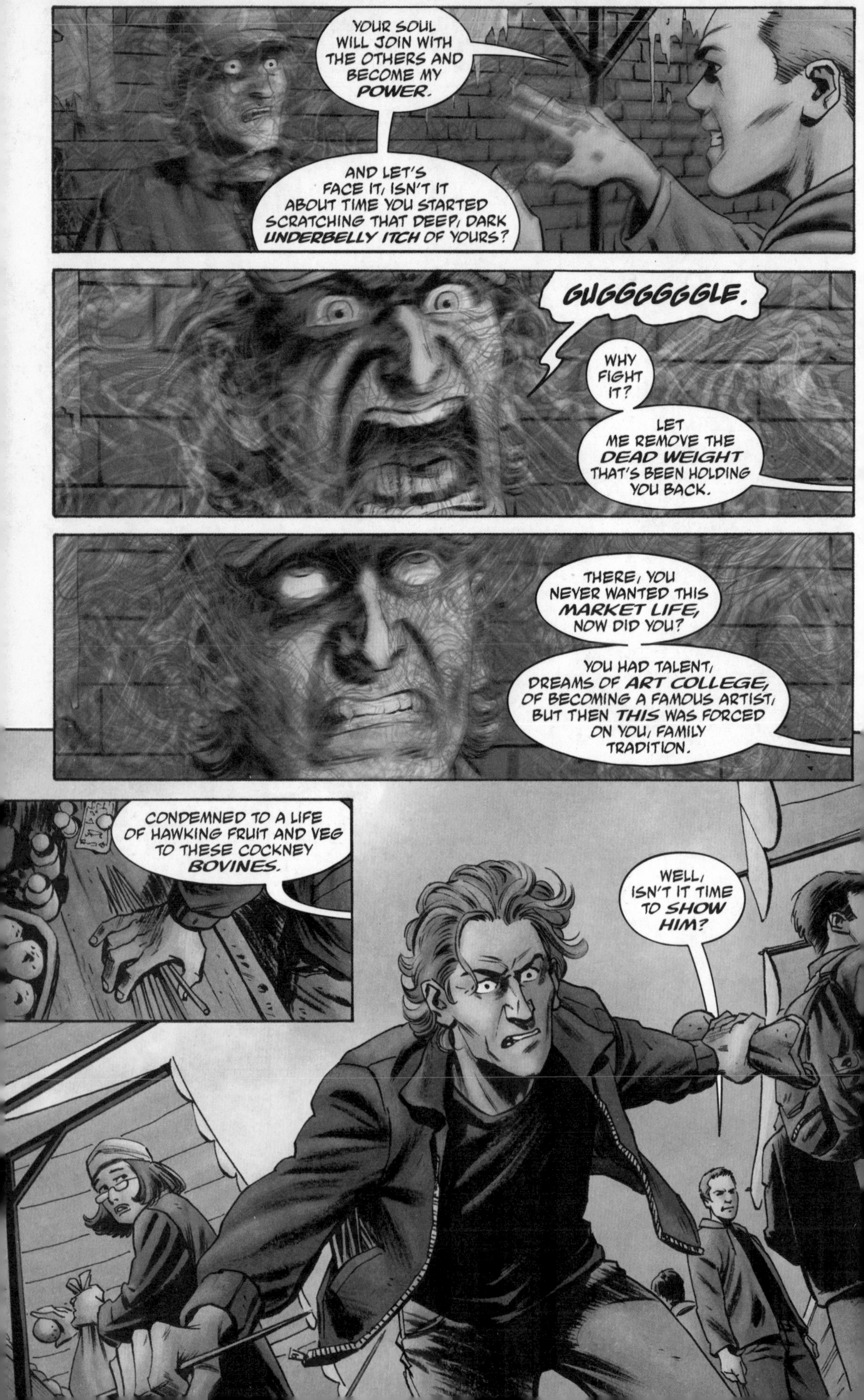
YOUR SOUL WILL JOIN WITH THE OTHERS AND BECOME MY *POWER*.
AND LET'S FACE IT, ISN'T IT ABOUT TIME YOU STARTED SCRATCHING THAT DEEP, DARK *UNDERBELLY ITCH* OF YOURS?
GUGGGGGGLE.
WHY FIGHT IT?
LET ME REMOVE THE *DEAD WEIGHT* THAT'S BEEN HOLDING YOU BACK.
THERE, YOU NEVER WANTED THIS *MARKET LIFE*, NOW DID YOU?
YOU HAD TALENT, DREAMS OF *ART COLLEGE*, OF BECOMING A FAMOUS ARTIST, BUT THEN *THIS* WAS FORCED ON YOU, FAMILY TRADITION.
CONDEMNED TO A LIFE OF HAWKING FRUIT AND VEG TO THESE COCKNEY *BOVINES*.
WELL, ISN'T IT TIME TO *SHOW HIM*?

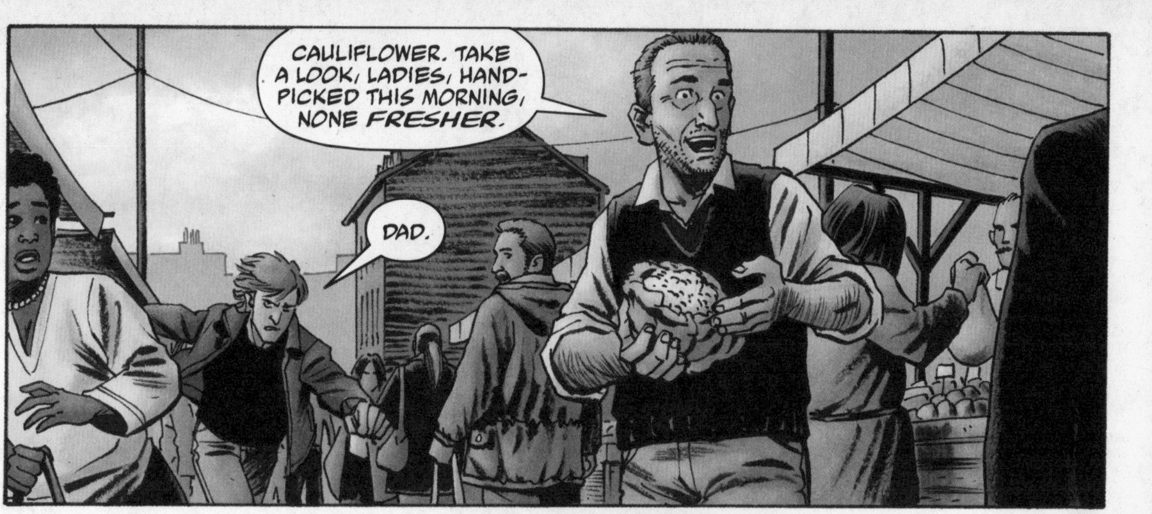
CAULIFLOWER. TAKE A LOOK, LADIES, HAND-PICKED THIS MORNING, NONE FRESHER.
DAD.

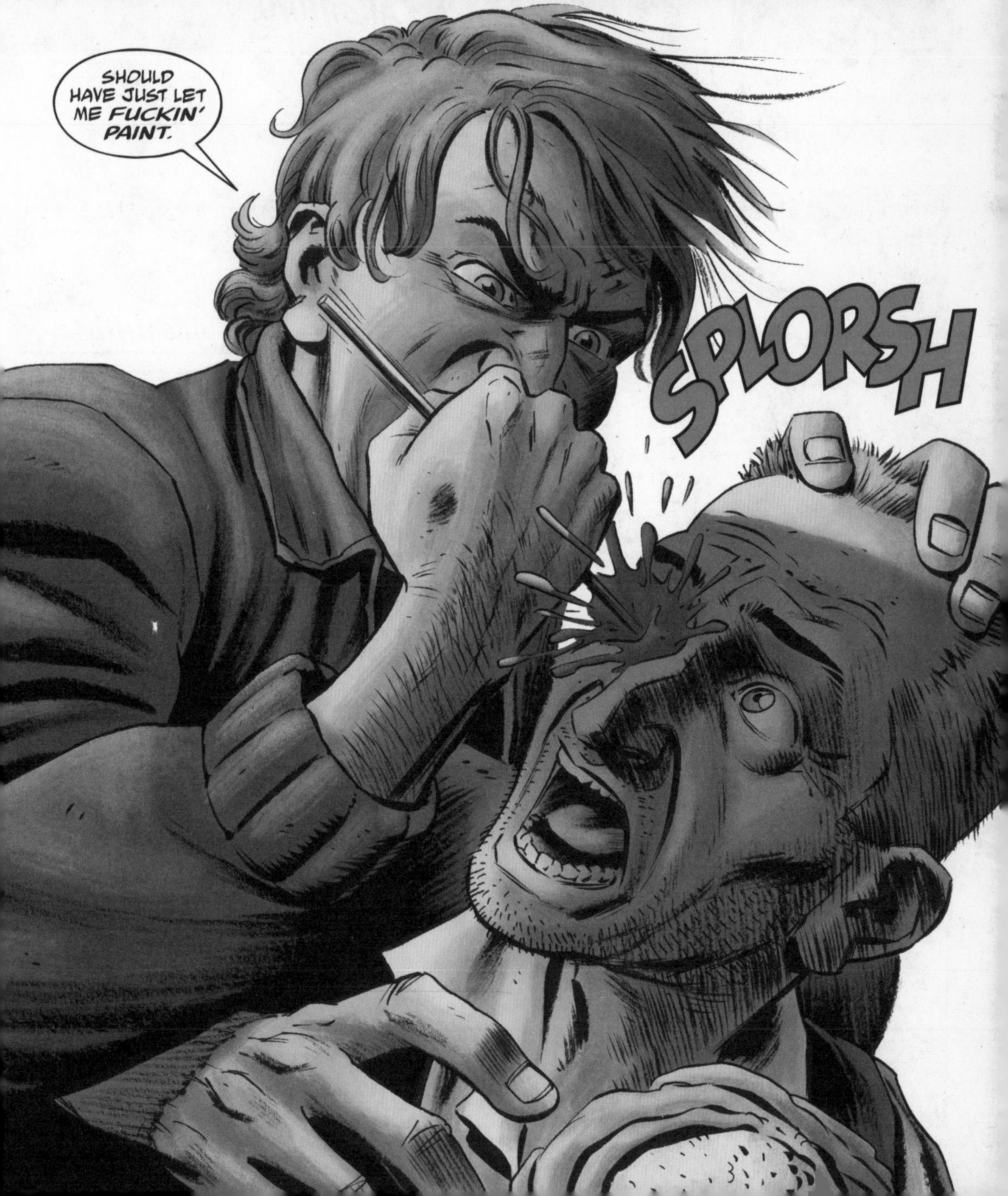
SHOULD HAVE JUST LET ME FUCKIN' PAINT.
SPLORSH

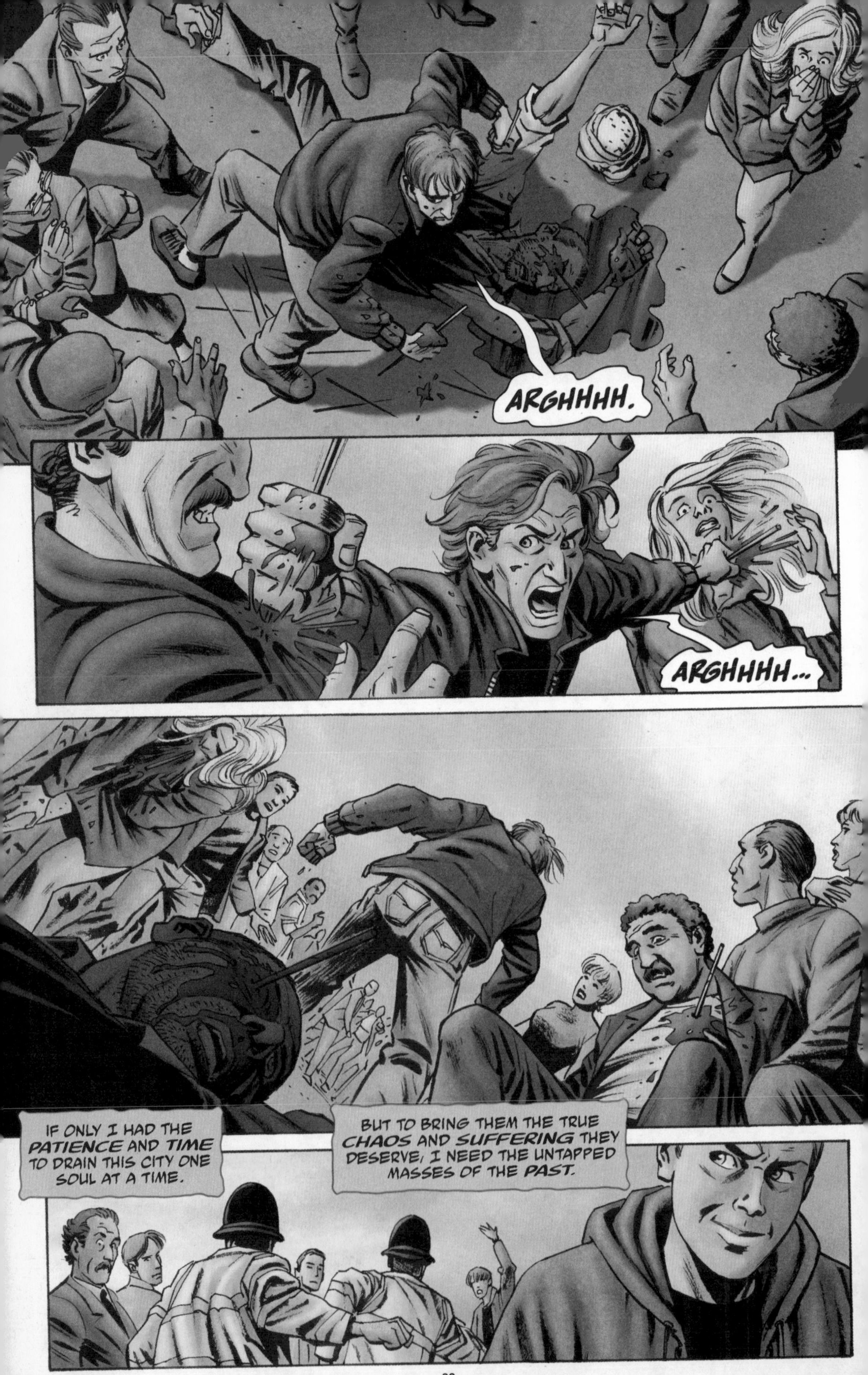
ARGHHHH.
ARGHHHH...
IF ONLY I HAD THE *PATIENCE* AND *TIME* TO DRAIN THIS CITY ONE SOUL AT A TIME.
BUT TO BRING THEM THE TRUE *CHAOS* AND *SUFFERING* THEY DESERVE, I NEED THE UNTAPPED MASSES OF THE *PAST*.

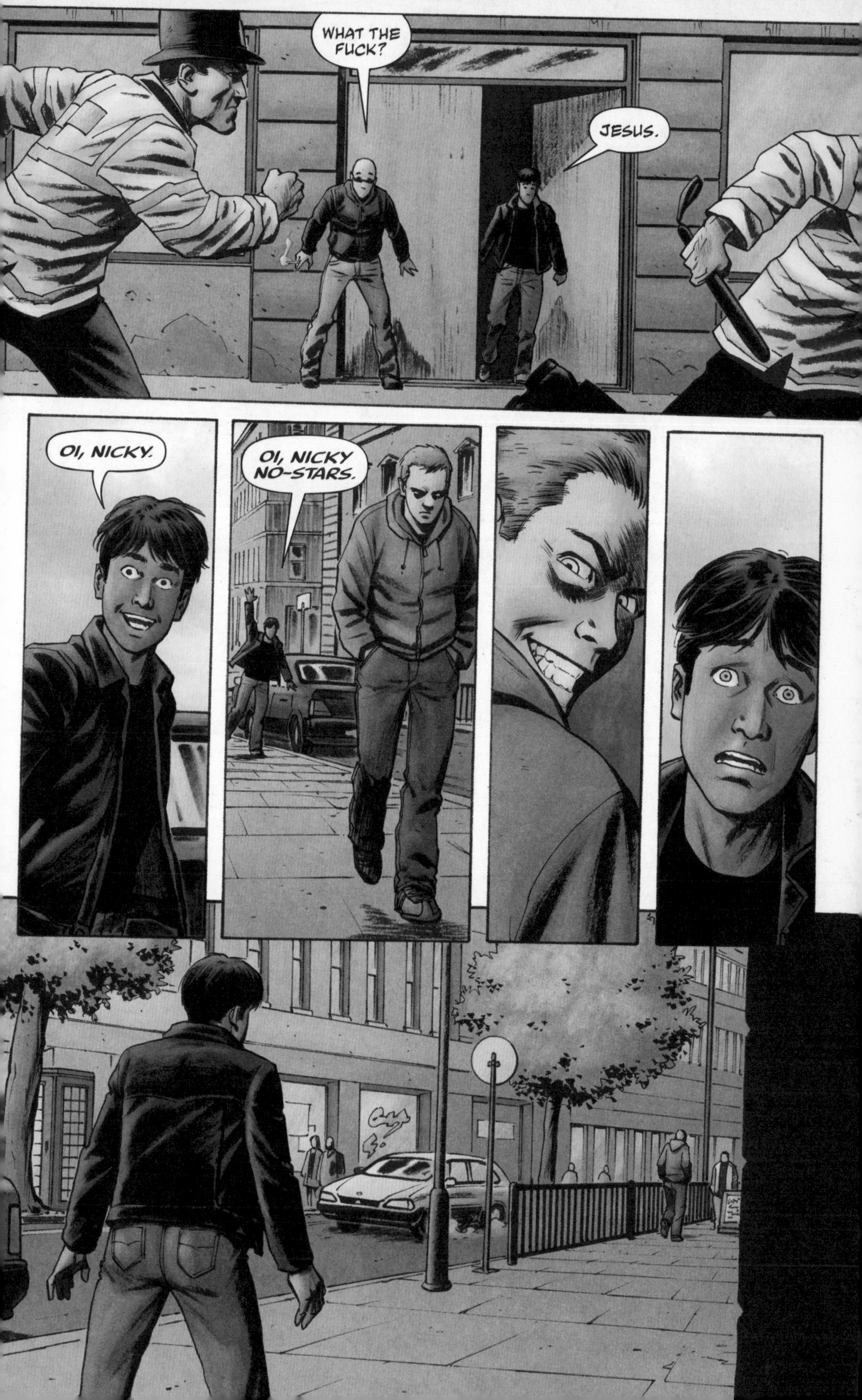
WHAT THE FUCK?
JESUS.
OI, NICKY.
OI, NICKY NO-STARS.

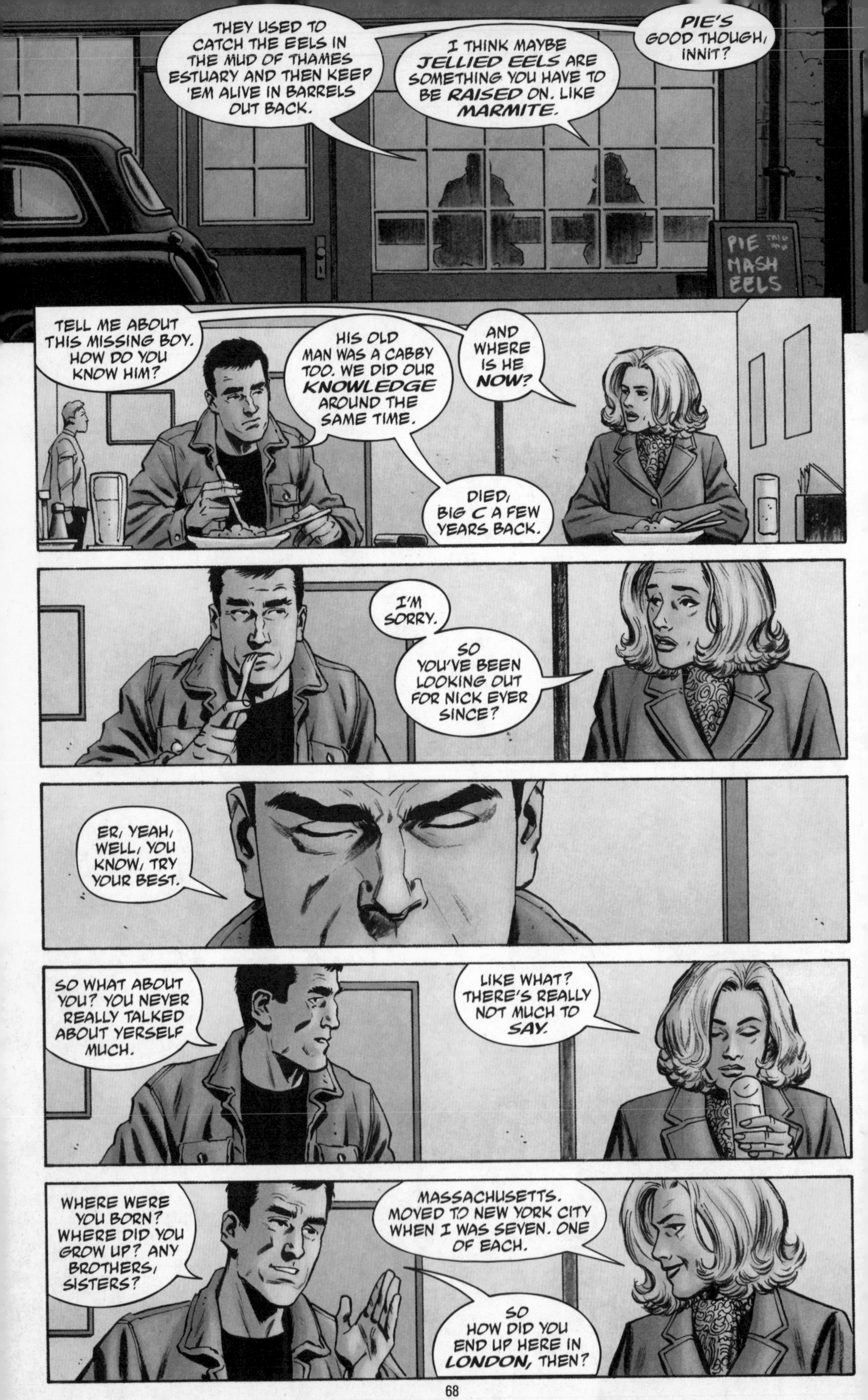

THEY USED TO CATCH THE EELS IN THE MUD OF THAMES ESTUARY AND THEN KEEP 'EM ALIVE IN BARRELS OUT BACK.
I THINK MAYBE JELLIED EELS ARE SOMETHING YOU HAVE TO BE RAISED ON. LIKE MARMITE.
PIE'S GOOD THOUGH, INNIT?
PIE
MASH
EELS
TELL ME ABOUT THIS MISSING BOY. HOW DO YOU KNOW HIM?
HIS OLD MAN WAS A CABBY TOO. WE DID OUR KNOWLEDGE AROUND THE SAME TIME.
AND WHERE IS HE NOW?
DIED, BIG C A FEW YEARS BACK.
I'M SORRY.
SO YOU'VE BEEN LOOKING OUT FOR NICK EVER SINCE?
ER, YEAH, WELL, YOU KNOW, TRY YOUR BEST.
SO WHAT ABOUT YOU? YOU NEVER REALLY TALKED ABOUT YERSELF MUCH.
LIKE WHAT? THERE'S REALLY NOT MUCH TO SAY.
WHERE WERE YOU BORN? WHERE DID YOU GROW UP? ANY BROTHERS, SISTERS?
MASSACHUSETTS. MOVED TO NEW YORK CITY WHEN I WAS SEVEN. ONE OF EACH.
SO HOW DID YOU END UP HERE IN LONDON, THEN?

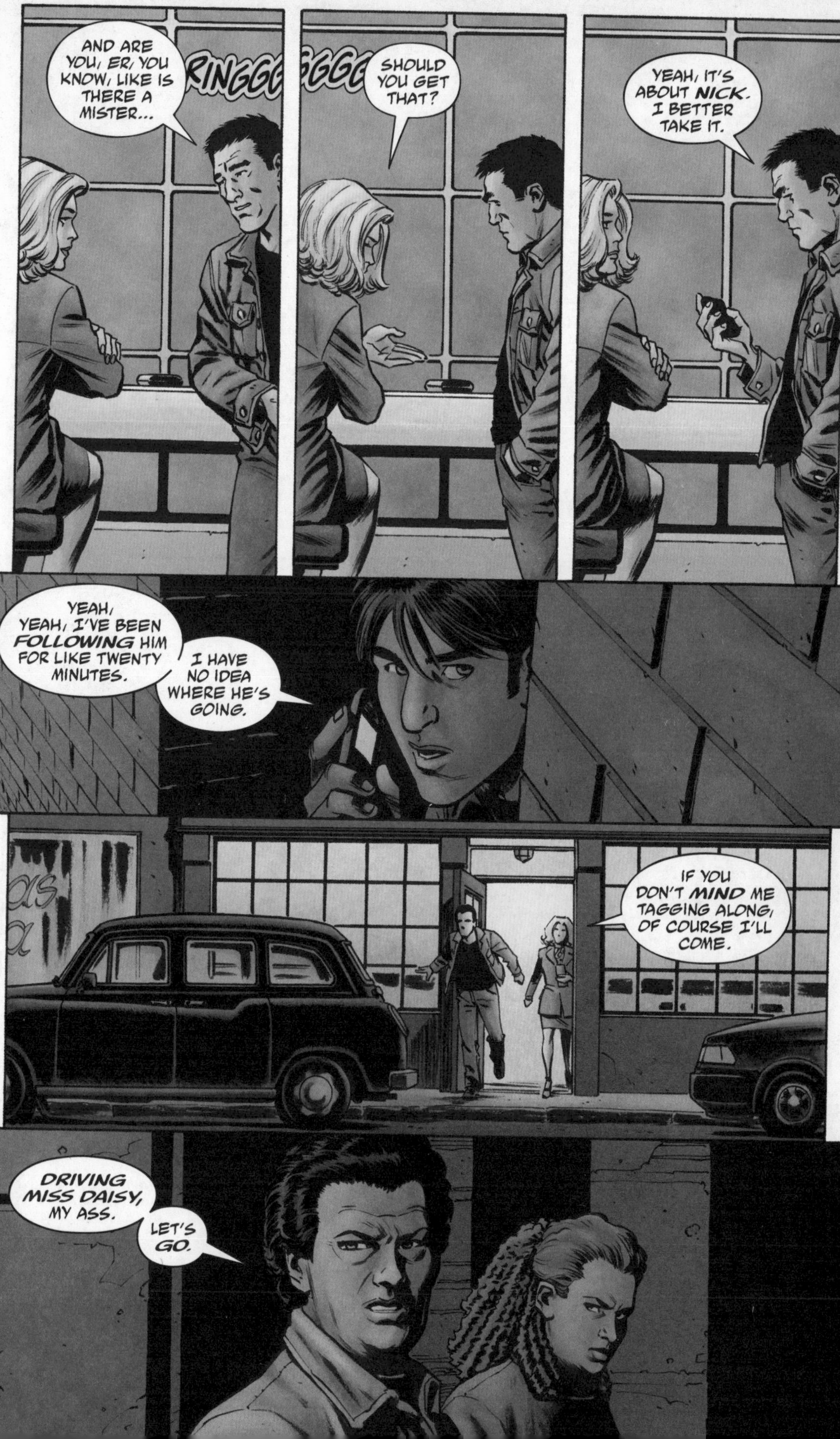
AND ARE YOU, ER, YOU KNOW, LIKE IS THERE A MISTER...
RINGGGGGGG
SHOULD YOU GET THAT?
YEAH, IT'S ABOUT NICK. I BETTER TAKE IT.
YEAH, YEAH, I'VE BEEN FOLLOWING HIM FOR LIKE TWENTY MINUTES.
I HAVE NO IDEA WHERE HE'S GOING.
IF YOU DON'T MIND ME TAGGING ALONG, OF COURSE I'LL COME.
DRIVING MISS DAISY, MY ASS.
LET'S GO.

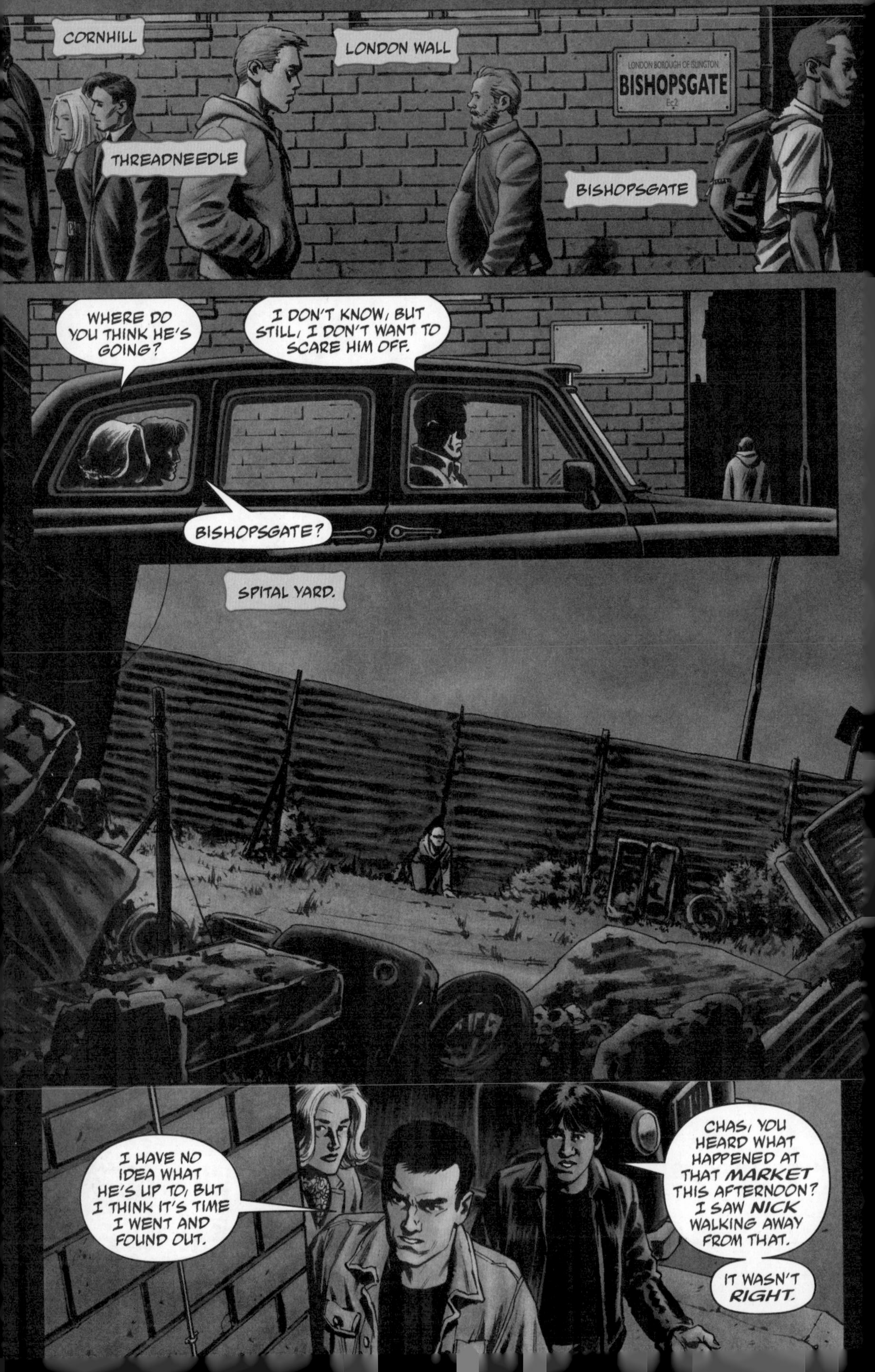
CORNHILL
LONDON WALL
LONDON BOROUGH OF ISLINGTON
BISHOPSGATE
THREADNEEDLE
BISHOPSGATE
WHERE DO YOU THINK HE'S GOING?
I DON'T KNOW, BUT STILL, I DON'T WANT TO SCARE HIM OFF.
BISHOPSGATE?
SPITAL YARD.
CHAS, YOU HEARD WHAT HAPPENED AT THAT MARKET THIS AFTERNOON? I SAW NICK WALKING AWAY FROM THAT.
IT WASN'T RIGHT.
I HAVE NO IDEA WHAT HE'S UP TO, BUT I THINK IT'S TIME I WENT AND FOUND OUT.

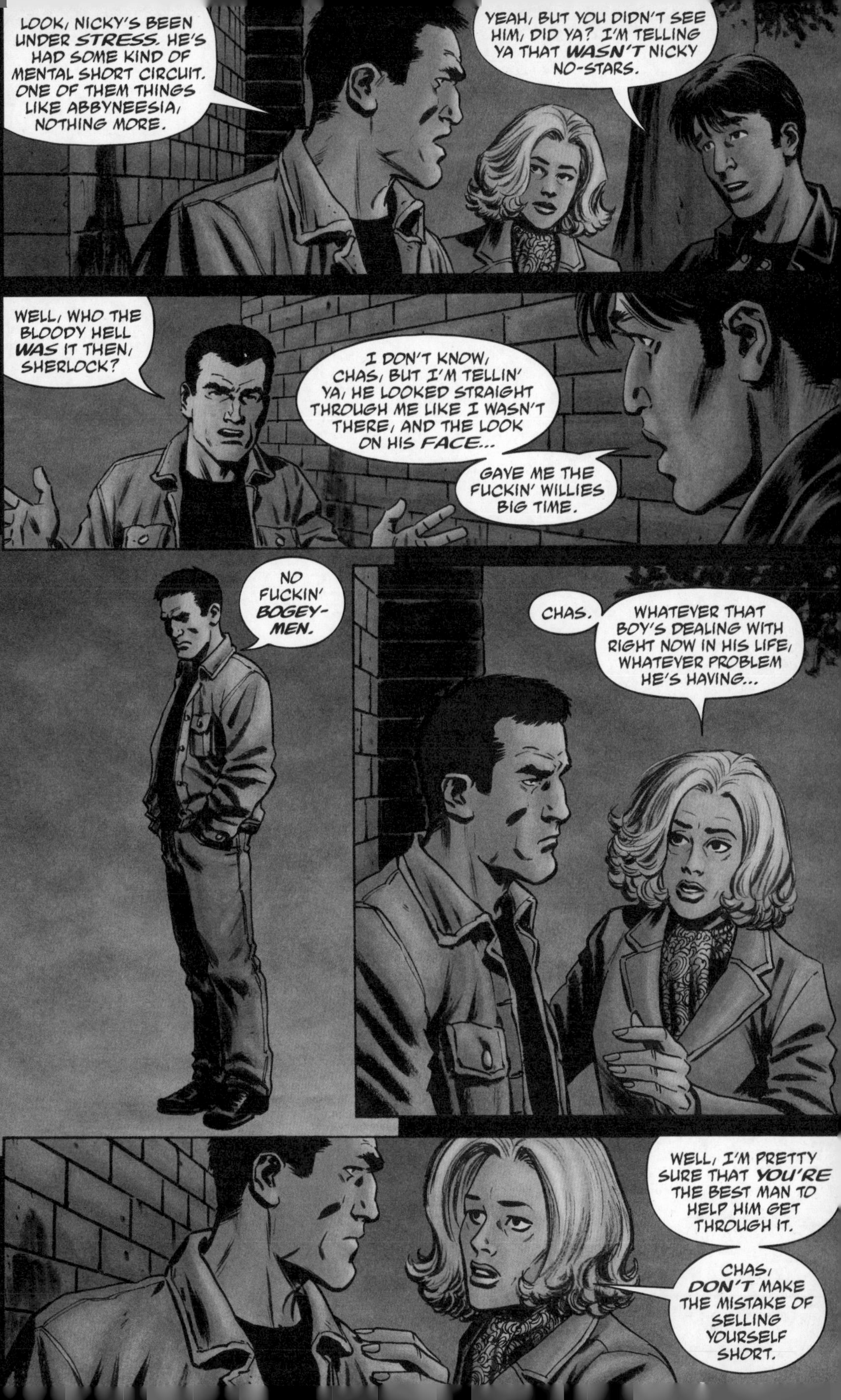
LOOK, NICKY'S BEEN UNDER STRESS. HE'S HAD SOME KIND OF MENTAL SHORT CIRCUIT. ONE OF THEM THINGS LIKE ABBYNEESIA, NOTHING MORE.
YEAH, BUT YOU DIDN'T SEE HIM, DID YA? I'M TELLING YA THAT WASN'T NICKY NO-STARS.
WELL, WHO THE BLOODY HELL WAS IT THEN, SHERLOCK?
I DON'T KNOW, CHAS, BUT I'M TELLIN' YA, HE LOOKED STRAIGHT THROUGH ME LIKE I WASN'T THERE, AND THE LOOK ON HIS FACE...
GAVE ME THE FUCKIN' WILLIES BIG TIME.
NO FUCKIN' BOGEY-MEN.
CHAS.
WHATEVER THAT BOY'S DEALING WITH RIGHT NOW IN HIS LIFE, WHATEVER PROBLEM HE'S HAVING...
WELL, I'M PRETTY SURE THAT YOU'RE THE BEST MAN TO HELP HIM GET THROUGH IT.
CHAS, DON'T MAKE THE MISTAKE OF SELLING YOURSELF SHORT.

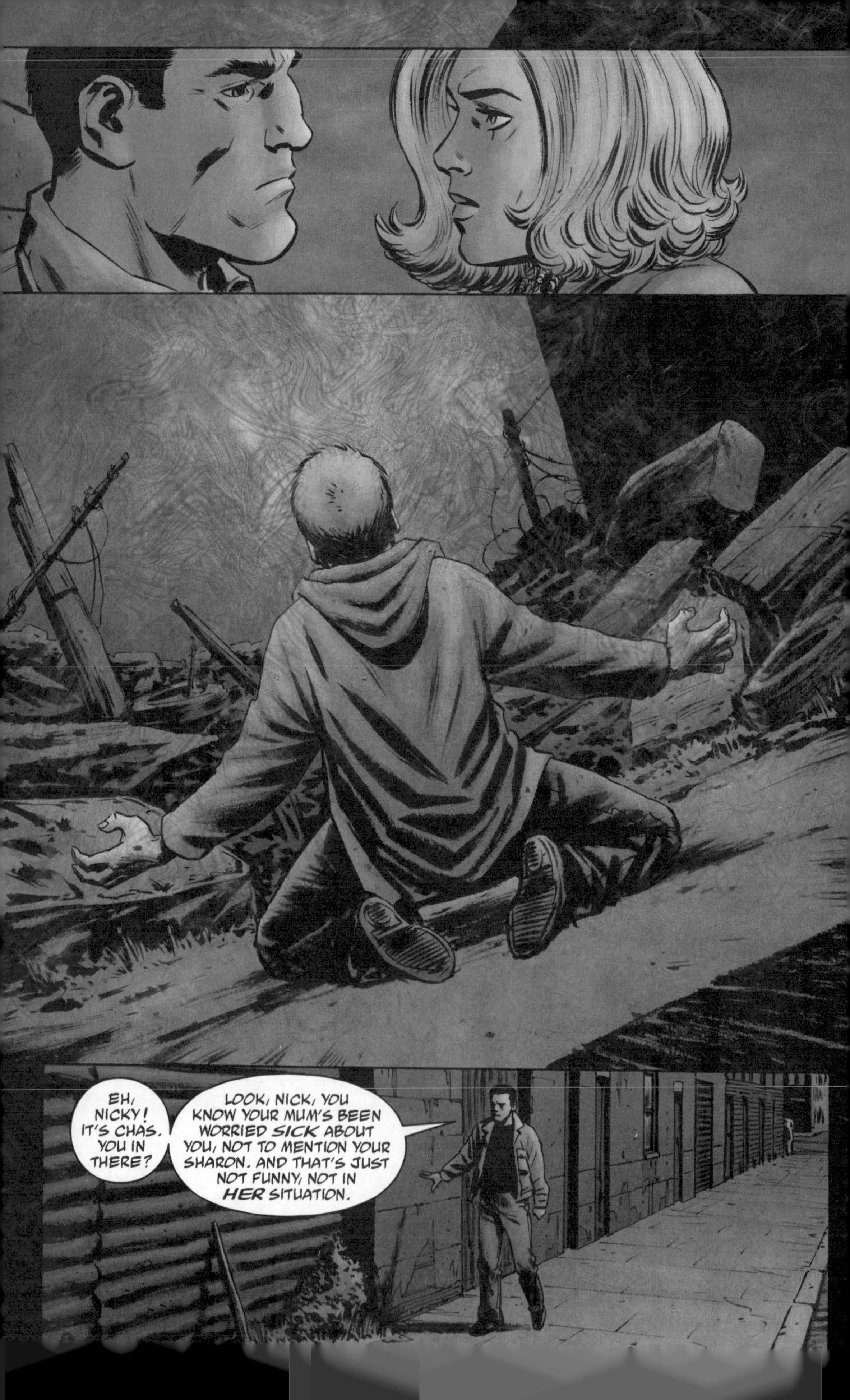
EH, NICKY! IT'S CHAS. YOU IN THERE?
LOOK, NICK, YOU KNOW YOUR MUM'S BEEN WORRIED SICK ABOUT YOU, NOT TO MENTION YOUR SHARON. AND THAT'S JUST NOT FUNNY, NOT IN HER SITUATION.

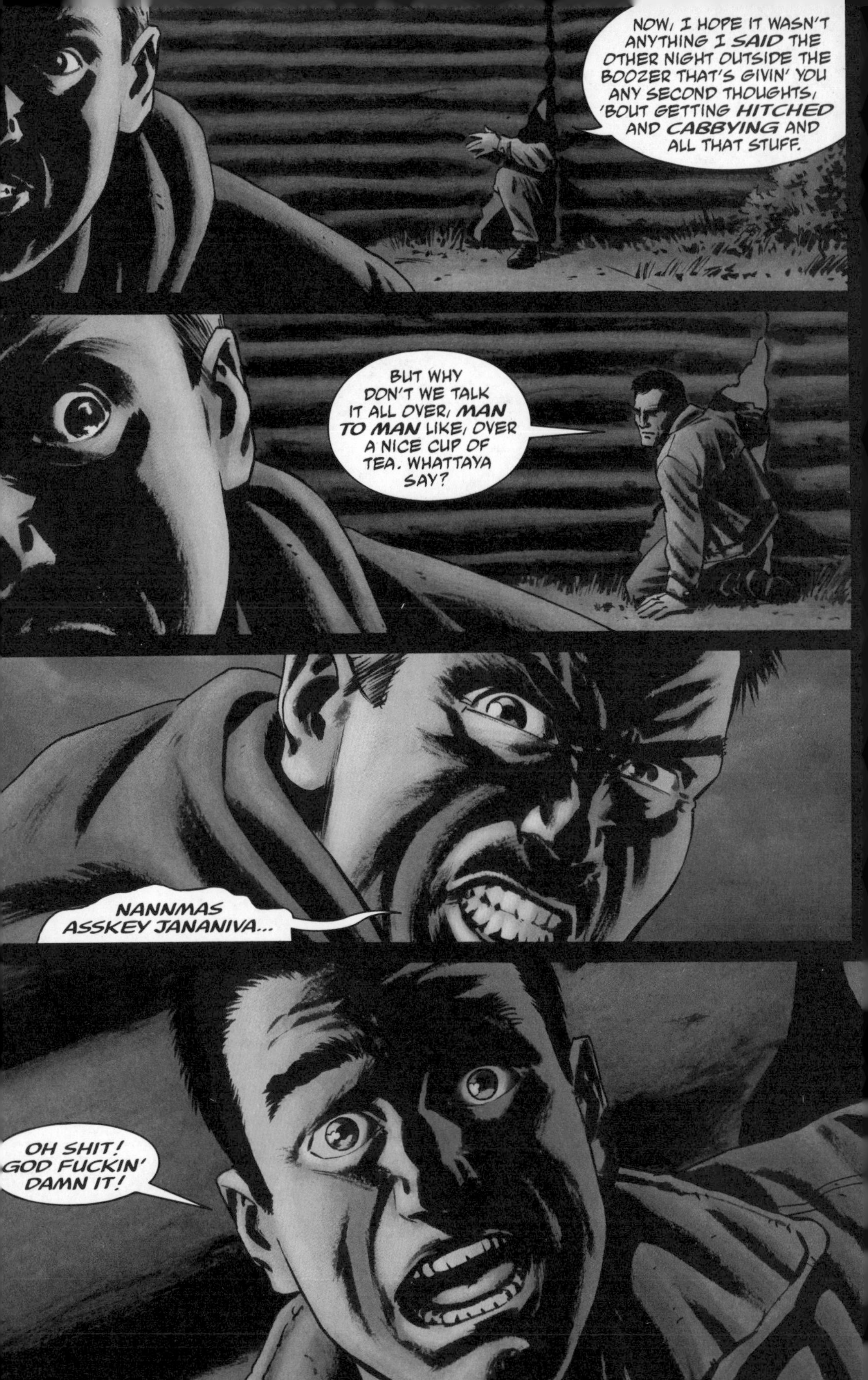
NOW, I HOPE IT WASN'T ANYTHING I *SAID* THE OTHER NIGHT OUTSIDE THE BOOZER THAT'S GIVIN' YOU ANY SECOND THOUGHTS, 'BOUT GETTING *HITCHED* AND *CABBYING* AND ALL THAT STUFF.
BUT WHY DON'T WE TALK IT ALL OVER, *MAN TO MAN* LIKE, OVER A NICE CUP OF TEA. WHATTAYA SAY?
NANNMAS ASSKEY JANANIVA...
OH SHIT! GOD FUCKIN' DAMN IT!

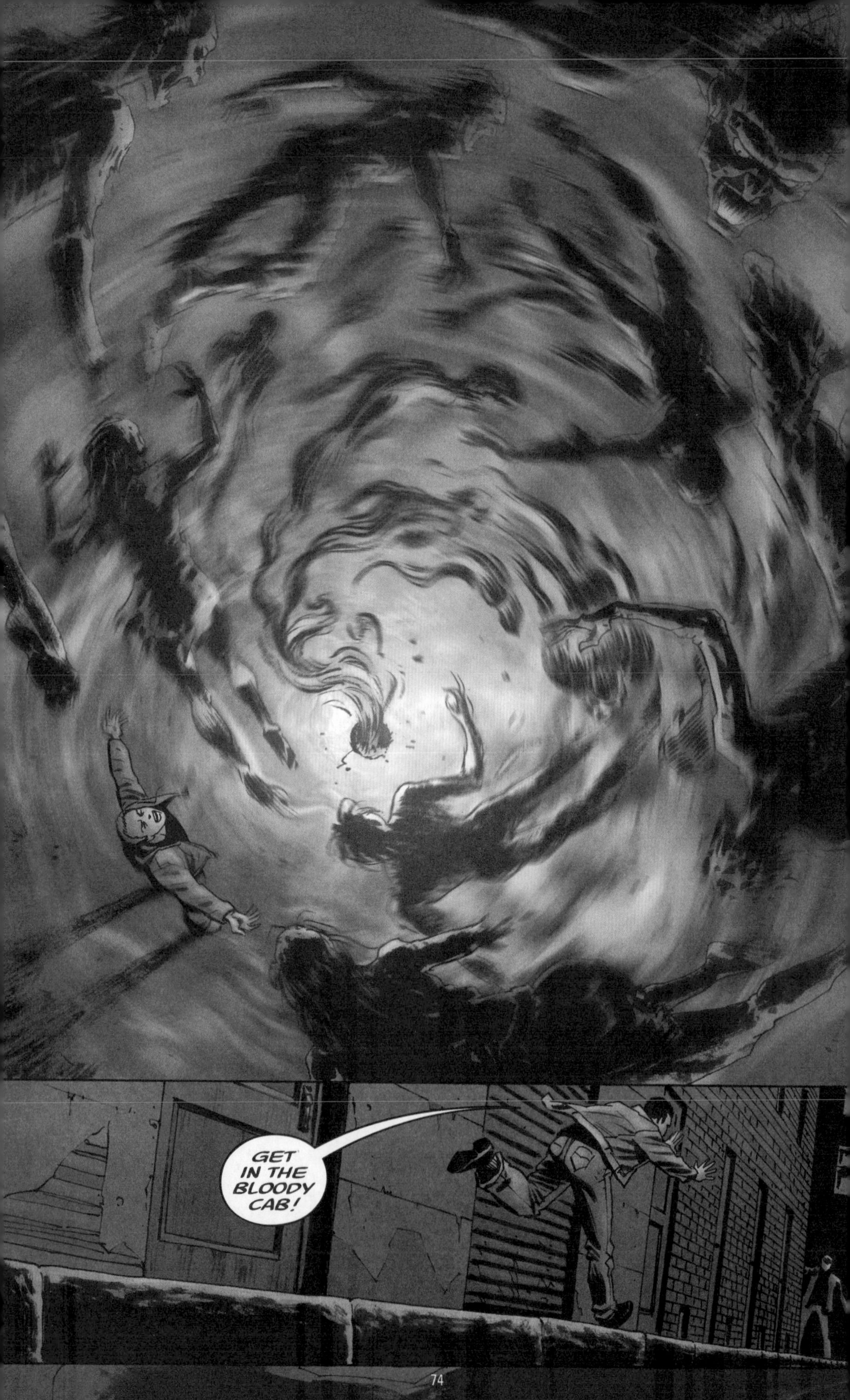
GET IN THE BLOODY CAB!

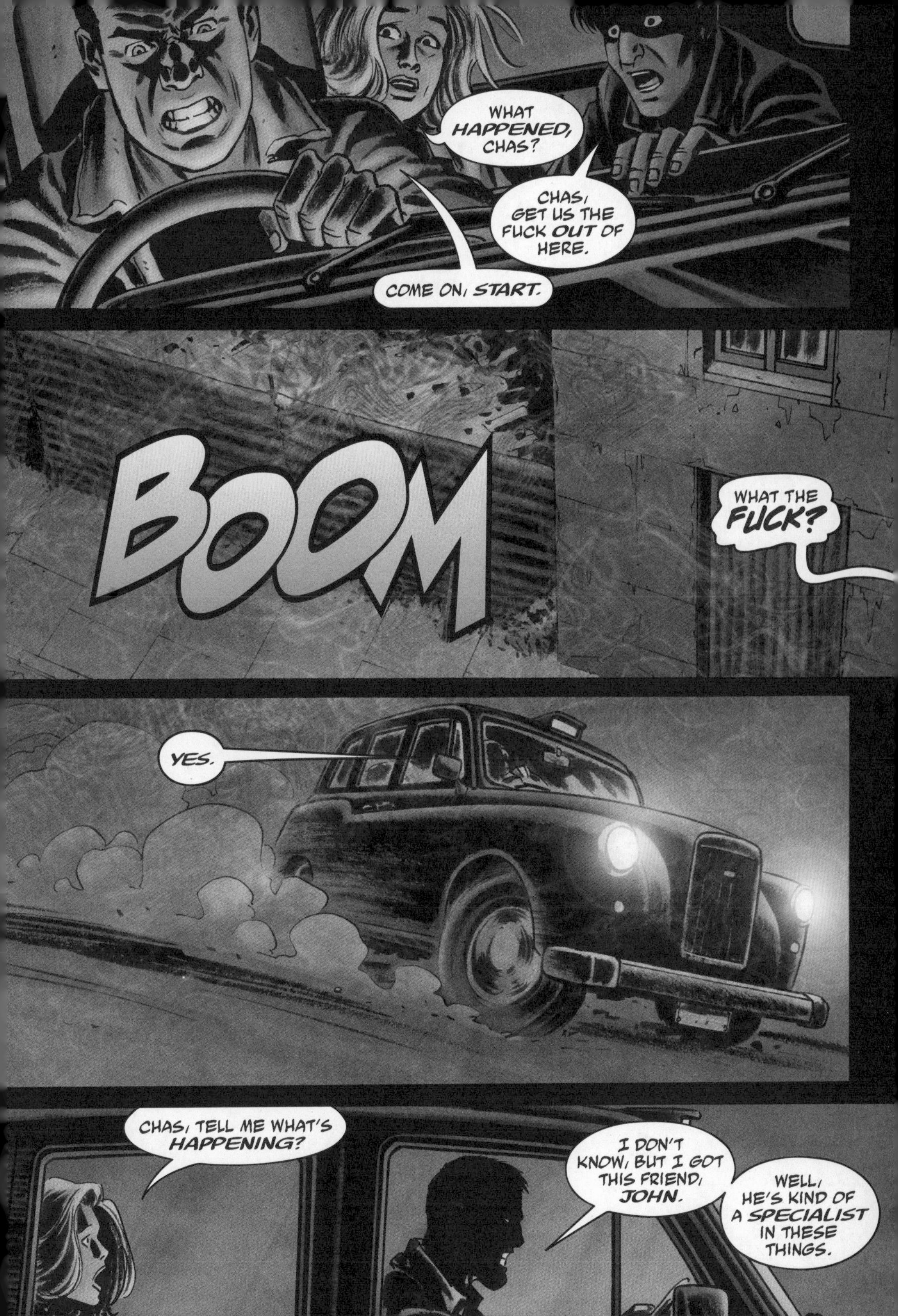

WHAT HAPPENED, CHAS?
CHAS, GET US THE FUCK OUT OF HERE.
COME ON, START.
BOOM
WHAT THE FUCK?
YES.
CHAS, TELL ME WHAT'S HAPPENING?
I DON'T KNOW, BUT I GOT THIS FRIEND, JOHN.
WELL, HE'S KIND OF A SPECIALIST IN THESE THINGS.

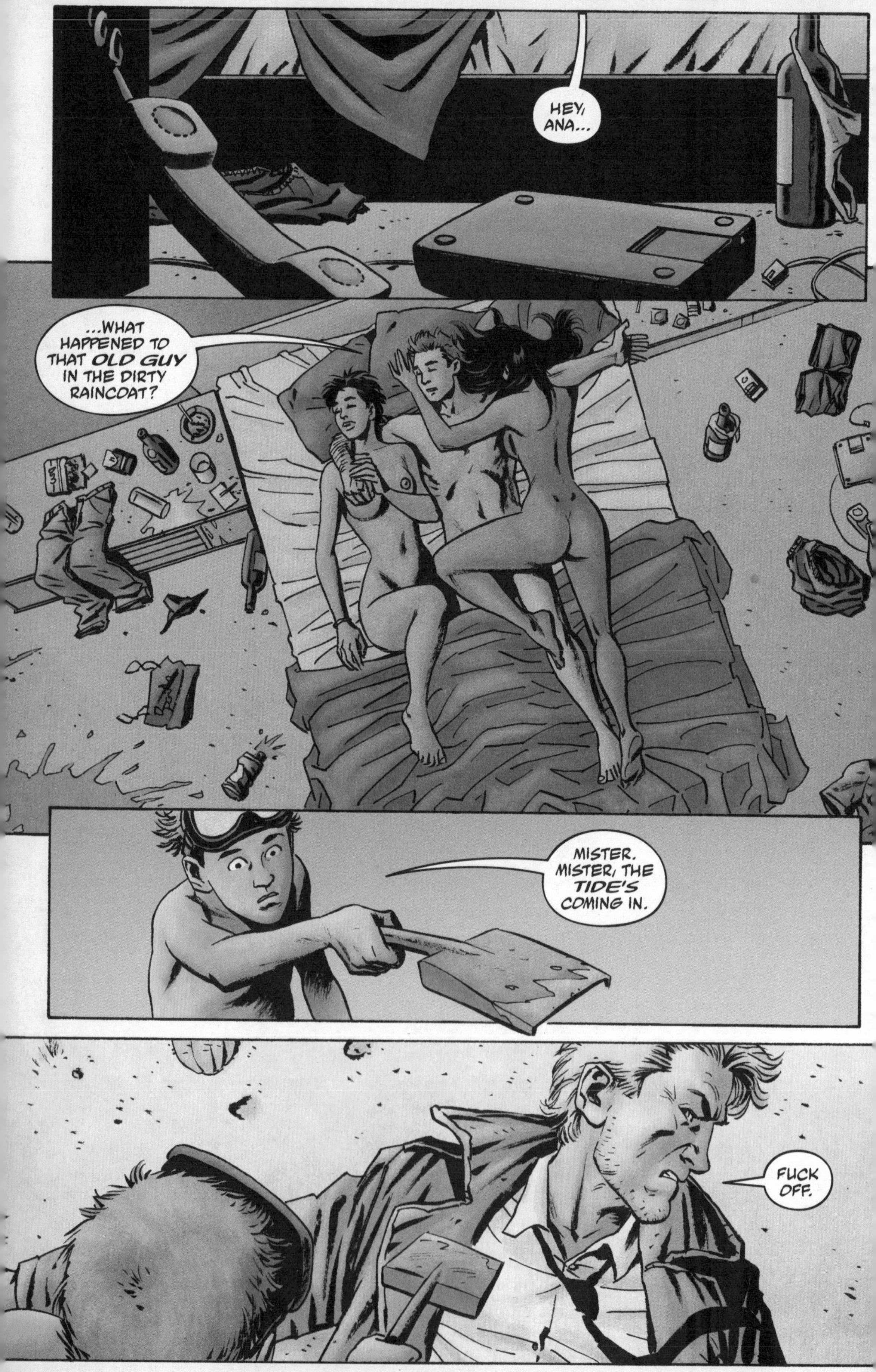
HEY, ANA...
...WHAT HAPPENED TO THAT OLD GUY IN THE DIRTY RAINCOAT?
MISTER. MISTER, THE TIDE'S COMING IN.
FUCK OFF.

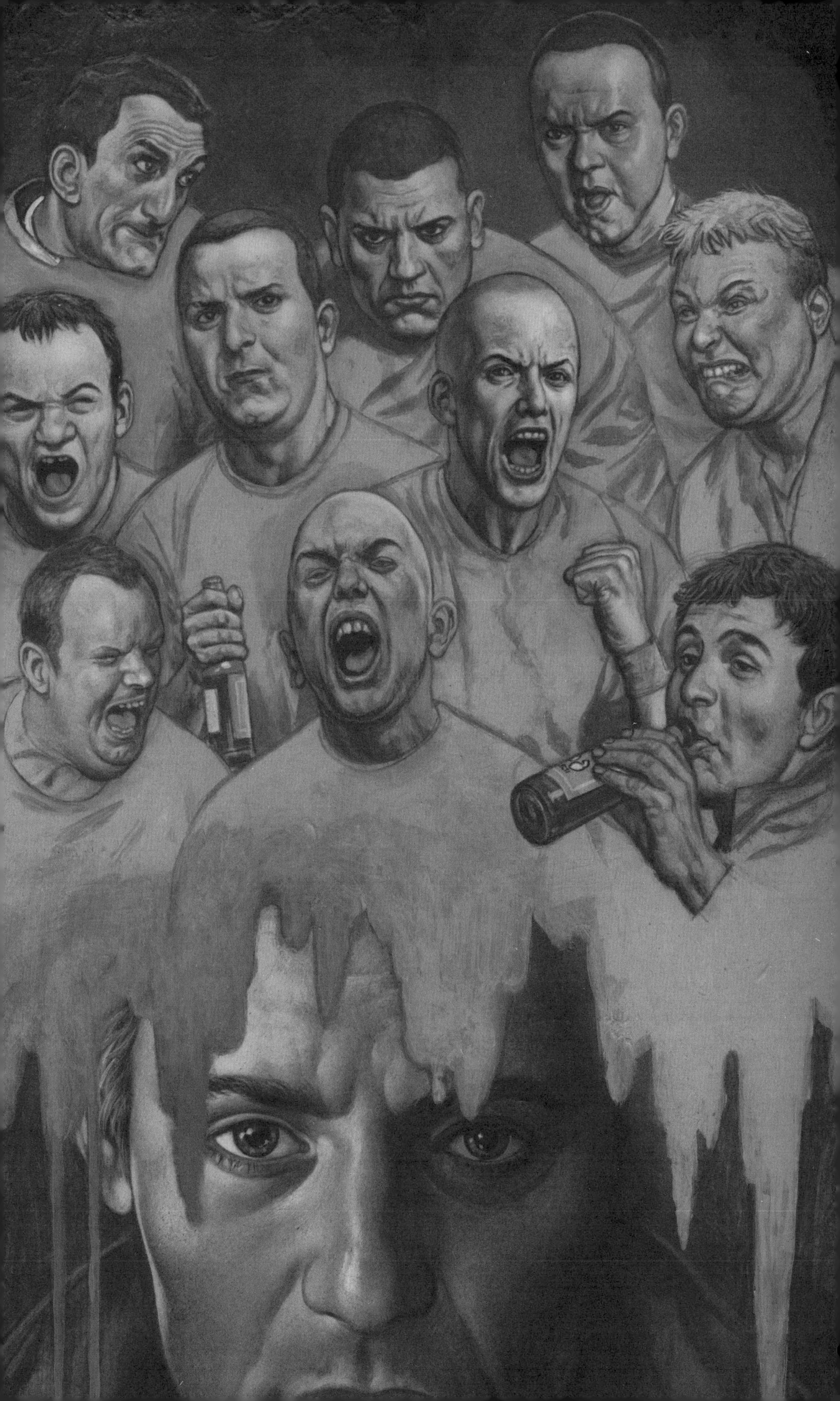

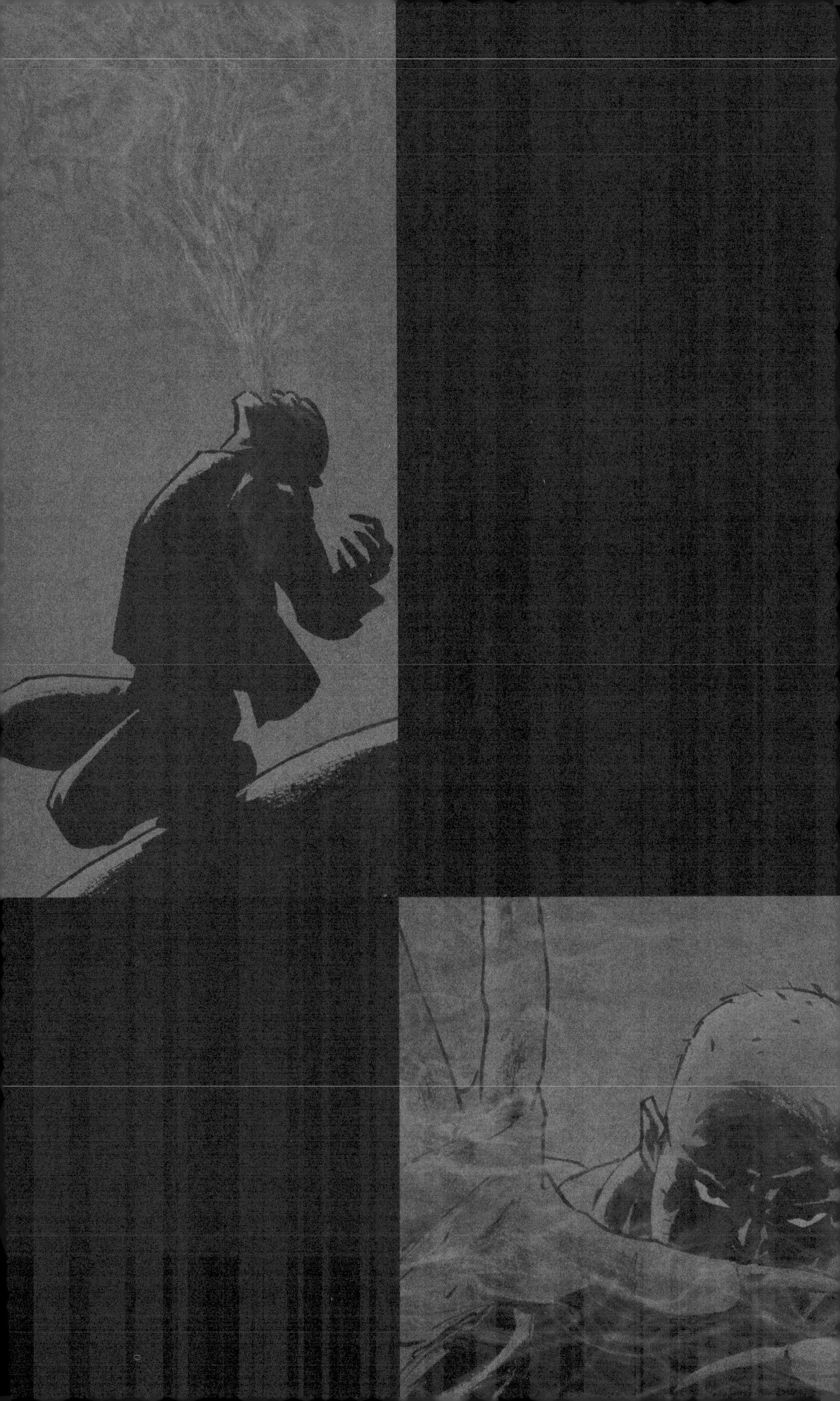

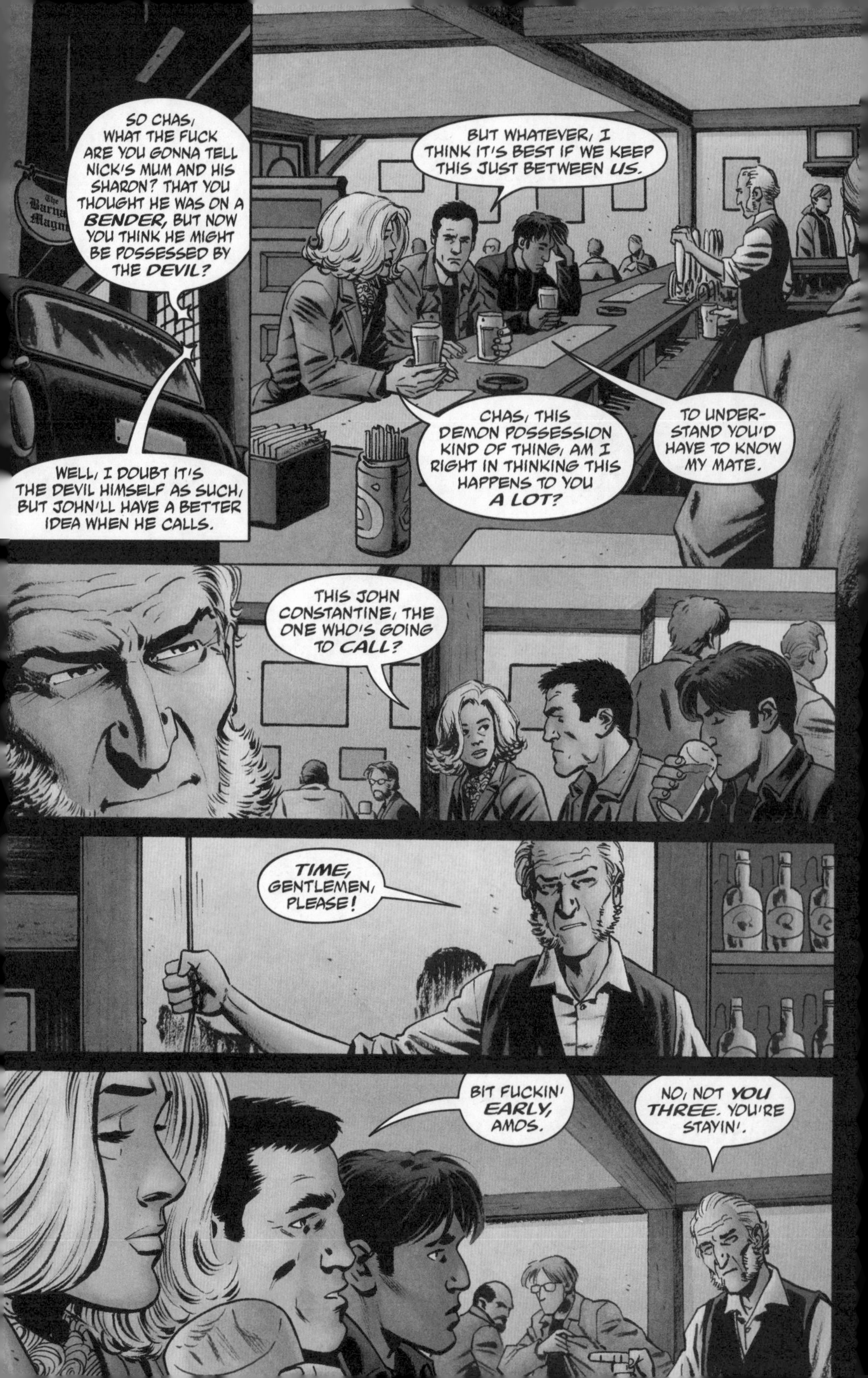
SO CHAS, WHAT THE FUCK ARE YOU GONNA TELL NICK'S MUM AND HIS SHARON? THAT YOU THOUGHT HE WAS ON A BENDER, BUT NOW YOU THINK HE MIGHT BE POSSESSED BY THE DEVIL?
WELL, I DOUBT IT'S THE DEVIL HIMSELF AS SUCH, BUT JOHN'LL HAVE A BETTER IDEA WHEN HE CALLS.
BUT WHATEVER, I THINK IT'S BEST IF WE KEEP THIS JUST BETWEEN US.
CHAS, THIS DEMON POSSESSION KIND OF THING, AM I RIGHT IN THINKING THIS HAPPENS TO YOU A LOT?
TO UNDER-STAND YOU'D HAVE TO KNOW MY MATE.
THIS JOHN CONSTANTINE, THE ONE WHO'S GOING TO CALL?
TIME, GENTLEMEN, PLEASE!
BIT FUCKIN' EARLY, AMOS.
NO, NOT YOU THREE. YOU'RE STAYIN'.

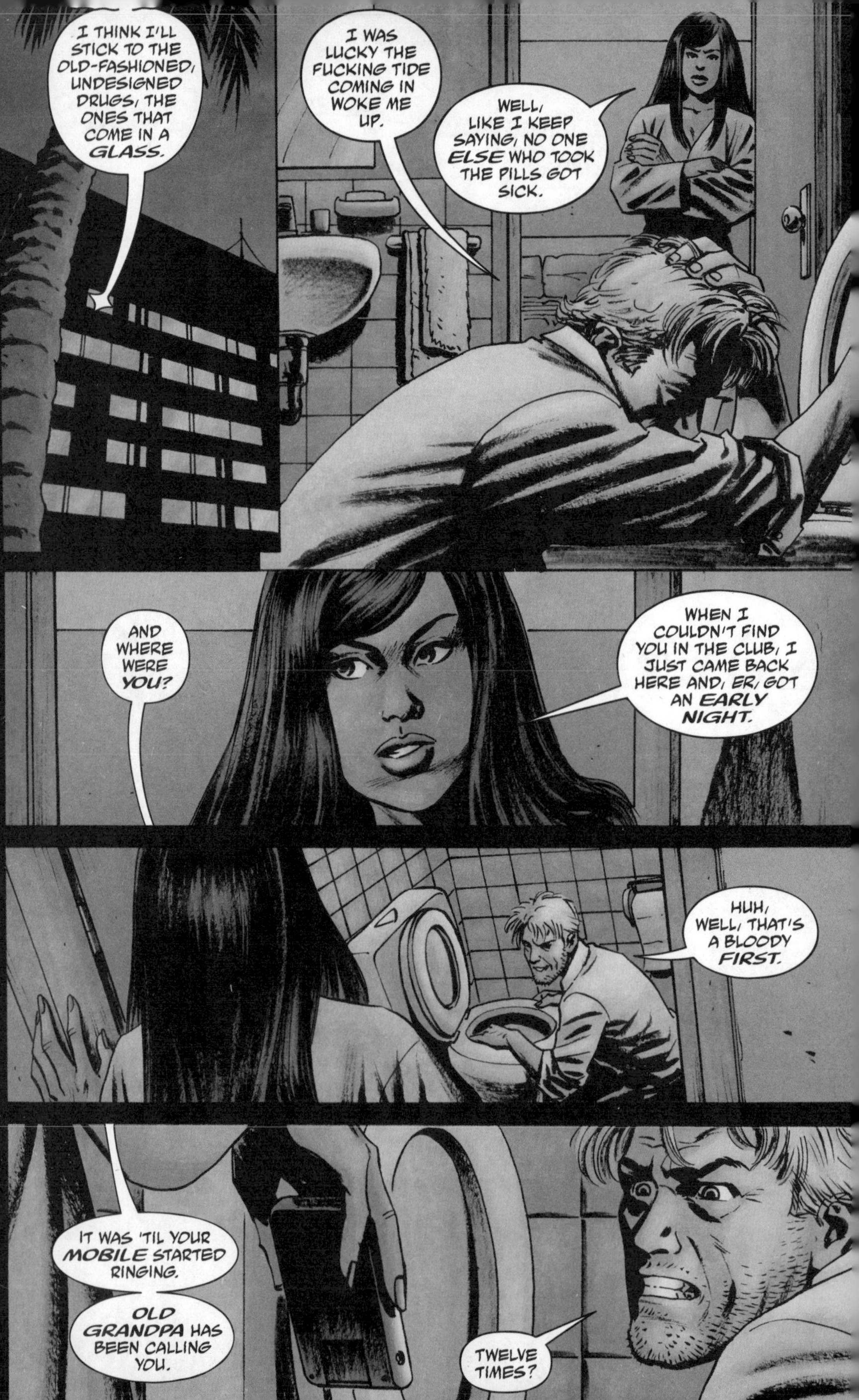
I THINK I'LL STICK TO THE OLD-FASHIONED, UNDESIGNED DRUGS, THE ONES THAT COME IN A GLASS.
I WAS LUCKY THE FUCKING TIDE COMING IN WOKE ME UP.
WELL, LIKE I KEEP SAYING, NO ONE ELSE WHO TOOK THE PILLS GOT SICK.
AND WHERE WERE YOU?
WHEN I COULDN'T FIND YOU IN THE CLUB, I JUST CAME BACK HERE AND, ER, GOT AN EARLY NIGHT.
HUH, WELL, THAT'S A BLOODY FIRST.
IT WAS 'TIL YOUR MOBILE STARTED RINGING.
OLD GRANDPA HAS BEEN CALLING YOU.
TWELVE TIMES?

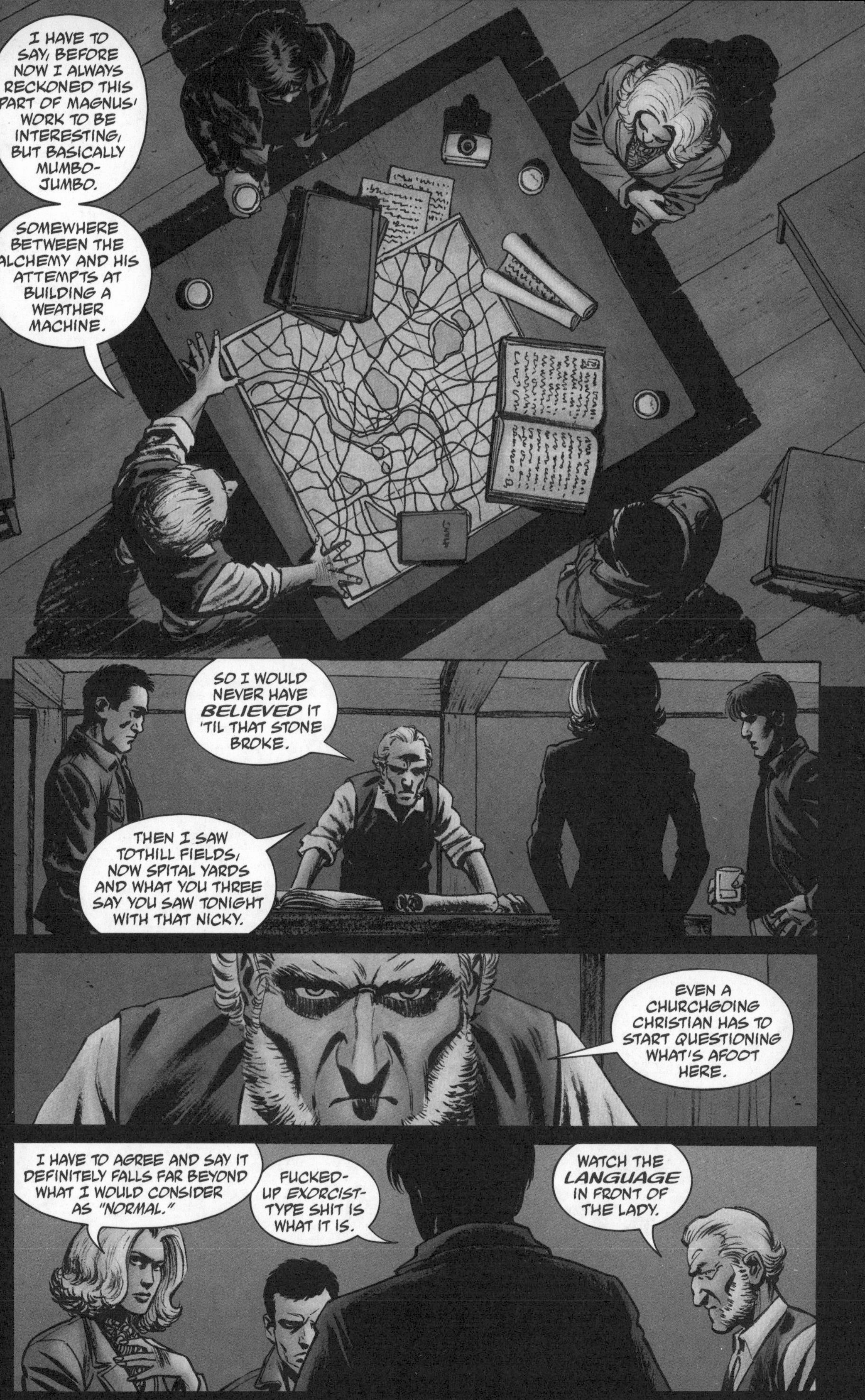

I HAVE TO SAY, BEFORE NOW I ALWAYS RECKONED THIS PART OF MAGNUS' WORK TO BE INTERESTING, BUT BASICALLY MUMBO-JUMBO.
SOMEWHERE BETWEEN THE ALCHEMY AND HIS ATTEMPTS AT BUILDING A WEATHER MACHINE.
SO I WOULD NEVER HAVE BELIEVED IT 'TIL THAT STONE BROKE.
THEN I SAW TOTHILL FIELDS, NOW SPITAL YARDS AND WHAT YOU THREE SAY YOU SAW TONIGHT WITH THAT NICKY.
EVEN A CHURCHGOING CHRISTIAN HAS TO START QUESTIONING WHAT'S AFOOT HERE.
I HAVE TO AGREE AND SAY IT DEFINITELY FALLS FAR BEYOND WHAT I WOULD CONSIDER AS "NORMAL."
FUCKED-UP EXORCIST-TYPE SHIT IS WHAT IT IS.
WATCH THE LANGUAGE IN FRONT OF THE LADY.

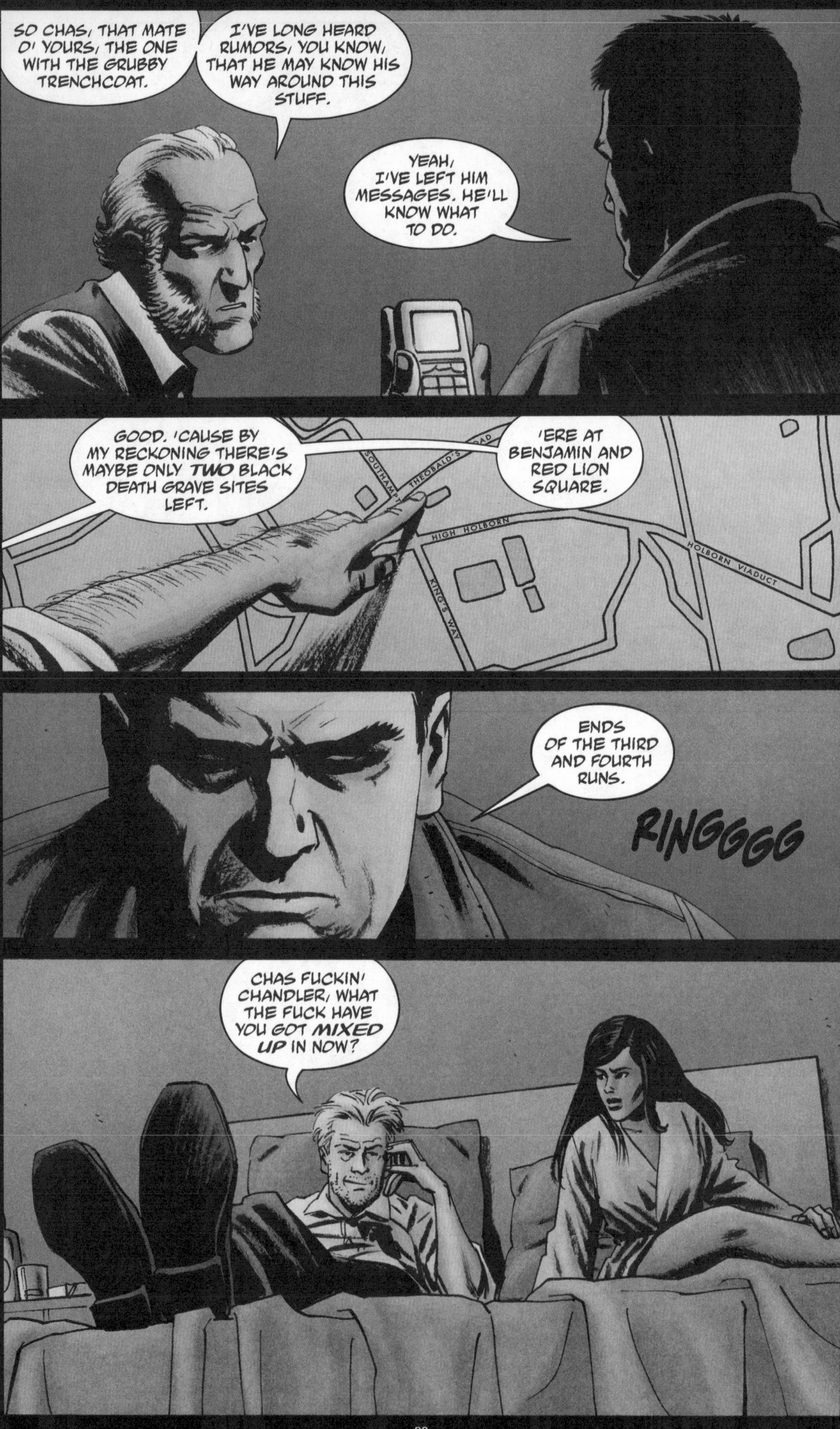

SO CHAS, THAT MATE O' YOURS, THE ONE WITH THE GRUBBY TRENCHCOAT.
I'VE LONG HEARD RUMORS, YOU KNOW, THAT HE MAY KNOW HIS WAY AROUND THIS STUFF.
YEAH, I'VE LEFT HIM MESSAGES. HE'LL KNOW WHAT TO DO.
GOOD. 'CAUSE BY MY RECKONING THERE'S MAYBE ONLY *TWO* BLACK DEATH GRAVE SITES LEFT.
'ERE AT BENJAMIN AND RED LION SQUARE.
THEOBALD'S
HIGH HOLBORN
KING'S WAY
HOLBORN VIADUCT
ENDS OF THE THIRD AND FOURTH RUNS.
RINGGGG
CHAS FUCKIN' CHANDLER, WHAT THE FUCK HAVE YOU GOT *MIXED UP* IN NOW?

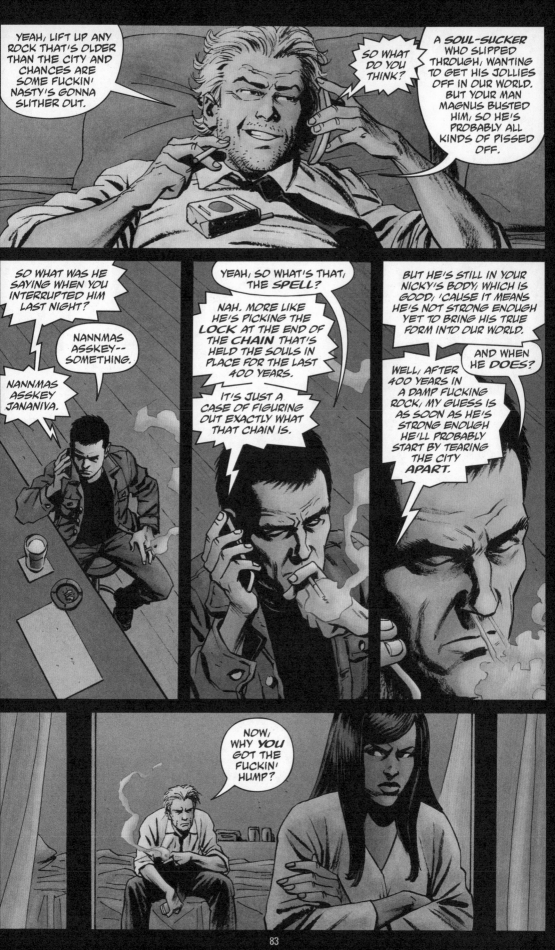

YEAH, LIFT UP ANY ROCK THAT'S OLDER THAN THE CITY AND CHANCES ARE SOME FUCKIN' NASTY'S GONNA SLITHER OUT.

SO WHAT DO YOU THINK?

A SOUL-SUCKER WHO SLIPPED THROUGH, WANTING TO GET HIS JOLLIES OFF IN OUR WORLD. BUT YOUR MAN MAGNUS BUSTED HIM, SO HE'S PROBABLY ALL KINDS OF PISSED OFF.

SO WHAT WAS HE SAYING WHEN YOU INTERRUPTED HIM LAST NIGHT?

NANNMAS ASSKEY-- SOMETHING.

NANNMAS ASSKEY JANANIVA.

YEAH, SO WHAT'S THAT, THE SPELL?

NAH. MORE LIKE HE'S PICKING THE LOCK AT THE END OF THE CHAIN THAT'S HELD THE SOULS IN PLACE FOR THE LAST 400 YEARS.

IT'S JUST A CASE OF FIGURING OUT EXACTLY WHAT THAT CHAIN IS.

BUT HE'S STILL IN YOUR NICKY'S BODY, WHICH IS GOOD, 'CAUSE IT MEANS HE'S NOT STRONG ENOUGH YET TO BRING HIS TRUE FORM INTO OUR WORLD.

AND WHEN HE DOES?

WELL, AFTER 400 YEARS IN A DAMP FUCKING ROCK, MY GUESS IS AS SOON AS HE'S STRONG ENOUGH HE'LL PROBABLY START BY TEARING THE CITY APART.

NOW, WHY YOU GOT THE FUCKIN' HUMP?

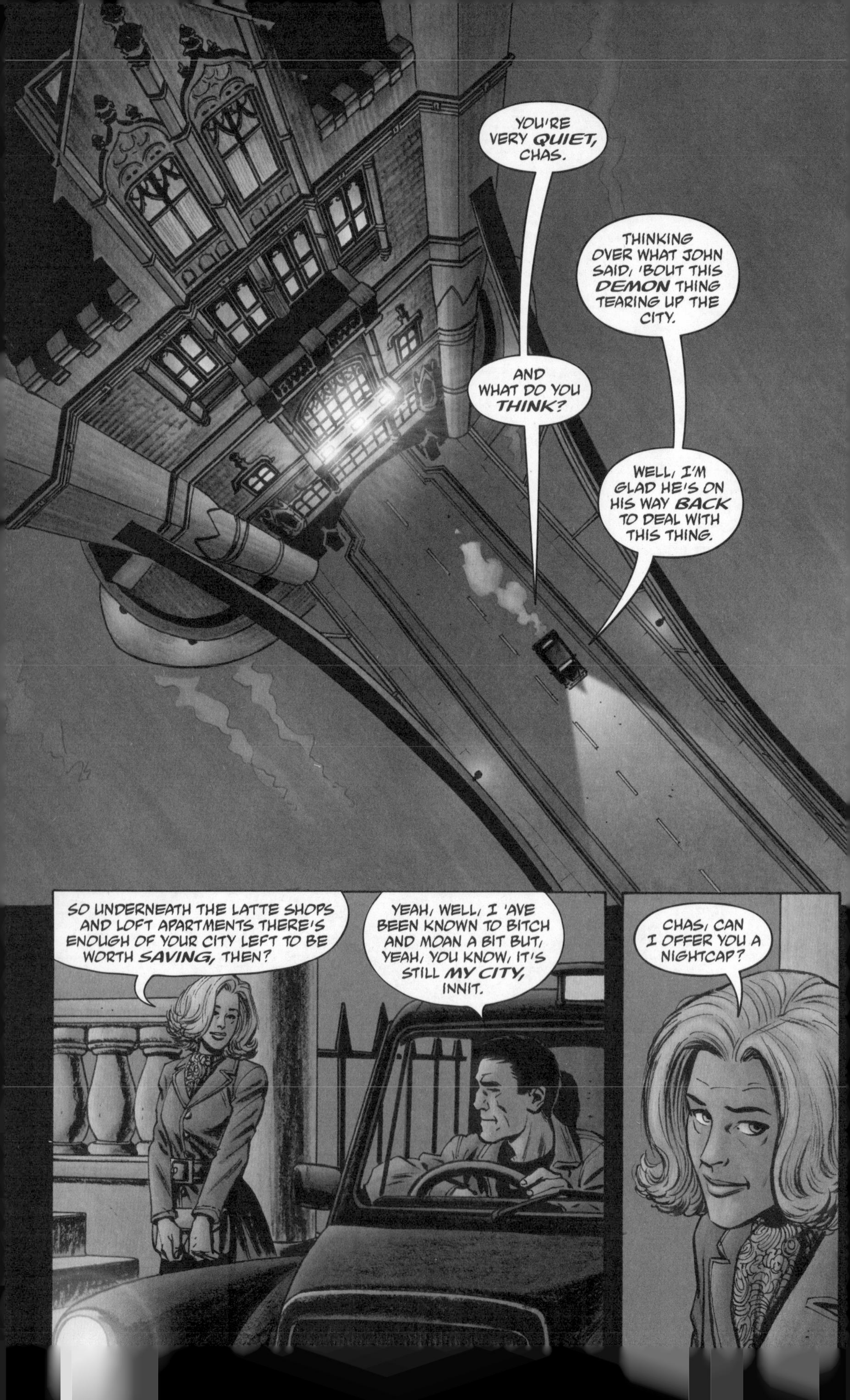
YOU'RE VERY QUIET, CHAS.
THINKING OVER WHAT JOHN SAID, 'BOUT THIS DEMON THING TEARING UP THE CITY.
AND WHAT DO YOU THINK?
WELL, I'M GLAD HE'S ON HIS WAY BACK TO DEAL WITH THIS THING.
SO UNDERNEATH THE LATTE SHOPS AND LOFT APARTMENTS THERE'S ENOUGH OF YOUR CITY LEFT TO BE WORTH SAVING, THEN?
YEAH, WELL, I 'AVE BEEN KNOWN TO BITCH AND MOAN A BIT BUT, YEAH, YOU KNOW, IT'S STILL MY CITY, INNIT.
CHAS, CAN I OFFER YOU A NIGHTCAP?

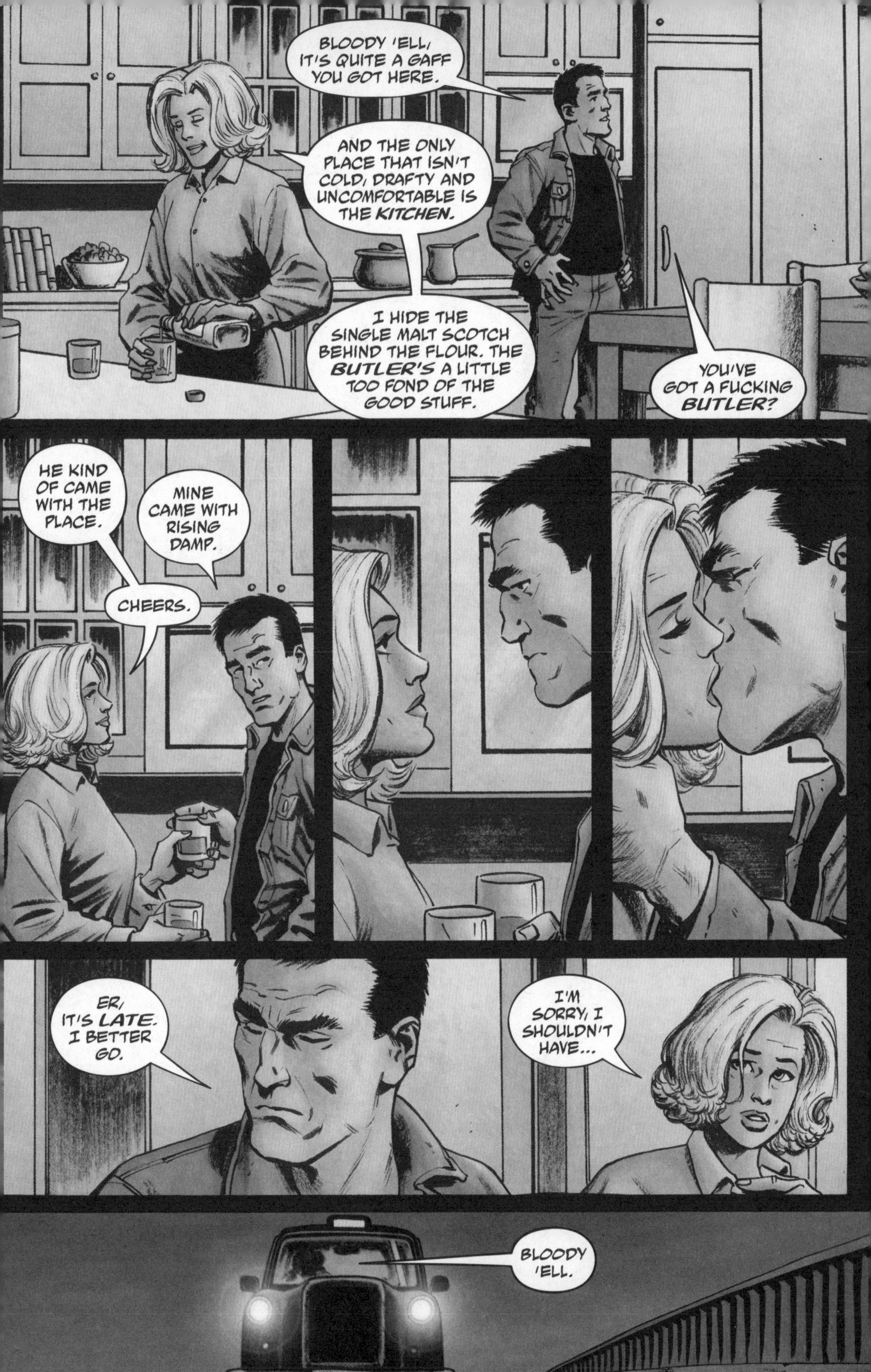
BLOODY 'ELL, IT'S QUITE A GAFF YOU GOT HERE.
AND THE ONLY PLACE THAT ISN'T COLD, DRAFTY AND UNCOMFORTABLE IS THE KITCHEN.
I HIDE THE SINGLE MALT SCOTCH BEHIND THE FLOUR. THE BUTLER'S A LITTLE TOO FOND OF THE GOOD STUFF.
YOU'VE GOT A FUCKING BUTLER?
HE KIND OF CAME WITH THE PLACE.
MINE CAME WITH RISING DAMP.
CHEERS.
ER, IT'S LATE. I BETTER GO.
I'M SORRY, I SHOULDN'T HAVE...
BLOODY 'ELL.

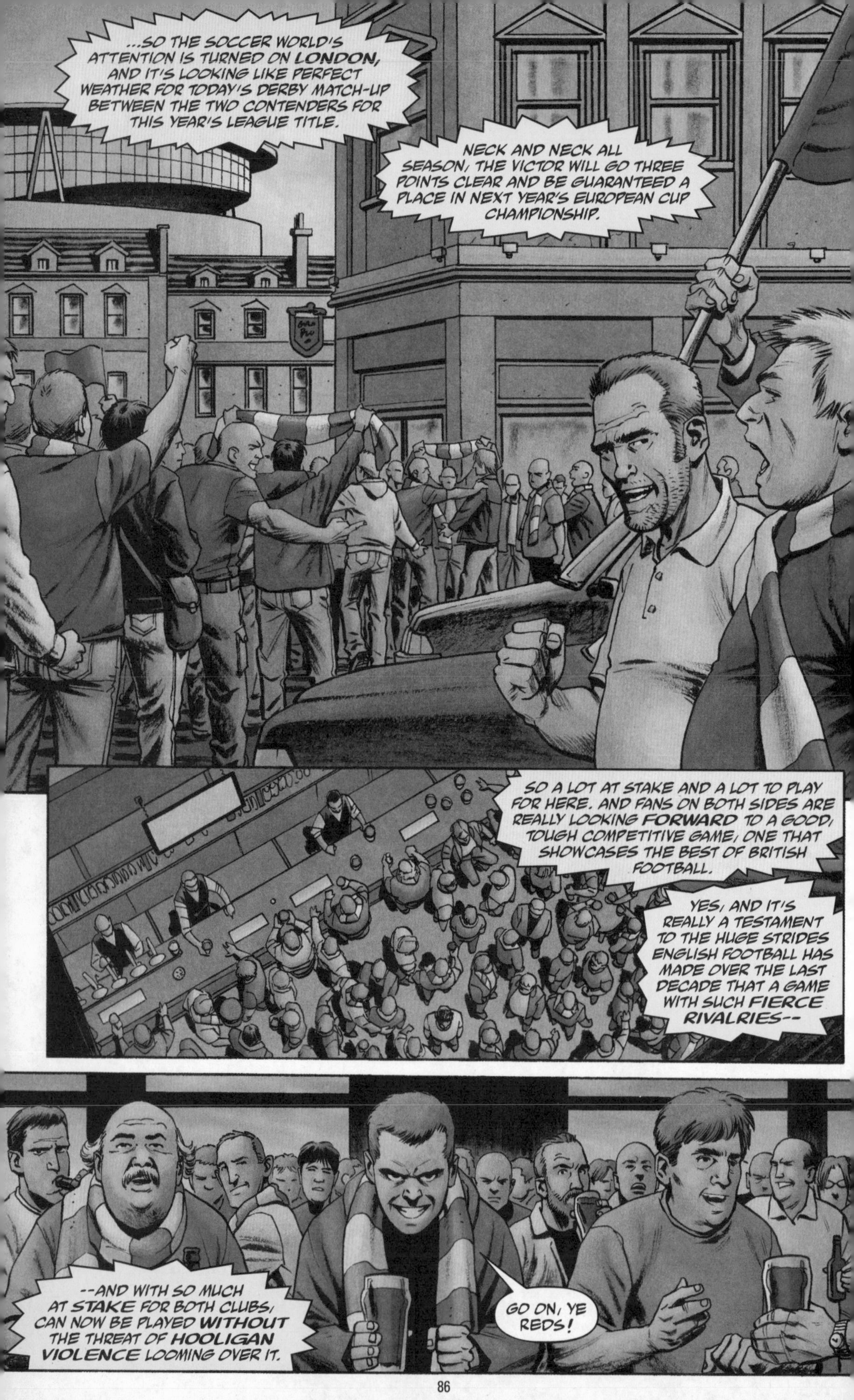
...SO THE SOCCER WORLD'S ATTENTION IS TURNED ON LONDON, AND IT'S LOOKING LIKE PERFECT WEATHER FOR TODAY'S DERBY MATCH-UP BETWEEN THE TWO CONTENDERS FOR THIS YEAR'S LEAGUE TITLE.
NECK AND NECK ALL SEASON, THE VICTOR WILL GO THREE POINTS CLEAR AND BE GUARANTEED A PLACE IN NEXT YEAR'S EUROPEAN CUP CHAMPIONSHIP.
SO A LOT AT STAKE AND A LOT TO PLAY FOR HERE. AND FANS ON BOTH SIDES ARE REALLY LOOKING FORWARD TO A GOOD, TOUGH COMPETITIVE GAME, ONE THAT SHOWCASES THE BEST OF BRITISH FOOTBALL.
YES, AND IT'S REALLY A TESTAMENT TO THE HUGE STRIDES ENGLISH FOOTBALL HAS MADE OVER THE LAST DECADE THAT A GAME WITH SUCH FIERCE RIVALRIES--
--AND WITH SO MUCH AT STAKE FOR BOTH CLUBS, CAN NOW BE PLAYED WITHOUT THE THREAT OF HOOLIGAN VIOLENCE LOOMING OVER IT.
GO ON, YE REDS!

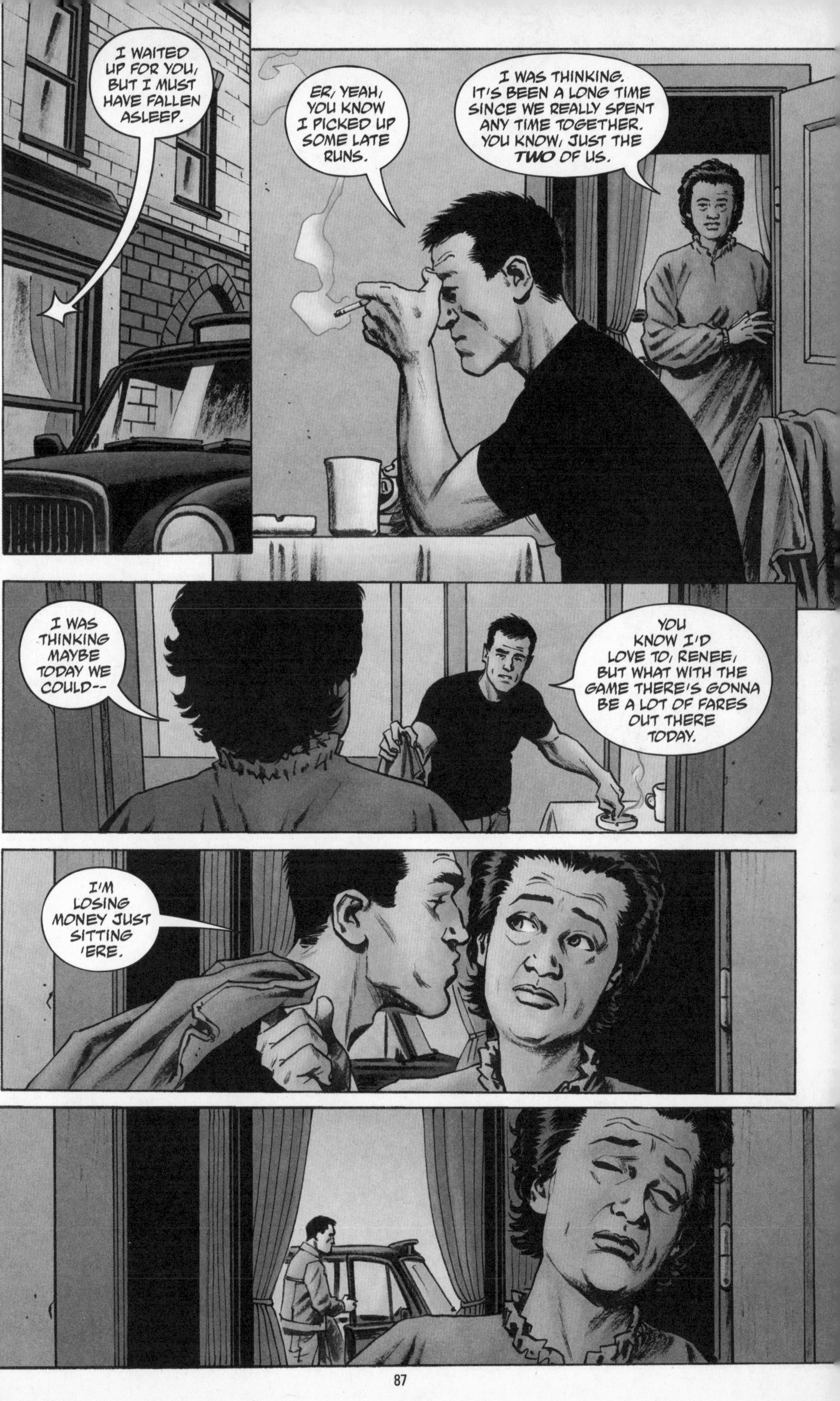
I WAITED UP FOR YOU, BUT I MUST HAVE FALLEN ASLEEP.
ER, YEAH, YOU KNOW I PICKED UP SOME LATE RUNS.
I WAS THINKING. IT'S BEEN A LONG TIME SINCE WE REALLY SPENT ANY TIME TOGETHER. YOU KNOW, JUST THE *TWO* OF US.
I WAS THINKING MAYBE TODAY WE COULD--
YOU KNOW I'D LOVE TO, RENEE, BUT WHAT WITH THE GAME THERE'S GONNA BE A LOT OF FARES OUT THERE TODAY.
I'M LOSING MONEY JUST SITTING 'ERE.

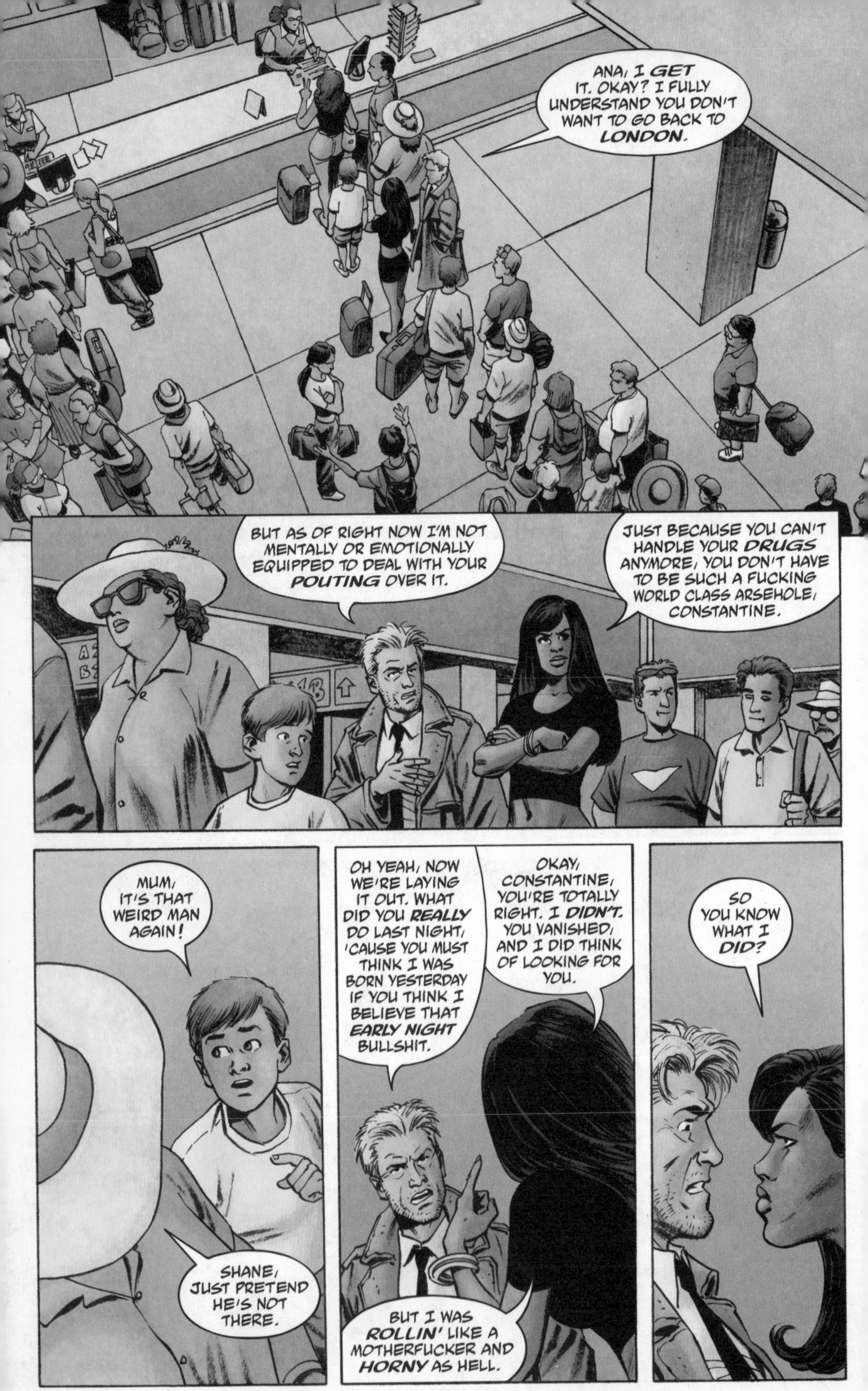
ANA, I GET IT. OKAY? I FULLY UNDERSTAND YOU DON'T WANT TO GO BACK TO LONDON.
BUT AS OF RIGHT NOW I'M NOT MENTALLY OR EMOTIONALLY EQUIPPED TO DEAL WITH YOUR POUTING OVER IT.
JUST BECAUSE YOU CAN'T HANDLE YOUR DRUGS ANYMORE, YOU DON'T HAVE TO BE SUCH A FUCKING WORLD CLASS ARSEHOLE, CONSTANTINE.
MUM, IT'S THAT WEIRD MAN AGAIN!
SHANE, JUST PRETEND HE'S NOT THERE.
OKAY, CONSTANTINE, YOU'RE TOTALLY RIGHT. I DIDN'T. YOU VANISHED, AND I DID THINK OF LOOKING FOR YOU.
BUT I WAS ROLLIN' LIKE A MOTHERFUCKER AND HORNY AS HELL.
OH YEAH, NOW WE'RE LAYING IT OUT. WHAT DID YOU REALLY DO LAST NIGHT, 'CAUSE YOU MUST THINK I WAS BORN YESTERDAY IF YOU THINK I BELIEVE THAT EARLY NIGHT BULLSHIT.
SO YOU KNOW WHAT I DID?

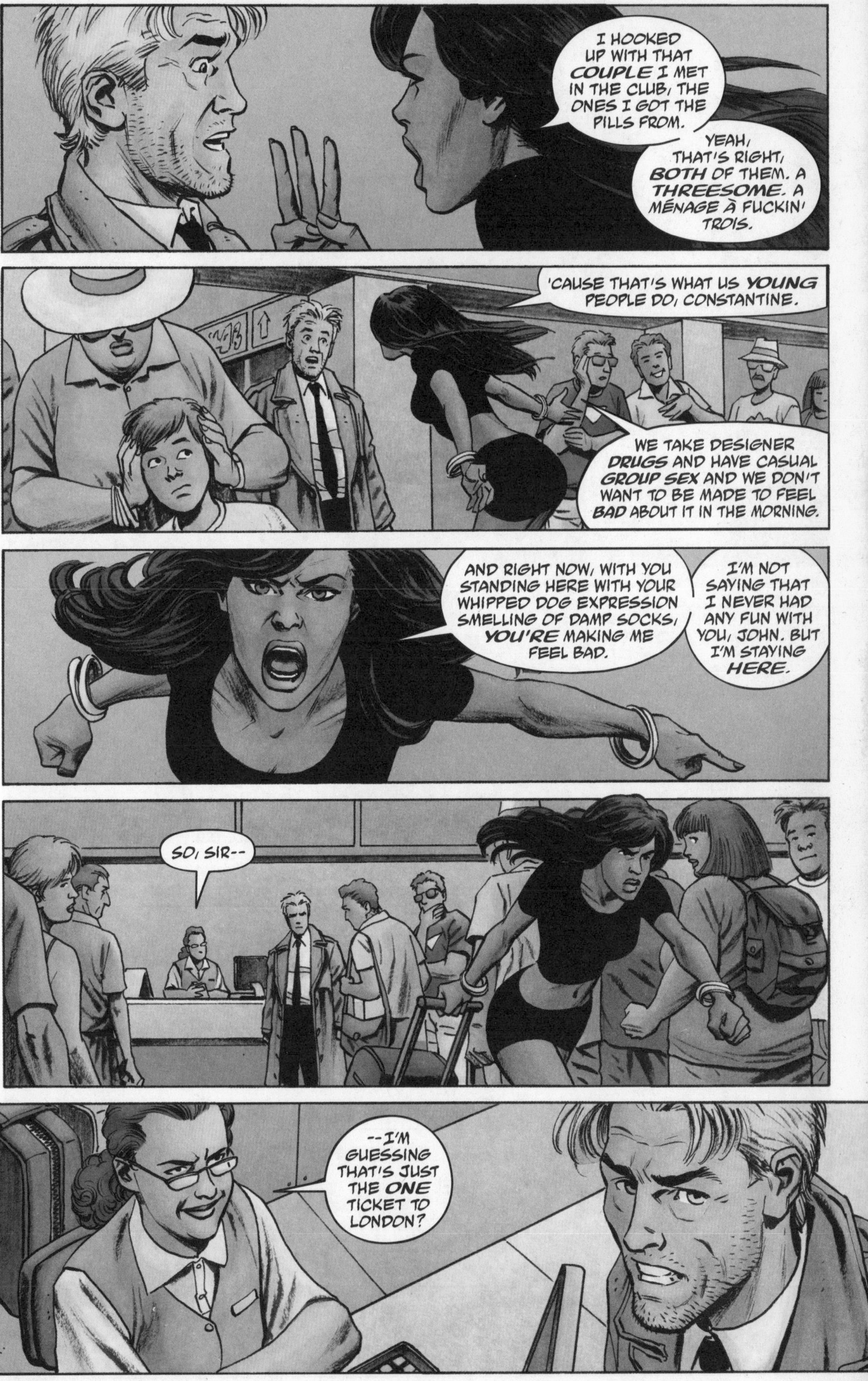
I HOOKED UP WITH THAT COUPLE I MET IN THE CLUB, THE ONES I GOT THE PILLS FROM.
YEAH, THAT'S RIGHT, BOTH OF THEM. A THREESOME. A MÉNAGE À FUCKIN' TROIS.
'CAUSE THAT'S WHAT US YOUNG PEOPLE DO, CONSTANTINE.
WE TAKE DESIGNER DRUGS AND HAVE CASUAL GROUP SEX AND WE DON'T WANT TO BE MADE TO FEEL BAD ABOUT IT IN THE MORNING.
AND RIGHT NOW, WITH YOU STANDING HERE WITH YOUR WHIPPED DOG EXPRESSION SMELLING OF DAMP SOCKS, YOU'RE MAKING ME FEEL BAD.
I'M NOT SAYING THAT I NEVER HAD ANY FUN WITH YOU, JOHN. BUT I'M STAYING HERE.
SO, SIR--
--I'M GUESSING THAT'S JUST THE ONE TICKET TO LONDON?

SO THAT'S SILVERJET FLIGHT 087, GETTING IN AT 8 P.M.

I'LL BE THERE TO PICK YOU BOTH UP.

OH, ER, OKAY.

NAH, IT'LL BE JUST ME, CHAS.

LOOK, I WAS THINKING, JOHN, ABOUT THIS **CHAIN** THING YOU NEED TO FIGURE OUT. I MEAN CAN I HELP OUT A BIT ON THAT, WHAT WITH ME BEING 'ERE?

YOU COULD GIVE ME SOME POINTERS AND I CAN GET A JUMP ON IT, SO YOU CAN HIT THE GROUND **RUNNING.**

I GO AWAY FOR A FEW DAYS AND WHAT, YOU TURN INTO FUCKIN' MISS MARPLE?

WELL, IT'S NOT EXACTLY LIKE THAT.

LOOK, CHAS, MAYBE WITH ANA I **WAS** THINKING WITH MY DICK, OKAY?

BUT WHEN I GET BACK TO LONDON, THINGS ARE GOING BACK TO HOW THEY'VE **ALWAYS** BEEN.

I DO MY THING AND YOU, CHAS--

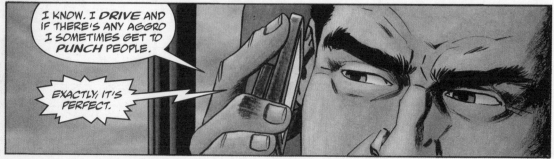

I KNOW. I **DRIVE** AND IF THERE'S ANY AGGRO I SOMETIMES GET TO **PUNCH** PEOPLE.

EXACTLY, IT'S PERFECT.

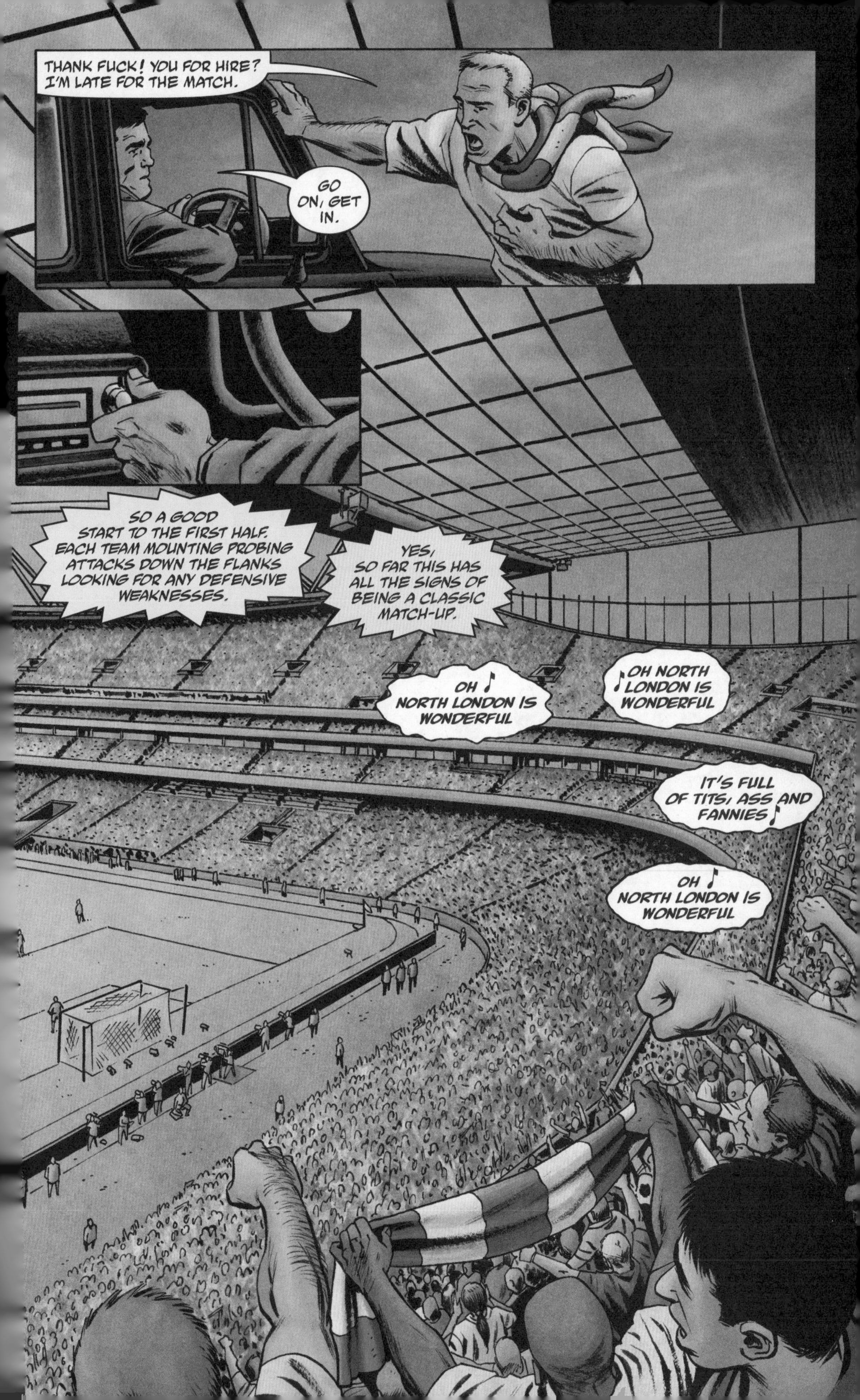
THANK FUCK! YOU FOR HIRE? I'M LATE FOR THE MATCH.
GO ON, GET IN.
SO A GOOD START TO THE FIRST HALF. EACH TEAM MOUNTING PROBING ATTACKS DOWN THE FLANKS LOOKING FOR ANY DEFENSIVE WEAKNESSES.
YES, SO FAR THIS HAS ALL THE SIGNS OF BEING A CLASSIC MATCH-UP.
OH ♪ NORTH LONDON IS WONDERFUL
♪ OH NORTH LONDON IS WONDERFUL
IT'S FULL OF TITS, ASS AND FANNIES ♪
OH ♪ NORTH LONDON IS WONDERFUL

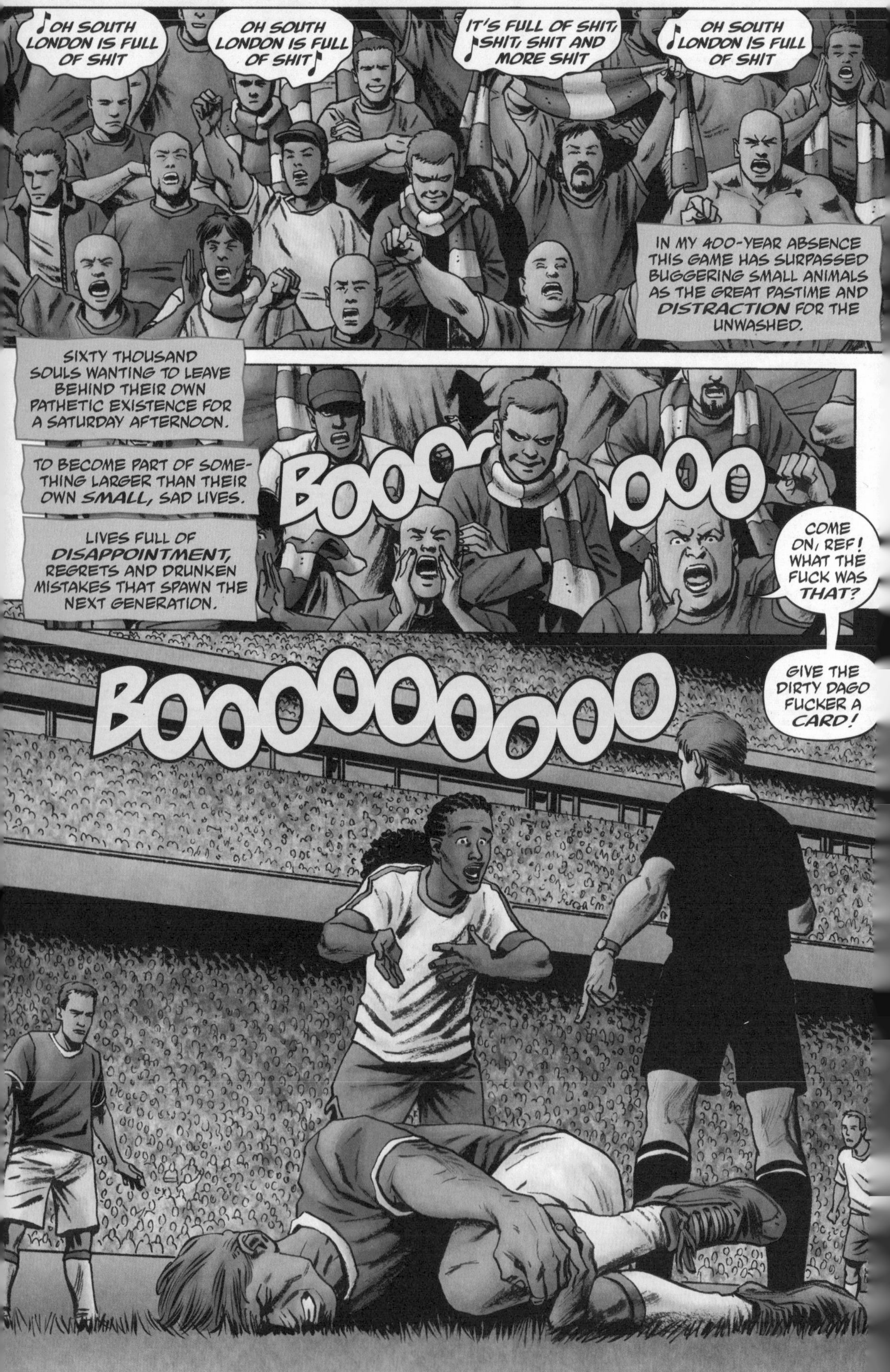

♪OH SOUTH LONDON IS FULL OF SHIT
OH SOUTH LONDON IS FULL OF SHIT♪
IT'S FULL OF SHIT, ♪SHIT, SHIT AND MORE SHIT
♪OH SOUTH LONDON IS FULL OF SHIT
IN MY 400-YEAR ABSENCE THIS GAME HAS SURPASSED BUGGERING SMALL ANIMALS AS THE GREAT PASTIME AND DISTRACTION FOR THE UNWASHED.
SIXTY THOUSAND SOULS WANTING TO LEAVE BEHIND THEIR OWN PATHETIC EXISTENCE FOR A SATURDAY AFTERNOON.
TO BECOME PART OF SOMETHING LARGER THAN THEIR OWN SMALL, SAD LIVES.
LIVES FULL OF DISAPPOINTMENT, REGRETS AND DRUNKEN MISTAKES THAT SPAWN THE NEXT GENERATION.
BOOO OOOO
COME ON, REF! WHAT THE FUCK WAS THAT?
GIVE THE DIRTY DAGO FUCKER A CARD!
BOOOOOOOOO

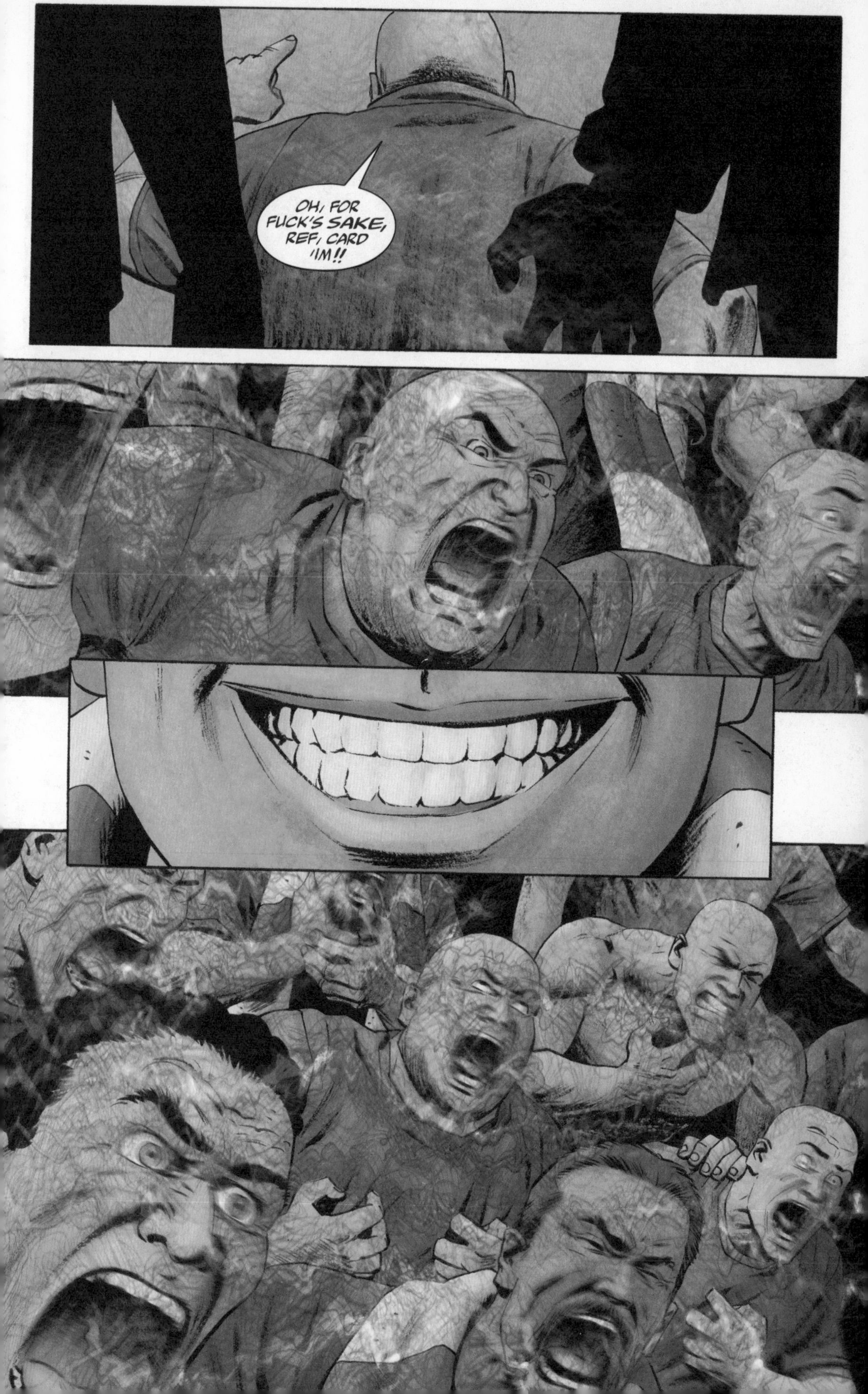
OH, FOR FUCK'S SAKE, REF, CARD 'IM!!

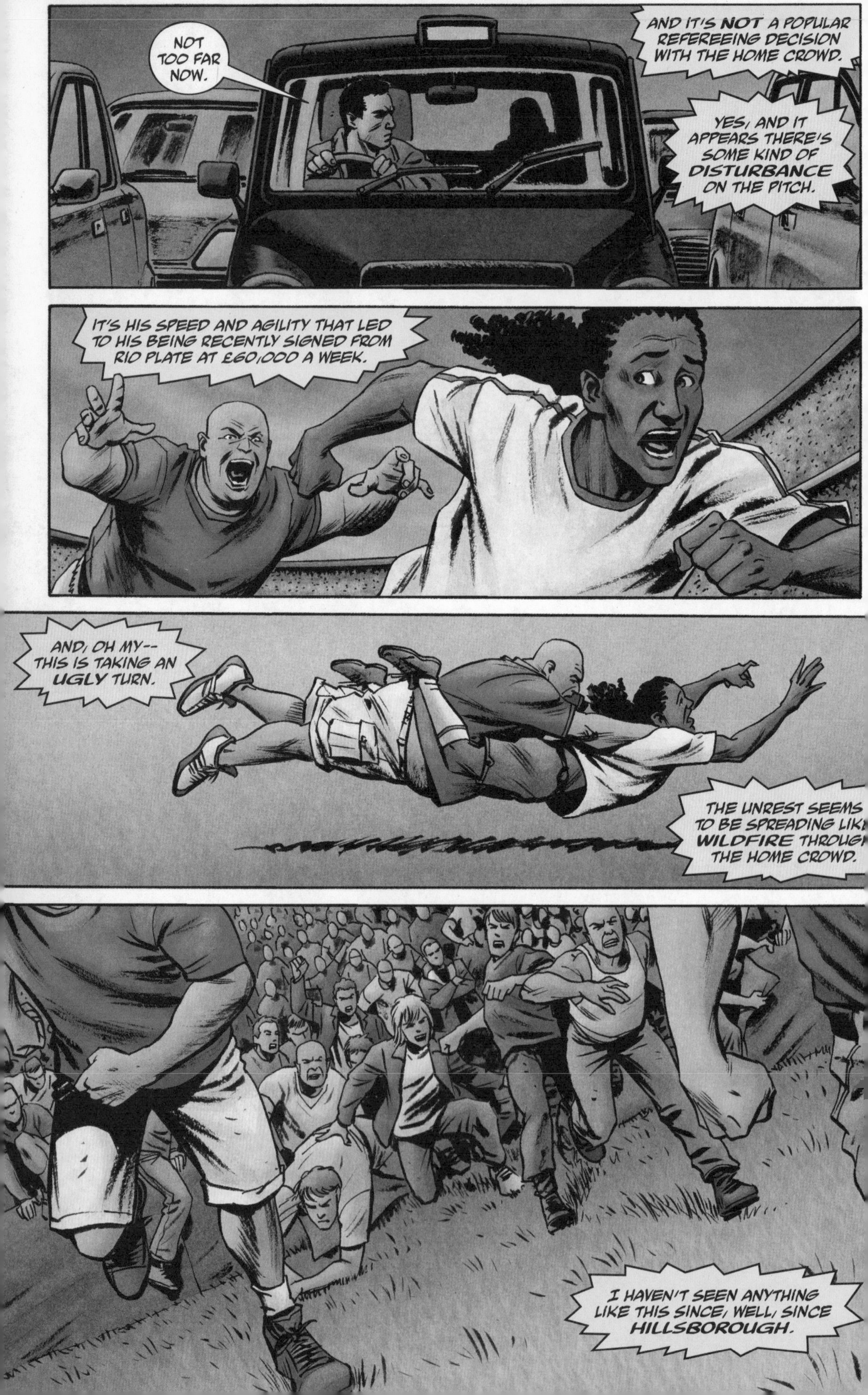
NOT TOO FAR NOW.
AND IT'S NOT A POPULAR REFEREEING DECISION WITH THE HOME CROWD.
YES, AND IT APPEARS THERE'S SOME KIND OF DISTURBANCE ON THE PITCH.
IT'S HIS SPEED AND AGILITY THAT LED TO HIS BEING RECENTLY SIGNED FROM RIO PLATE AT £60,000 A WEEK.
AND, OH MY-- THIS IS TAKING AN UGLY TURN.
THE UNREST SEEMS TO BE SPREADING LIKE WILDFIRE THROUGH THE HOME CROWD.
I HAVEN'T SEEN ANYTHING LIKE THIS SINCE, WELL, SINCE HILLSBOROUGH.

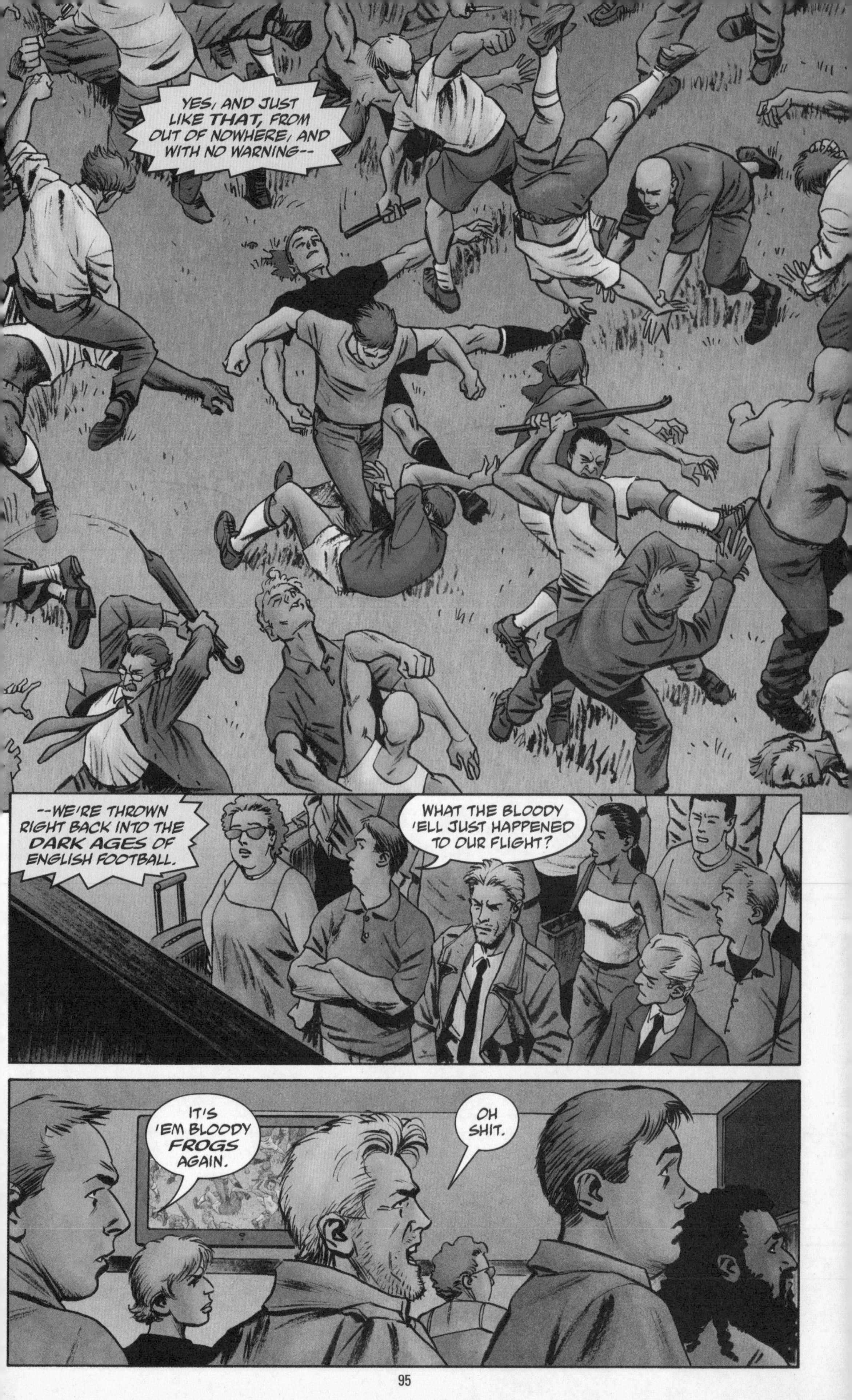
YES, AND JUST LIKE THAT, FROM OUT OF NOWHERE, AND WITH NO WARNING--
--WE'RE THROWN RIGHT BACK INTO THE DARK AGES OF ENGLISH FOOTBALL.
WHAT THE BLOODY 'ELL JUST HAPPENED TO OUR FLIGHT?
IT'S 'EM BLOODY FROGS AGAIN.
OH SHIT.

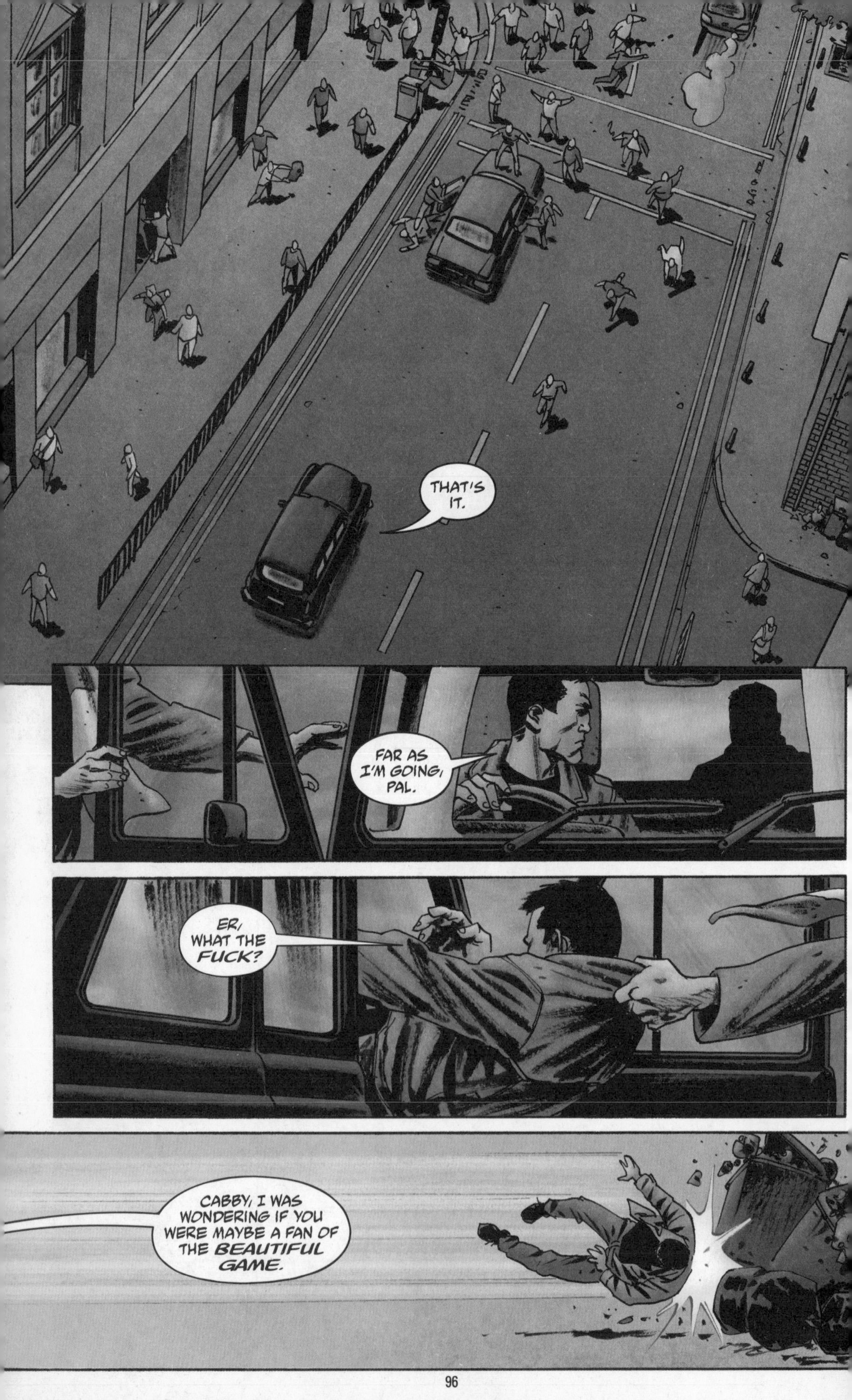
THAT'S IT.
FAR AS I'M GOING, PAL.
ER, WHAT THE FUCK?
CABBY, I WAS WONDERING IF YOU WERE MAYBE A FAN OF THE BEAUTIFUL GAME.

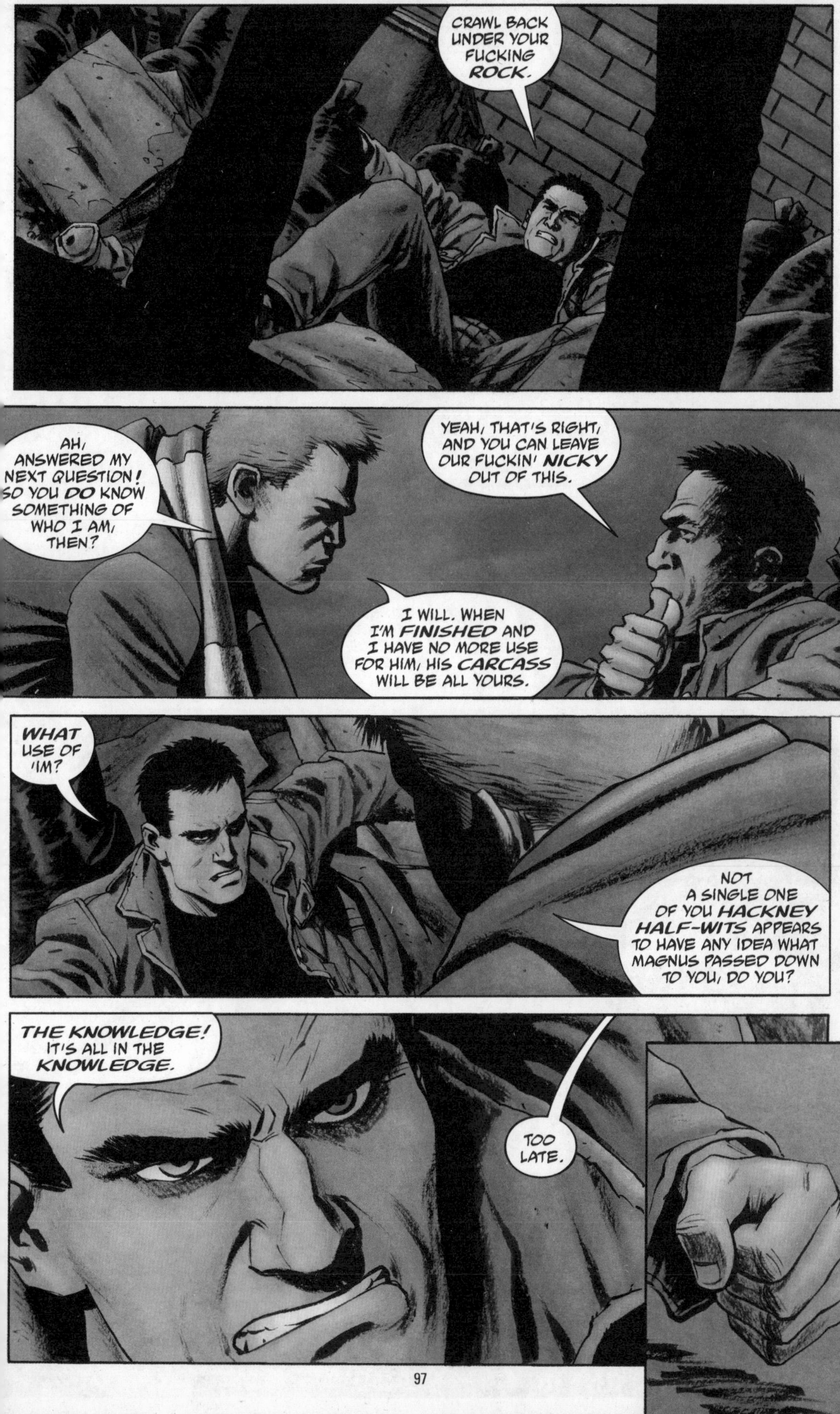
CRAWL BACK UNDER YOUR FUCKING ROCK.
AH, ANSWERED MY NEXT QUESTION! SO YOU DO KNOW SOMETHING OF WHO I AM, THEN?
YEAH, THAT'S RIGHT, AND YOU CAN LEAVE OUR FUCKIN' NICKY OUT OF THIS.
I WILL. WHEN I'M FINISHED AND I HAVE NO MORE USE FOR HIM, HIS CARCASS WILL BE ALL YOURS.
WHAT USE OF 'IM?
NOT A SINGLE ONE OF YOU HACKNEY HALF-WITS APPEARS TO HAVE ANY IDEA WHAT MAGNUS PASSED DOWN TO YOU, DO YOU?
THE KNOWLEDGE! IT'S ALL IN THE KNOWLEDGE.
TOO LATE.

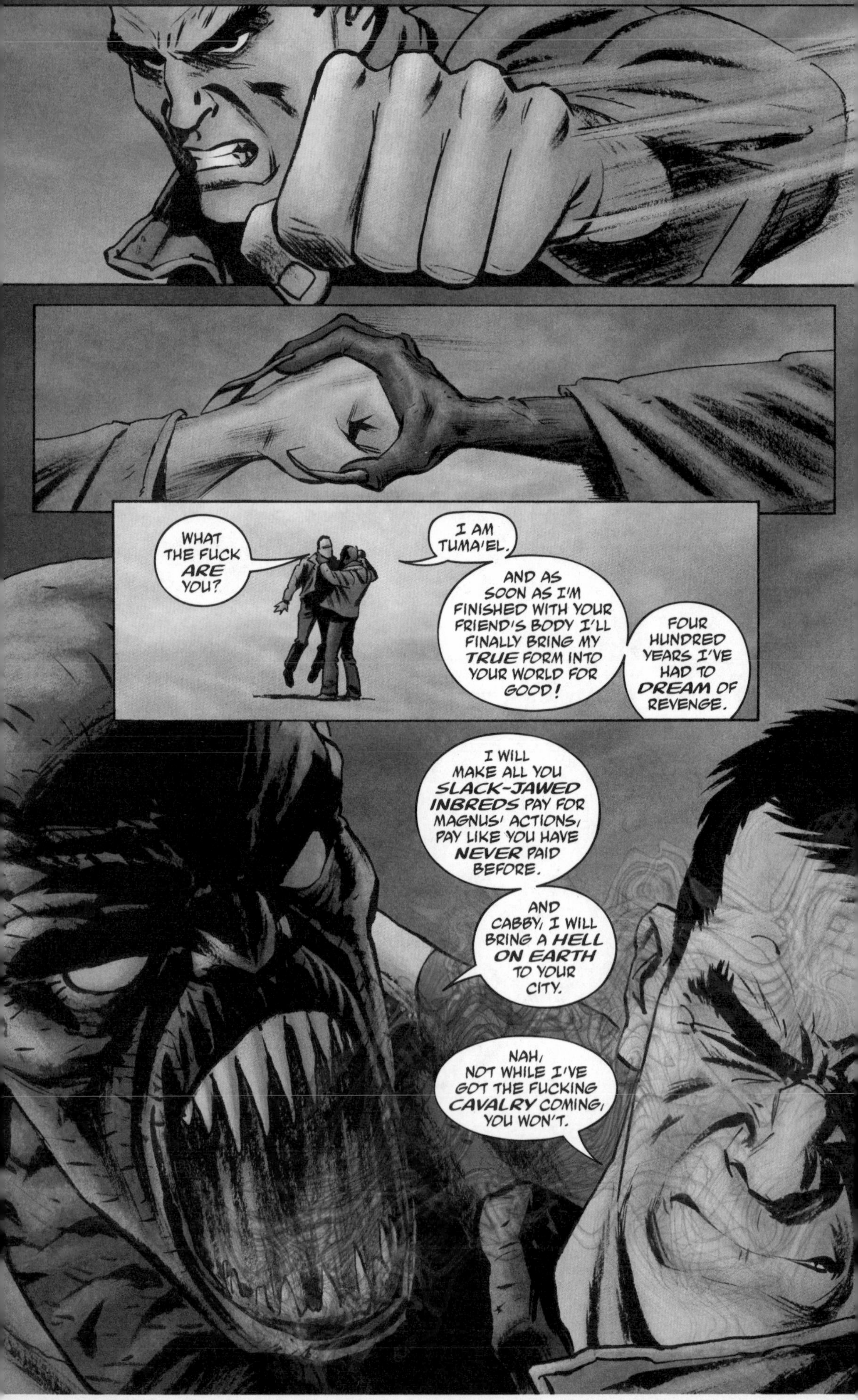
WHAT THE FUCK ARE YOU?
I AM TUMA'EL.
AND AS SOON AS I'M FINISHED WITH YOUR FRIEND'S BODY I'LL FINALLY BRING MY TRUE FORM INTO YOUR WORLD FOR GOOD!
FOUR HUNDRED YEARS I'VE HAD TO DREAM OF REVENGE.
I WILL MAKE ALL YOU SLACK-JAWED INBREDS PAY FOR MAGNUS' ACTIONS, PAY LIKE YOU HAVE NEVER PAID BEFORE.
AND CABBY, I WILL BRING A HELL ON EARTH TO YOUR CITY.
NAH, NOT WHILE I'VE GOT THE FUCKING CAVALRY COMING, YOU WON'T.

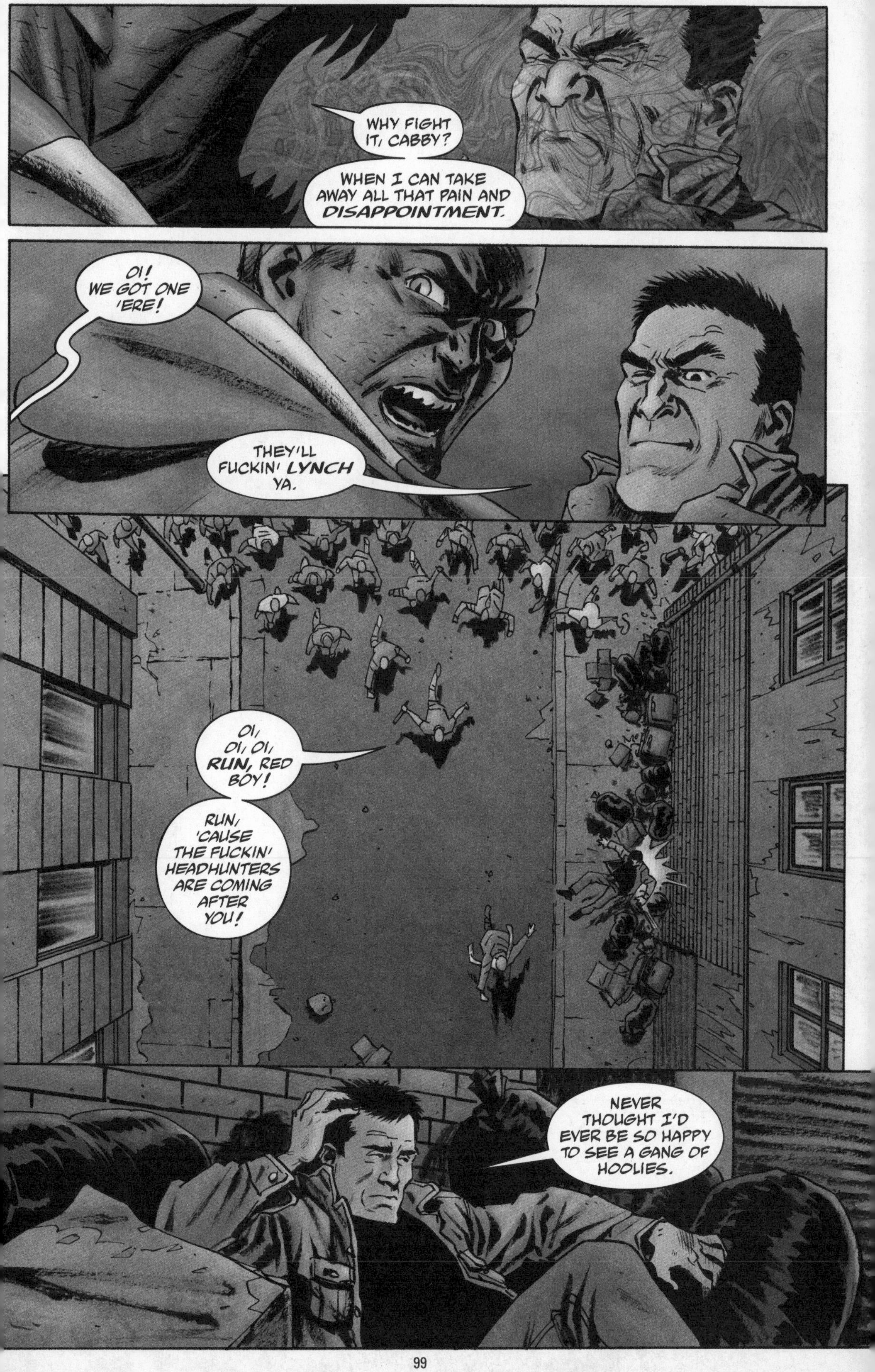
WHY FIGHT IT, CABBY?
WHEN I CAN TAKE AWAY ALL THAT PAIN AND DISAPPOINTMENT.
OI! WE GOT ONE 'ERE!
THEY'LL FUCKIN' LYNCH YA.
OI, OI, OI, RUN, RED BOY!
RUN, 'CAUSE THE FUCKIN' HEADHUNTERS ARE COMING AFTER YOU!
NEVER THOUGHT I'D EVER BE SO HAPPY TO SEE A GANG OF HOOLIES.

JOHN, I **SAW** 'IM, AND HE MUST BE GETTING STRONGER LIKE YOU SAID, 'CAUSE HE CHANGED TO WHAT MUST BE HIS **REAL** BODY.

SO I DON'T THINK WE'VE GOT MUCH **TIME.**

HOLD ON, CONSTANTINE, WHY AIN'T YOU ON THE FUCKING **PLANE?**

SLIGHT PROBLEM THERE.

2618	BONN	
6008	BUDAPEST	CANCELLED
5388	GENEVA	CANCELLED
3819	HELSINKI	CANCELLED
8734	LONDON	CANCELLED
2077	MOSCOW	CANCELLED
3167	NEW YORK	CANCELLED

453	NICE
9386	ST. PET
860	TRIEST
4308	ULM
2288	VIENNA
	WASHINGTON DC

FUCKING FRENCH AIR TRAFFIC CONTROLLERS.

CHAS, I THINK YOU'RE GONN HAVE TO TAKE CARE OF THIS WITHOUT ME.

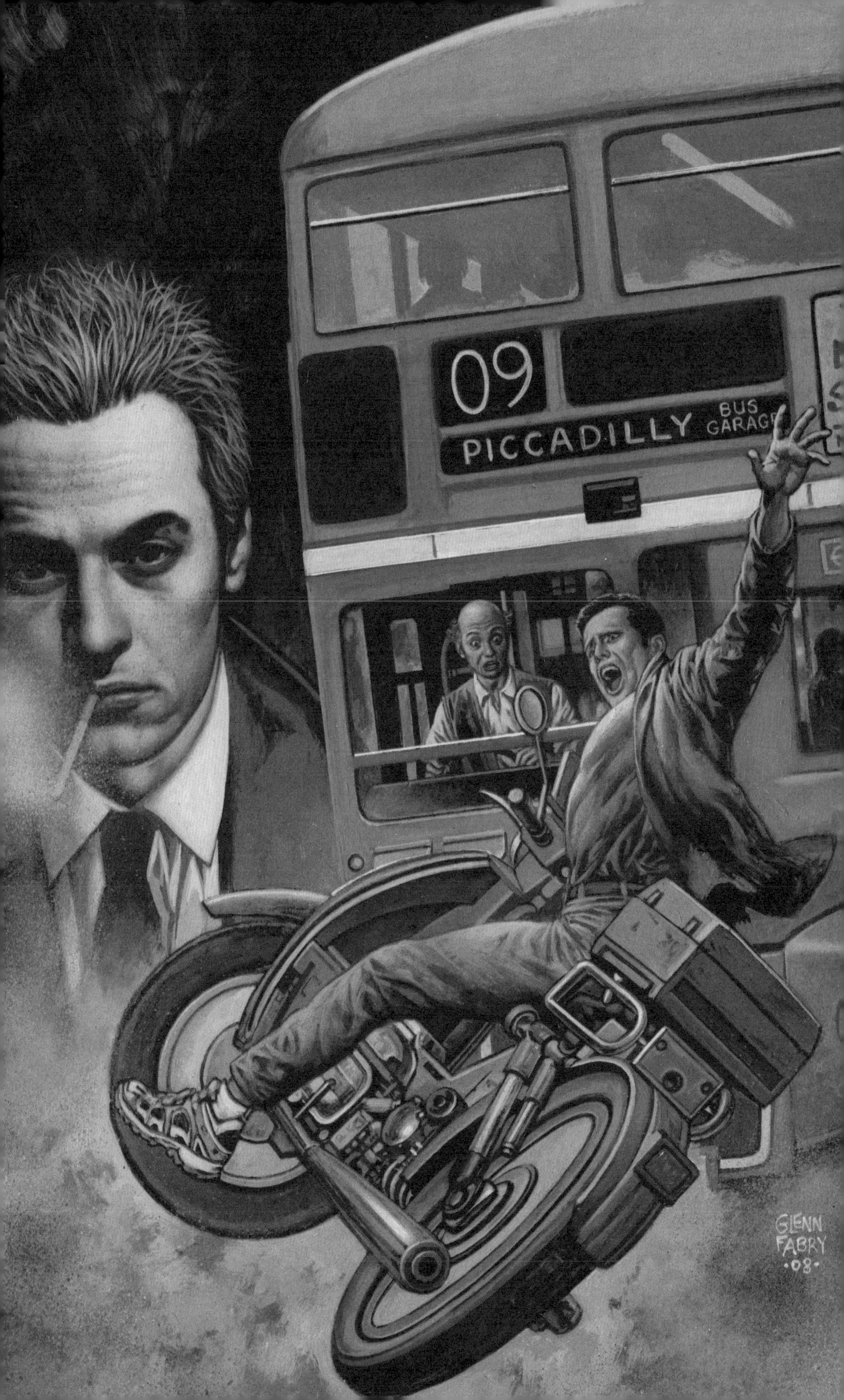
09
PICCADILLY
BUS
GARAGE
GLENN
FABRY
·08·

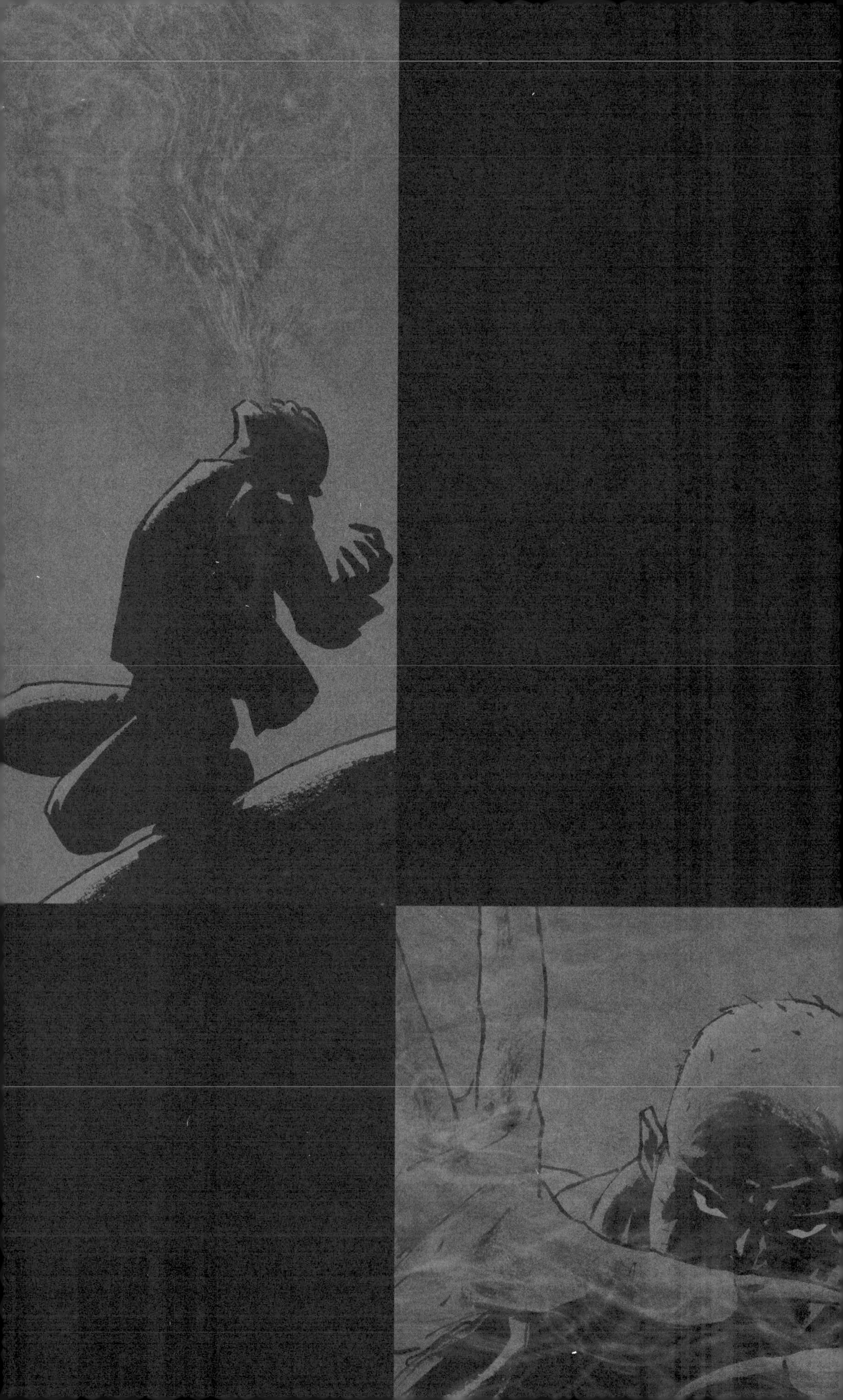

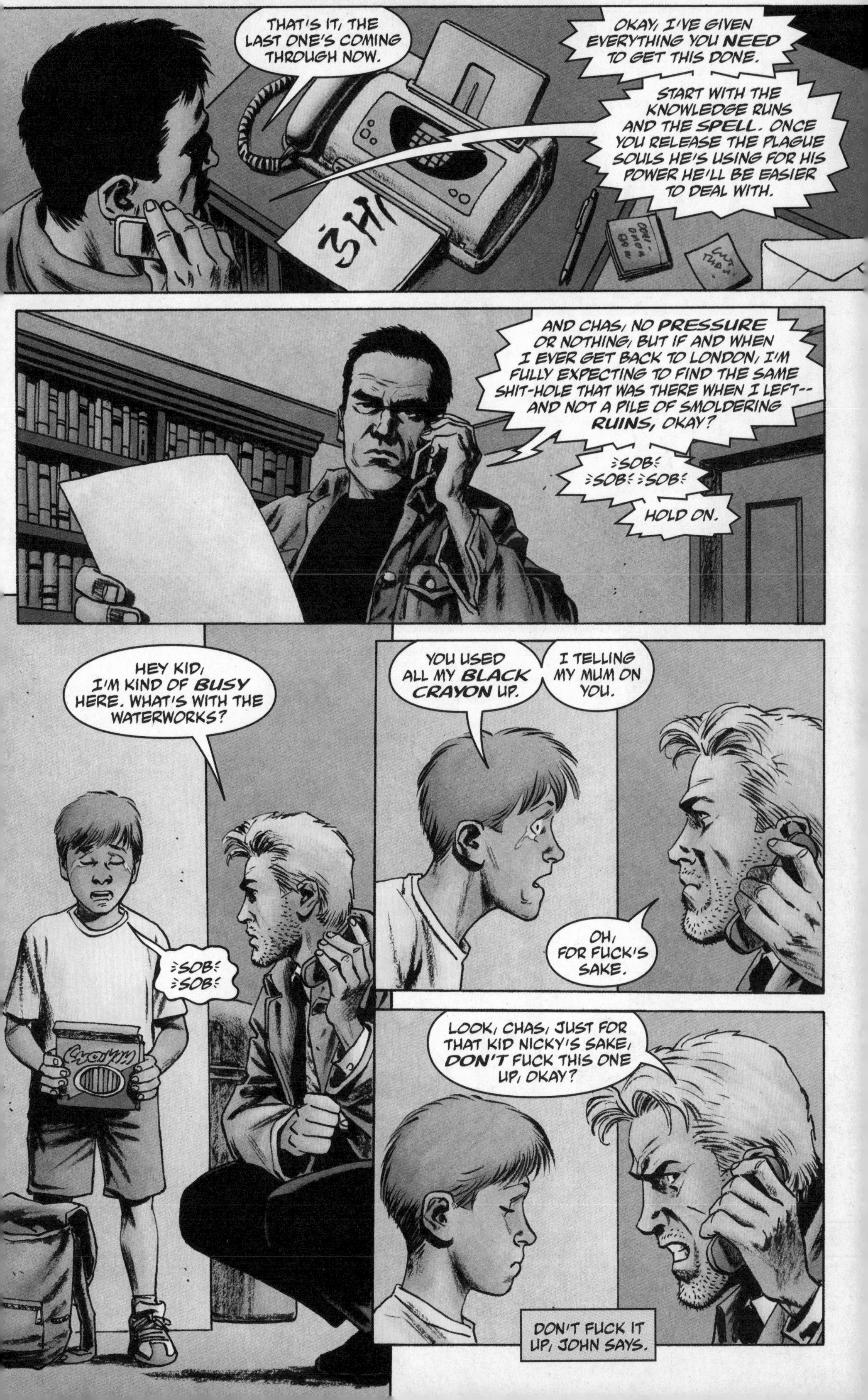

THAT'S IT, THE LAST ONE'S COMING THROUGH NOW.
OKAY, I'VE GIVEN EVERYTHING YOU NEED TO GET THIS DONE.
START WITH THE KNOWLEDGE RUNS AND THE SPELL. ONCE YOU RELEASE THE PLAGUE SOULS HE'S USING FOR HIS POWER HE'LL BE EASIER TO DEAL WITH.
AND CHAS, NO PRESSURE OR NOTHING, BUT IF AND WHEN I EVER GET BACK TO LONDON, I'M FULLY EXPECTING TO FIND THE SAME SHIT-HOLE THAT WAS THERE WHEN I LEFT-- AND NOT A PILE OF SMOLDERING RUINS, OKAY?
SOB
SOB SOB
HOLD ON.
HEY KID, I'M KIND OF BUSY HERE. WHAT'S WITH THE WATERWORKS?
SOB SOB
YOU USED ALL MY BLACK CRAYON UP.
I TELLING MY MUM ON YOU.
OH, FOR FUCK'S SAKE.
LOOK, CHAS, JUST FOR THAT KID NICKY'S SAKE, DON'T FUCK THIS ONE UP, OKAY?
DON'T FUCK IT UP, JOHN SAYS.

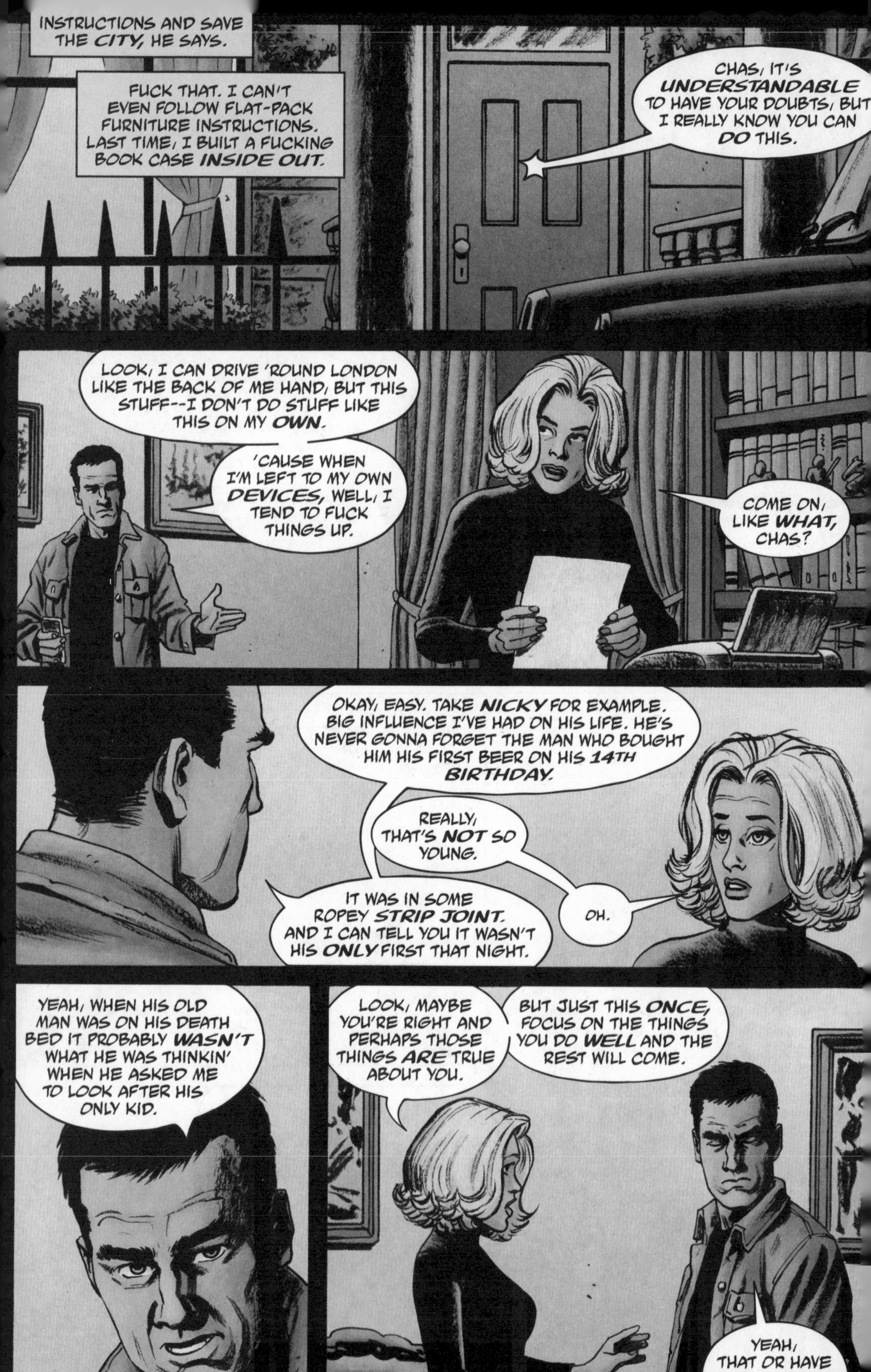
INSTRUCTIONS AND SAVE THE CITY, HE SAYS.
FUCK THAT. I CAN'T EVEN FOLLOW FLAT-PACK FURNITURE INSTRUCTIONS. LAST TIME, I BUILT A FUCKING BOOK CASE INSIDE OUT.
CHAS, IT'S UNDERSTANDABLE TO HAVE YOUR DOUBTS, BUT I REALLY KNOW YOU CAN DO THIS.
LOOK, I CAN DRIVE 'ROUND LONDON LIKE THE BACK OF ME HAND, BUT THIS STUFF--I DON'T DO STUFF LIKE THIS ON MY OWN.
'CAUSE WHEN I'M LEFT TO MY OWN DEVICES, WELL, I TEND TO FUCK THINGS UP.
COME ON, LIKE WHAT, CHAS?
OKAY, EASY. TAKE NICKY FOR EXAMPLE. BIG INFLUENCE I'VE HAD ON HIS LIFE. HE'S NEVER GONNA FORGET THE MAN WHO BOUGHT HIM HIS FIRST BEER ON HIS 14TH BIRTHDAY.
REALLY, THAT'S NOT SO YOUNG.
IT WAS IN SOME ROPEY STRIP JOINT. AND I CAN TELL YOU IT WASN'T HIS ONLY FIRST THAT NIGHT.
OH.
YEAH, WHEN HIS OLD MAN WAS ON HIS DEATH BED IT PROBABLY WASN'T WHAT HE WAS THINKIN' WHEN HE ASKED ME TO LOOK AFTER HIS ONLY KID.
LOOK, MAYBE YOU'RE RIGHT AND PERHAPS THOSE THINGS ARE TRUE ABOUT YOU.
BUT JUST THIS ONCE, FOCUS ON THE THINGS YOU DO WELL AND THE REST WILL COME.
YEAH, THAT OR HAVE IT GO BIG TIME PEAR-SHAPED ON ME.

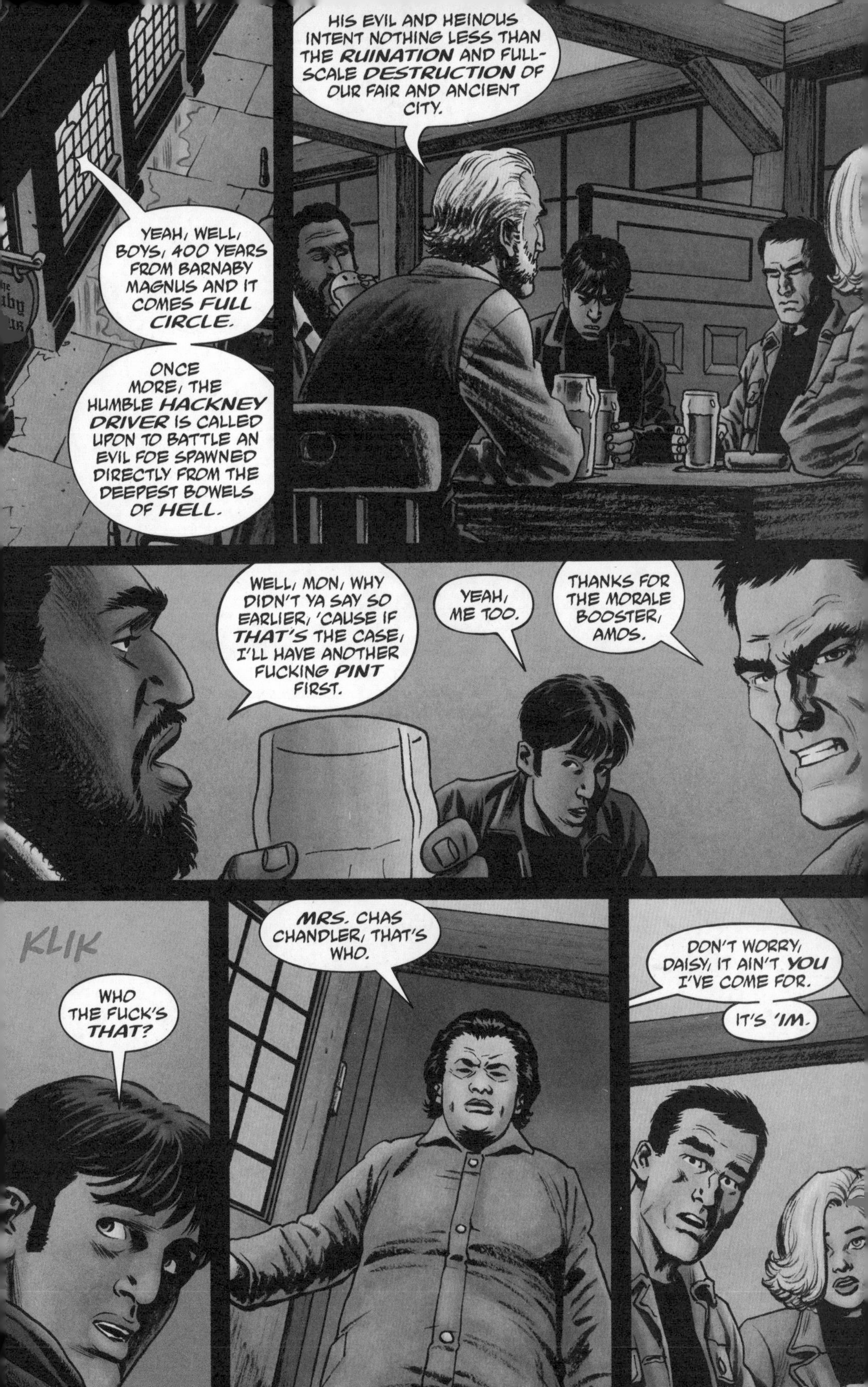
HIS EVIL AND HEINOUS INTENT NOTHING LESS THAN THE RUINATION AND FULL-SCALE DESTRUCTION OF OUR FAIR AND ANCIENT CITY.
YEAH, WELL, BOYS, 400 YEARS FROM BARNABY MAGNUS AND IT COMES FULL CIRCLE.
ONCE MORE, THE HUMBLE HACKNEY DRIVER IS CALLED UPON TO BATTLE AN EVIL FOE SPAWNED DIRECTLY FROM THE DEEPEST BOWELS OF HELL.
WELL, MON, WHY DIDN'T YA SAY SO EARLIER, 'CAUSE IF THAT'S THE CASE, I'LL HAVE ANOTHER FUCKING PINT FIRST.
YEAH, ME TOO.
THANKS FOR THE MORALE BOOSTER, AMOS.
KLIK
WHO THE FUCK'S THAT?
MRS. CHAS CHANDLER, THAT'S WHO.
DON'T WORRY, DAISY, IT AIN'T YOU I'VE COME FOR.
IT'S 'IM.

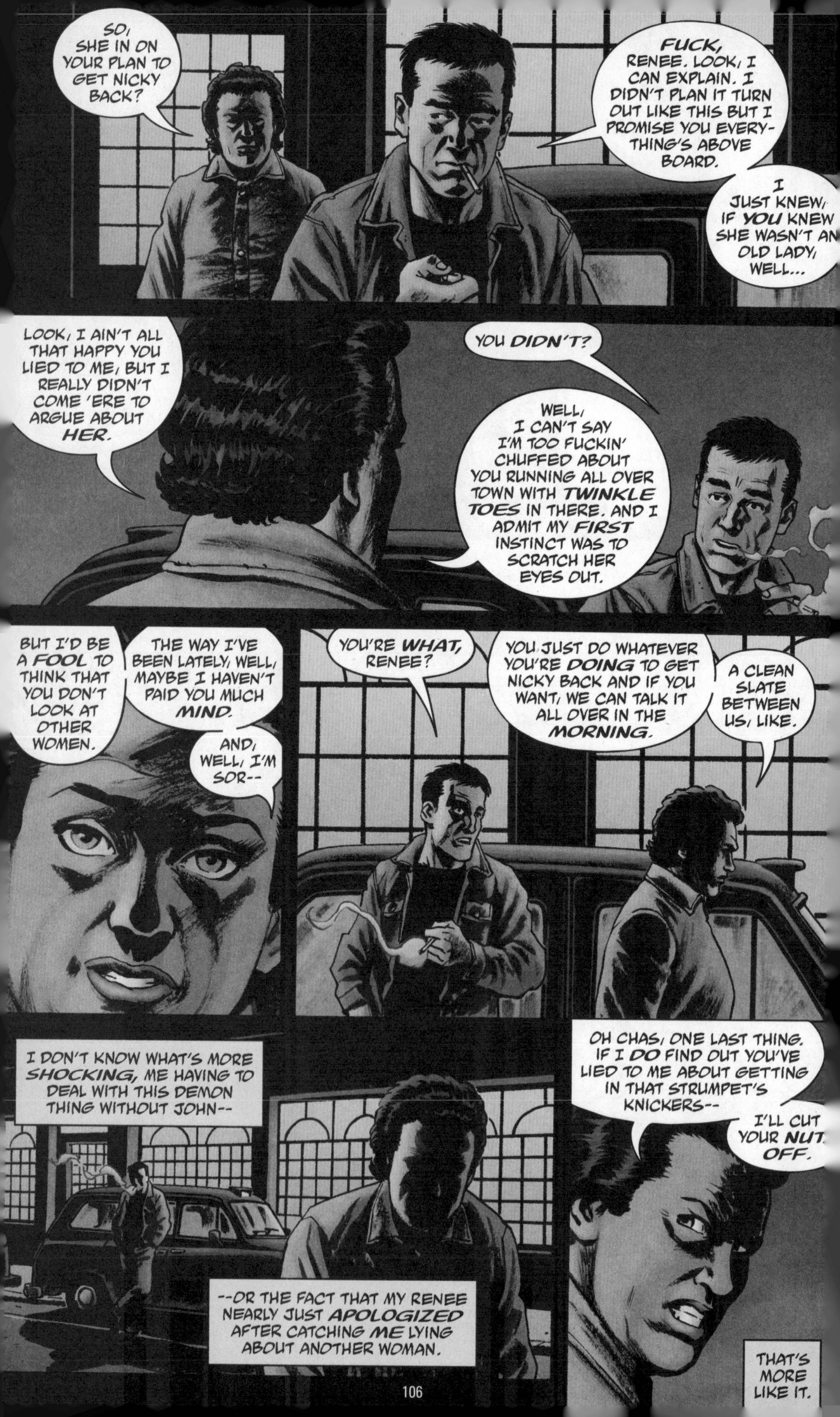

SO, SHE IN ON YOUR PLAN TO GET NICKY BACK?
FUCK, RENEE. LOOK, I CAN EXPLAIN. I DIDN'T PLAN IT TURN OUT LIKE THIS BUT I PROMISE YOU EVERY-THING'S ABOVE BOARD.
I JUST KNEW, IF YOU KNEW SHE WASN'T AN OLD LADY, WELL...
LOOK, I AIN'T ALL THAT HAPPY YOU LIED TO ME, BUT I REALLY DIDN'T COME 'ERE TO ARGUE ABOUT HER.
YOU DIDN'T?
WELL, I CAN'T SAY I'M TOO FUCKIN' CHUFFED ABOUT YOU RUNNING ALL OVER TOWN WITH TWINKLE TOES IN THERE. AND I ADMIT MY FIRST INSTINCT WAS TO SCRATCH HER EYES OUT.
BUT I'D BE A FOOL TO THINK THAT YOU DON'T LOOK AT OTHER WOMEN.
THE WAY I'VE BEEN LATELY, WELL, MAYBE I HAVEN'T PAID YOU MUCH MIND.
AND, WELL, I'M SOR--
YOU'RE WHAT, RENEE?
YOU JUST DO WHATEVER YOU'RE DOING TO GET NICKY BACK AND IF YOU WANT, WE CAN TALK IT ALL OVER IN THE MORNING.
A CLEAN SLATE BETWEEN US, LIKE.
I DON'T KNOW WHAT'S MORE SHOCKING, ME HAVING TO DEAL WITH THIS DEMON THING WITHOUT JOHN--
--OR THE FACT THAT MY RENEE NEARLY JUST APOLOGIZED AFTER CATCHING ME LYING ABOUT ANOTHER WOMAN.
OH CHAS, ONE LAST THING. IF I DO FIND OUT YOU'VE LIED TO ME ABOUT GETTING IN THAT STRUMPET'S KNICKERS--
I'LL CUT YOUR NUT OFF.
THAT'S MORE LIKE IT.

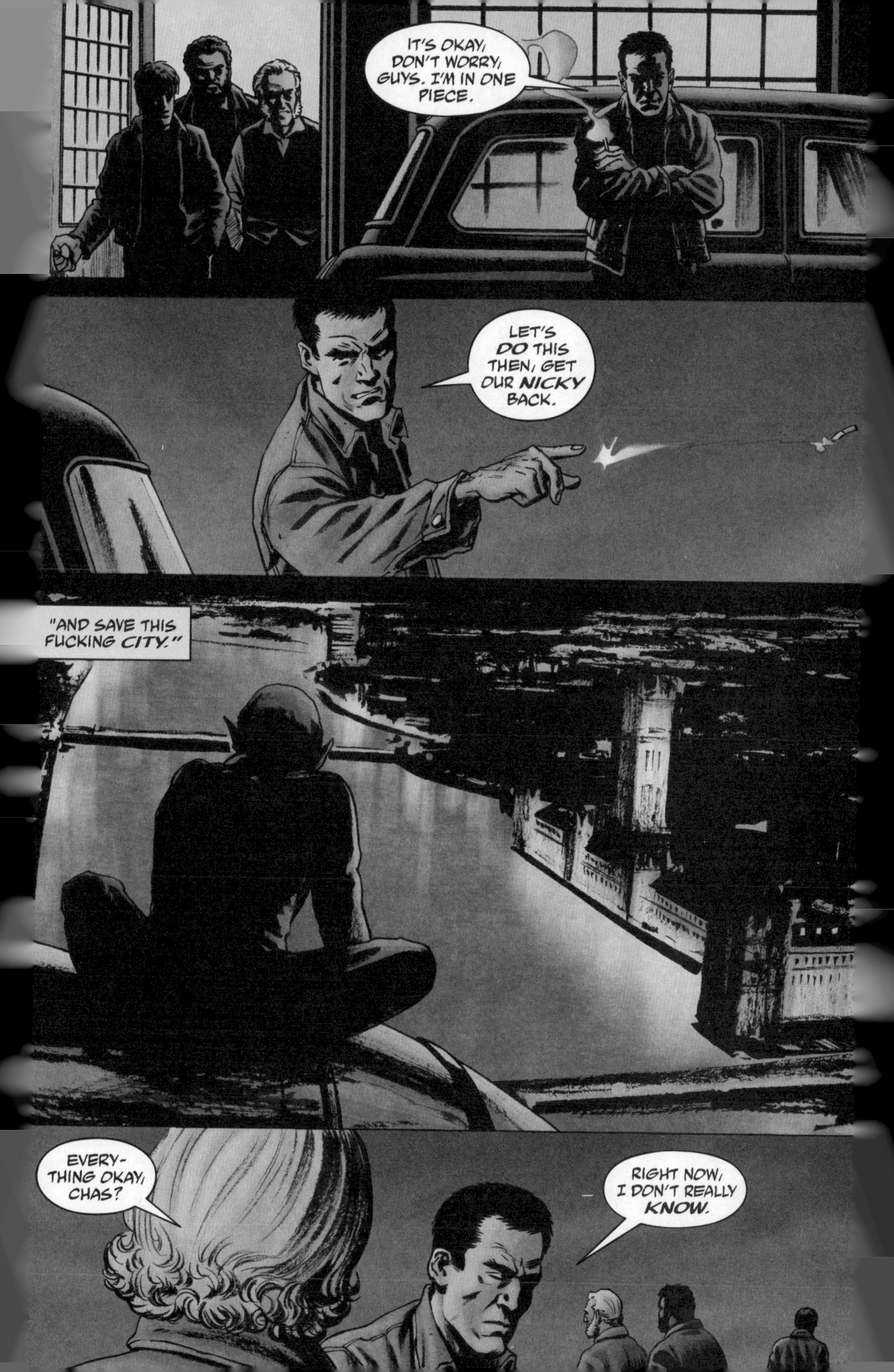
IT'S OKAY, DON'T WORRY, GUYS. I'M IN ONE PIECE.
LET'S DO THIS THEN, GET OUR NICKY BACK.
"AND SAVE THIS FUCKING CITY."
EVERY-THING OKAY, CHAS?
RIGHT NOW, I DON'T REALLY KNOW.

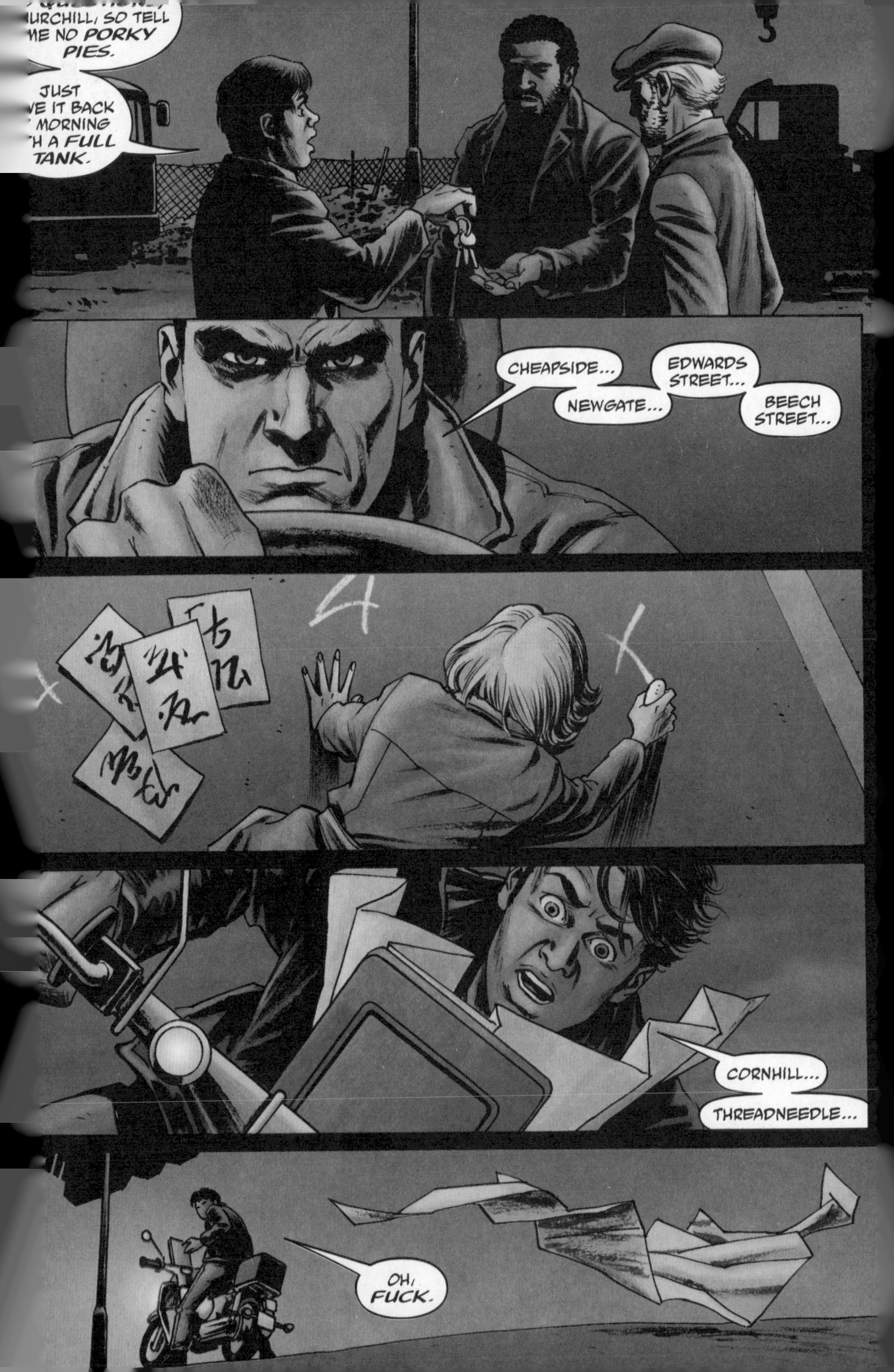
SO TELL ME NO PORKY PIES.
JUST ... IT BACK ... MORNING ... A FULL TANK.
CHEAPSIDE...
EDWARDS STREET...
NEWGATE...
BEECH STREET...
CORNHILL...
THREADNEEDLE...
OH, FUCK.

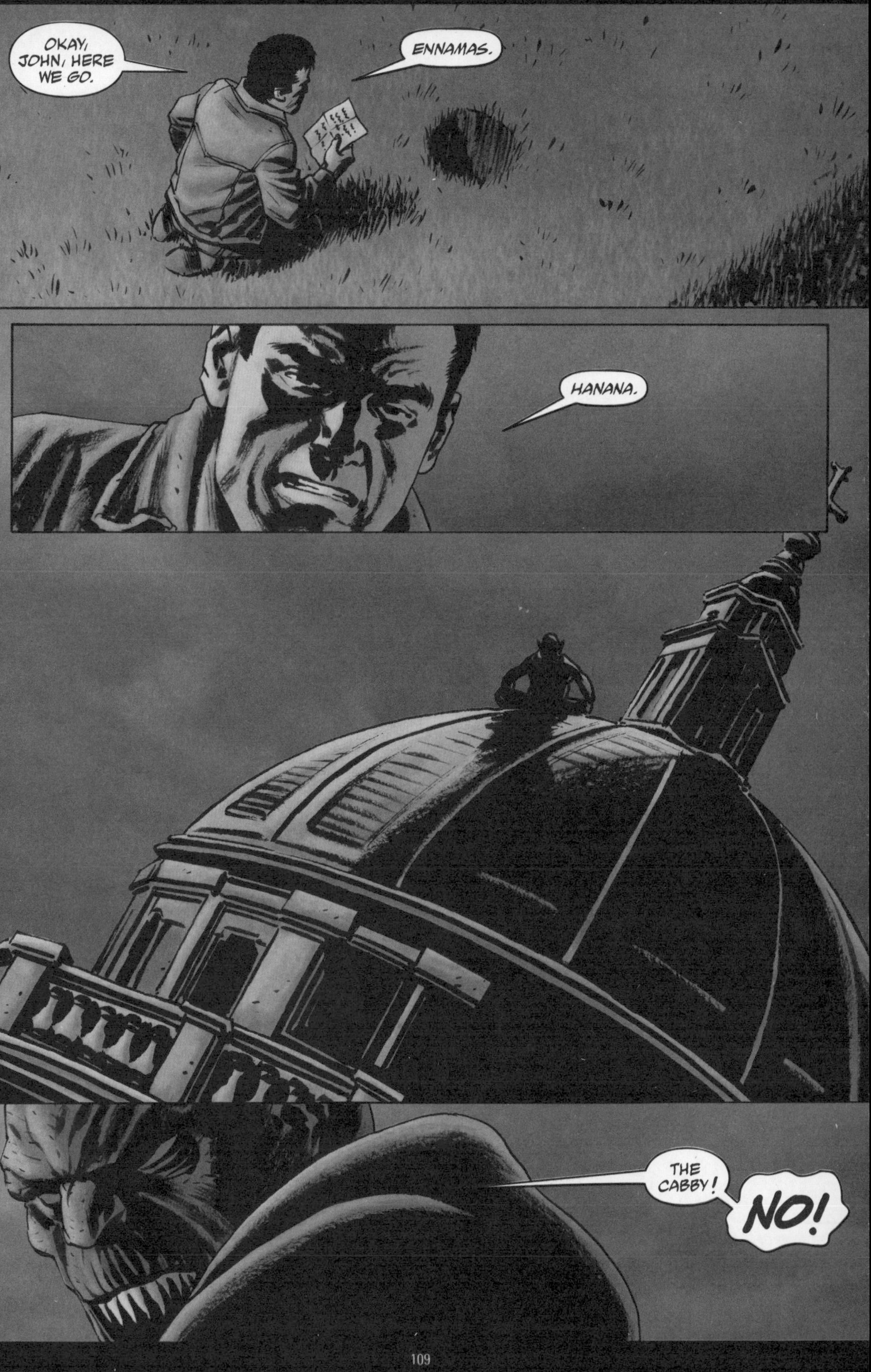
OKAY, JOHN, HERE WE GO.
ENNAMAS.
HANANA.
THE CABBY!
NO!

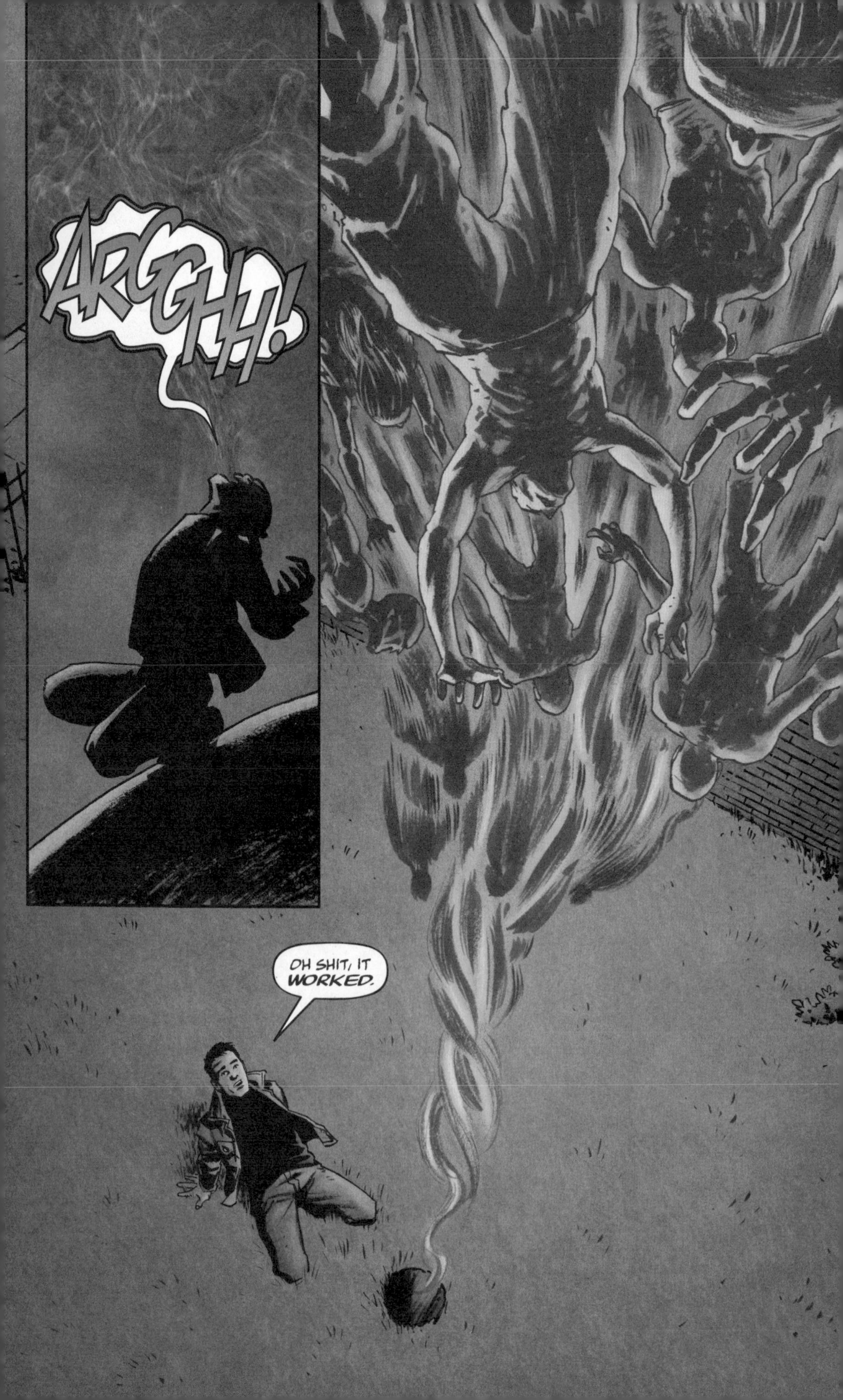
ARGGHH!
OH SHIT, IT WORKED.

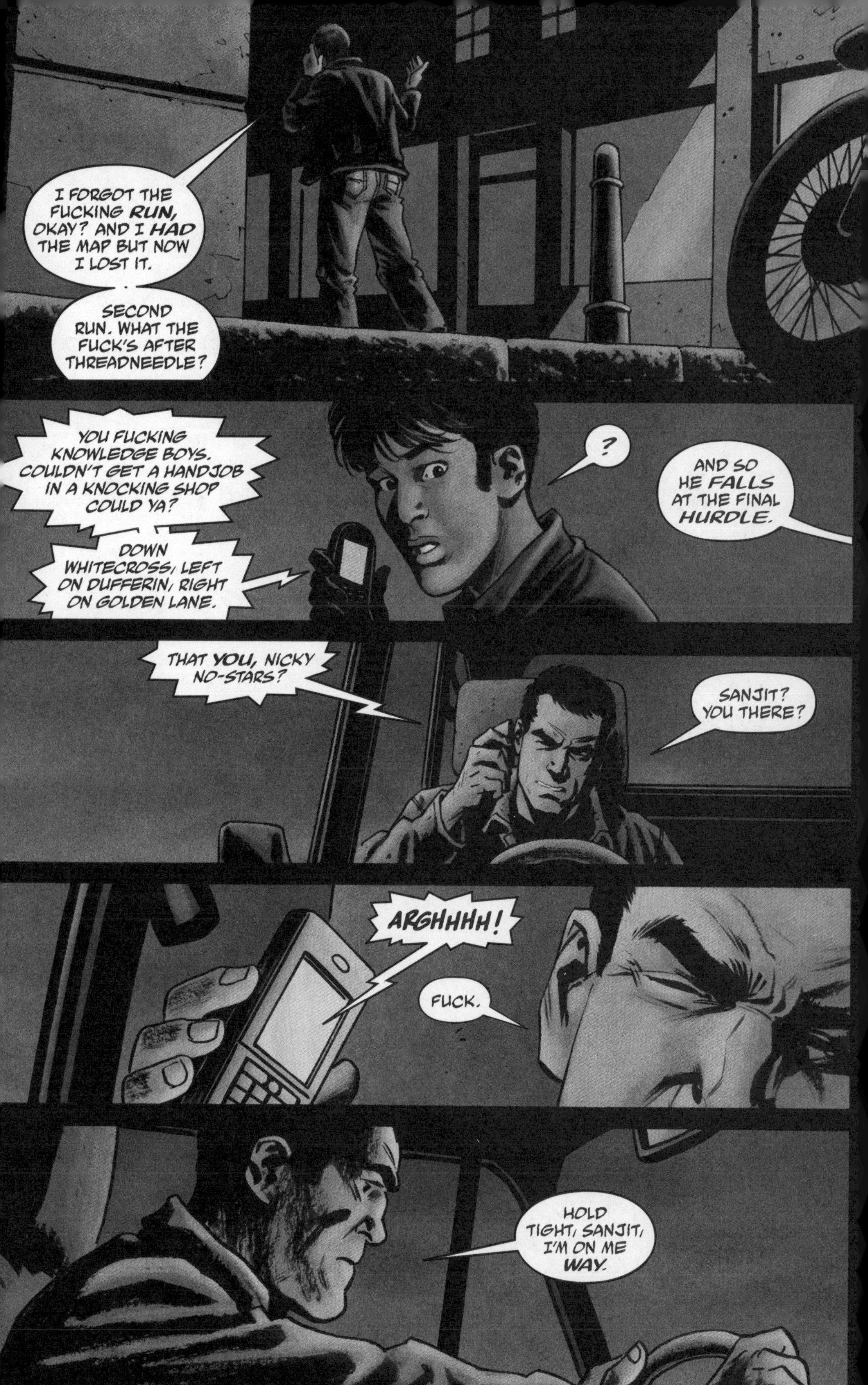

I FORGOT THE FUCKING RUN, OKAY? AND I HAD THE MAP BUT NOW I LOST IT.
SECOND RUN. WHAT THE FUCK'S AFTER THREADNEEDLE?
YOU FUCKING KNOWLEDGE BOYS. COULDN'T GET A HANDJOB IN A KNOCKING SHOP COULD YA?
DOWN WHITECROSS, LEFT ON DUFFERIN, RIGHT ON GOLDEN LANE.
?
AND SO HE FALLS AT THE FINAL HURDLE.
THAT YOU, NICKY NO-STARS?
SANJIT? YOU THERE?
ARGHHHH!
FUCK.
HOLD TIGHT, SANJIT, I'M ON ME WAY.

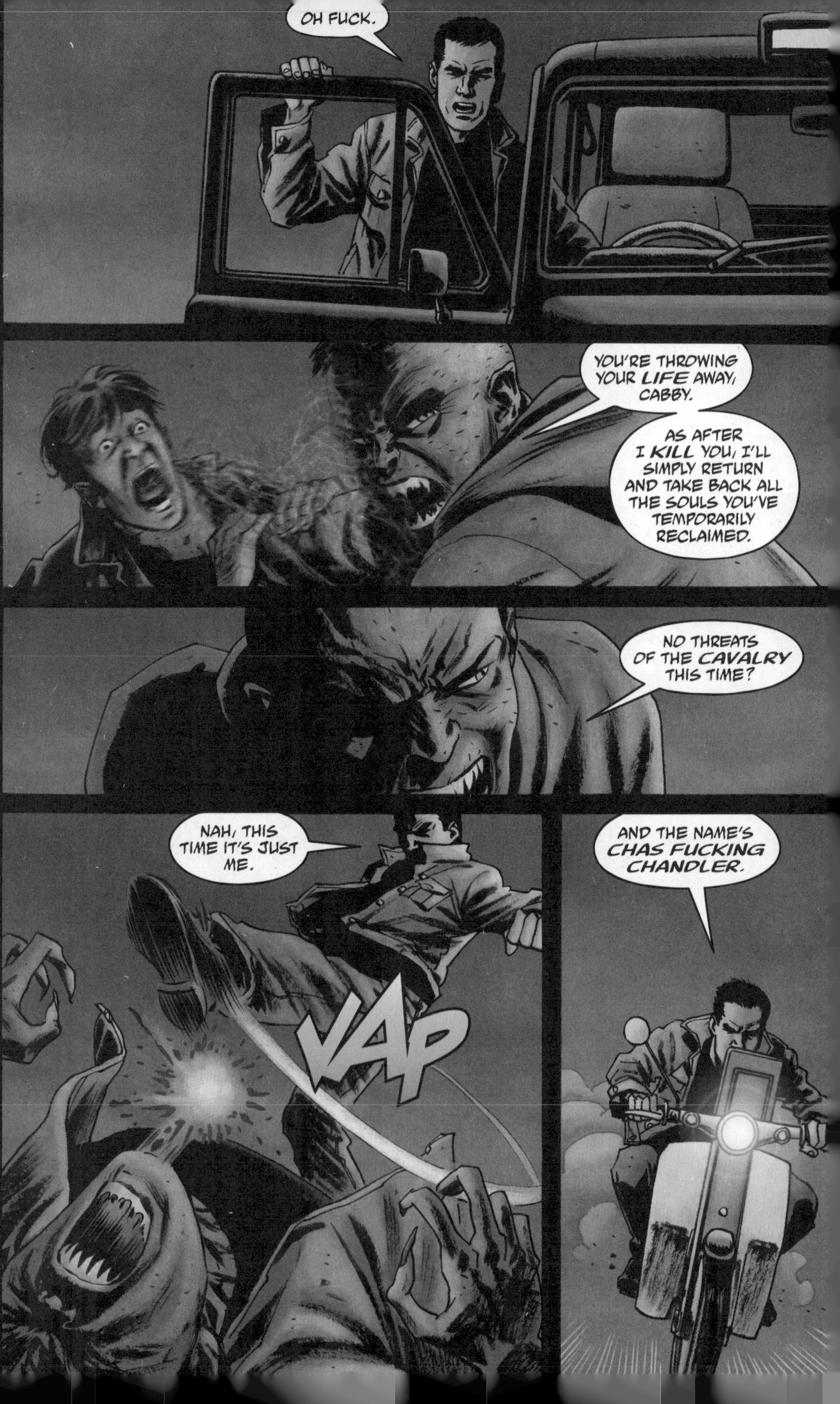
OH FUCK.
YOU'RE THROWING YOUR LIFE AWAY, CABBY.
AS AFTER I KILL YOU, I'LL SIMPLY RETURN AND TAKE BACK ALL THE SOULS YOU'VE TEMPORARILY RECLAIMED.
NO THREATS OF THE CAVALRY THIS TIME?
NAH, THIS TIME IT'S JUST ME.
VAP
AND THE NAME'S CHAS FUCKING CHANDLER.

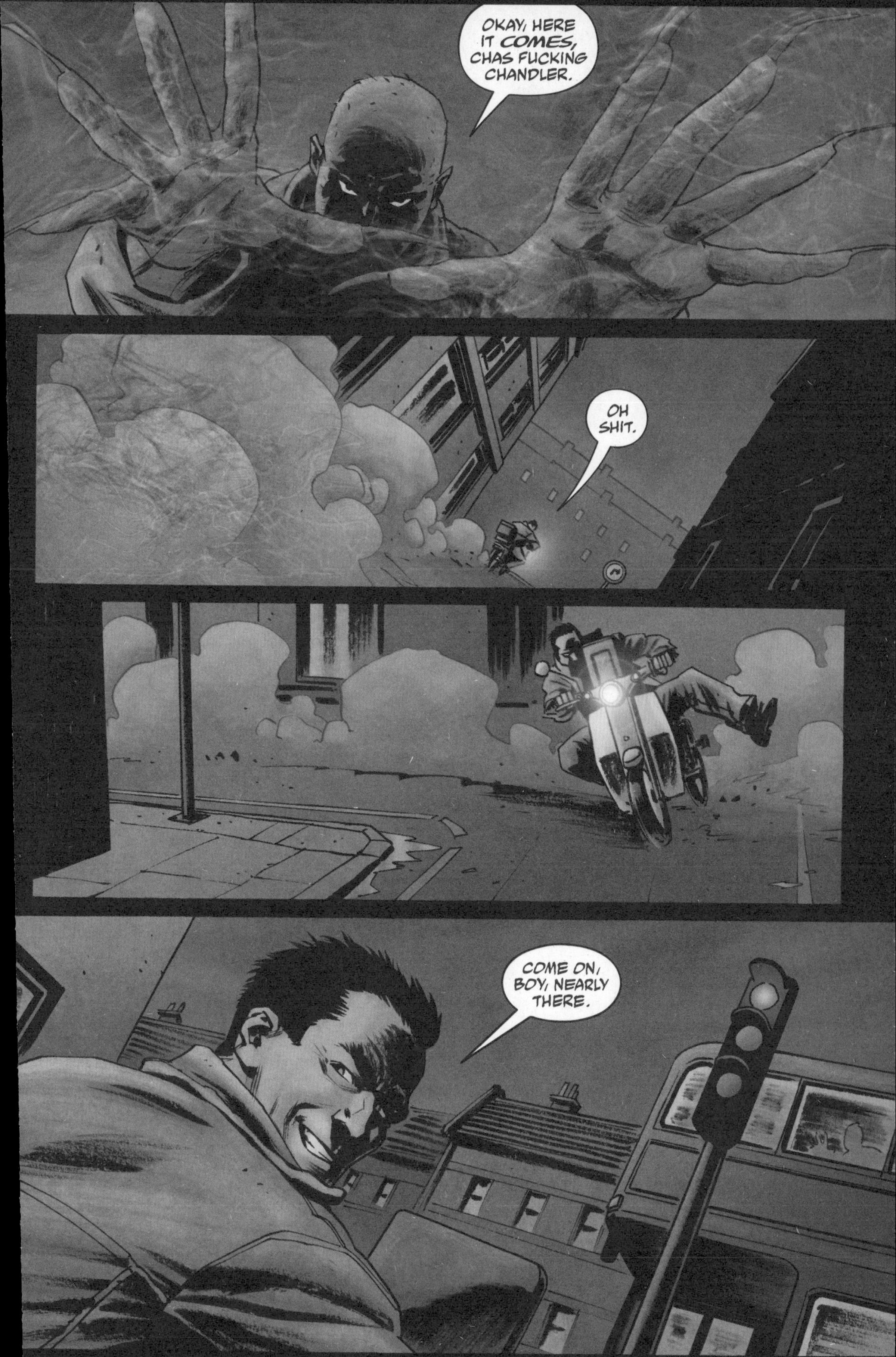
OKAY, HERE IT COMES, CHAS FUCKING CHANDLER.
OH SHIT.
COME ON, BOY, NEARLY THERE.

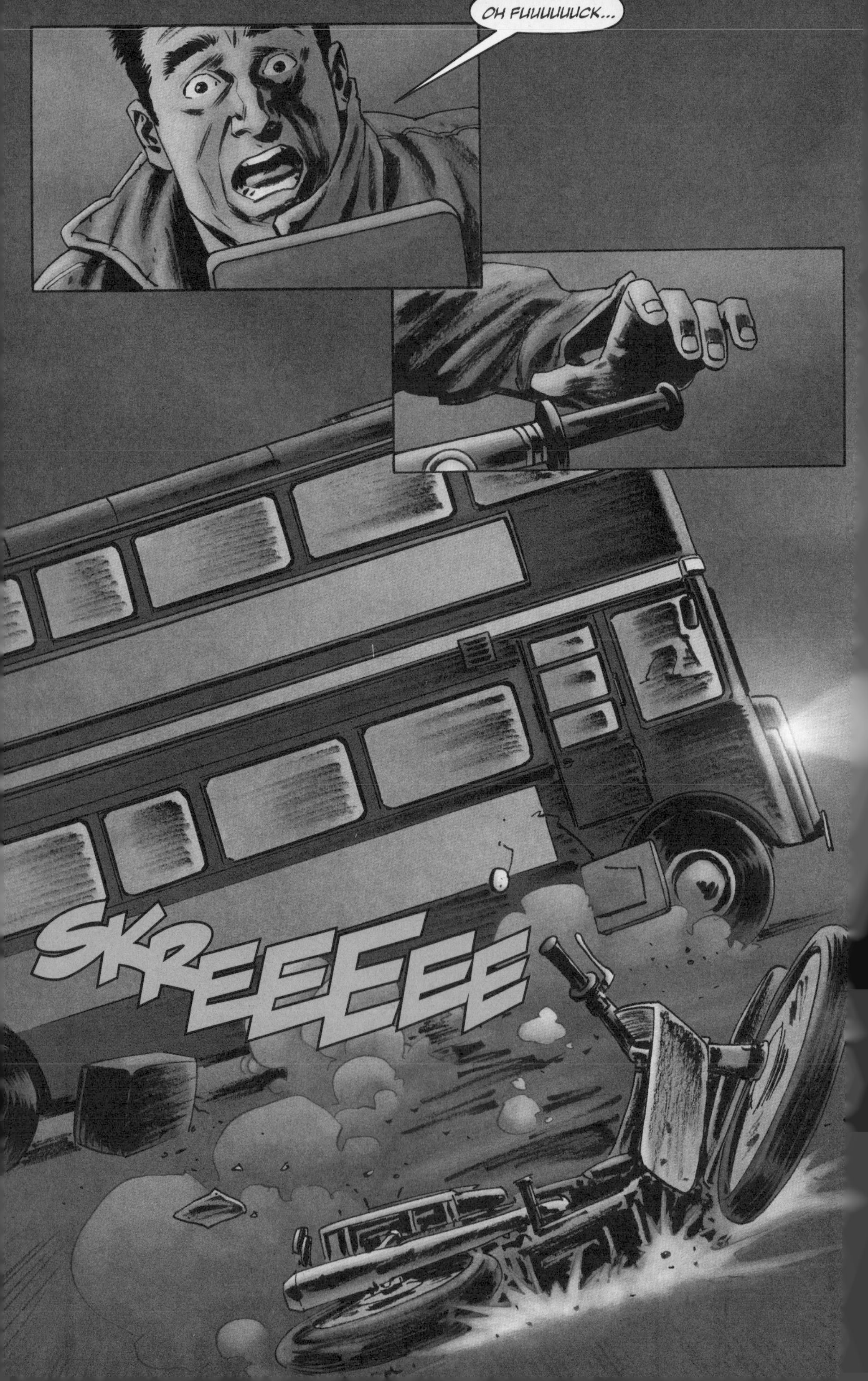
OH FUUUUUUCK...
SKREEEEEE

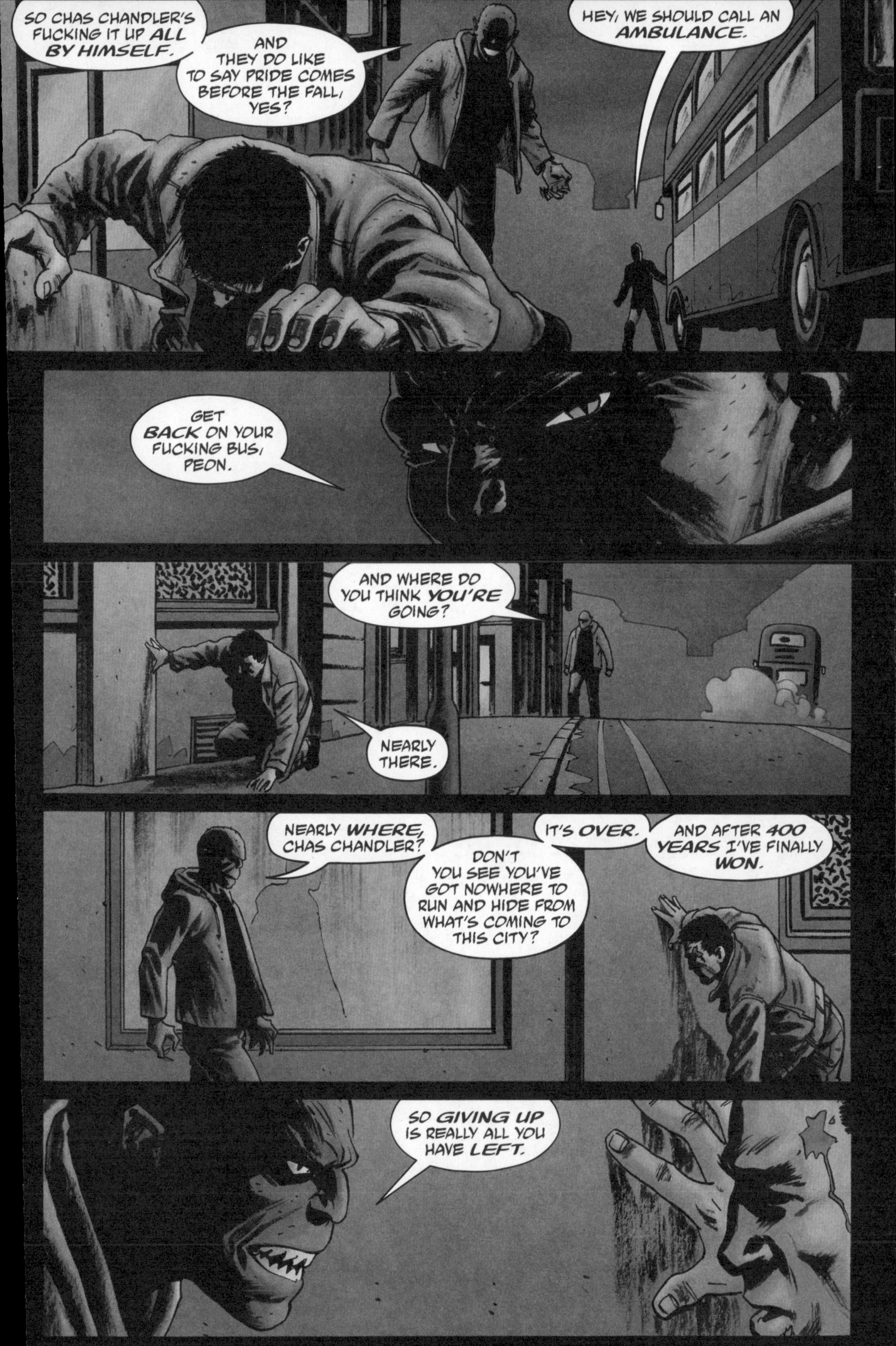
SO CHAS CHANDLER'S FUCKING IT UP ALL BY HIMSELF.
AND THEY DO LIKE TO SAY PRIDE COMES BEFORE THE FALL, YES?
HEY, WE SHOULD CALL AN AMBULANCE.
GET BACK ON YOUR FUCKING BUS, PEON.
AND WHERE DO YOU THINK YOU'RE GOING?
NEARLY THERE.
NEARLY WHERE, CHAS CHANDLER?
DON'T YOU SEE YOU'VE GOT NOWHERE TO RUN AND HIDE FROM WHAT'S COMING TO THIS CITY?
IT'S OVER.
AND AFTER 400 YEARS I'VE FINALLY WON.
SO GIVING UP IS REALLY ALL YOU HAVE LEFT.

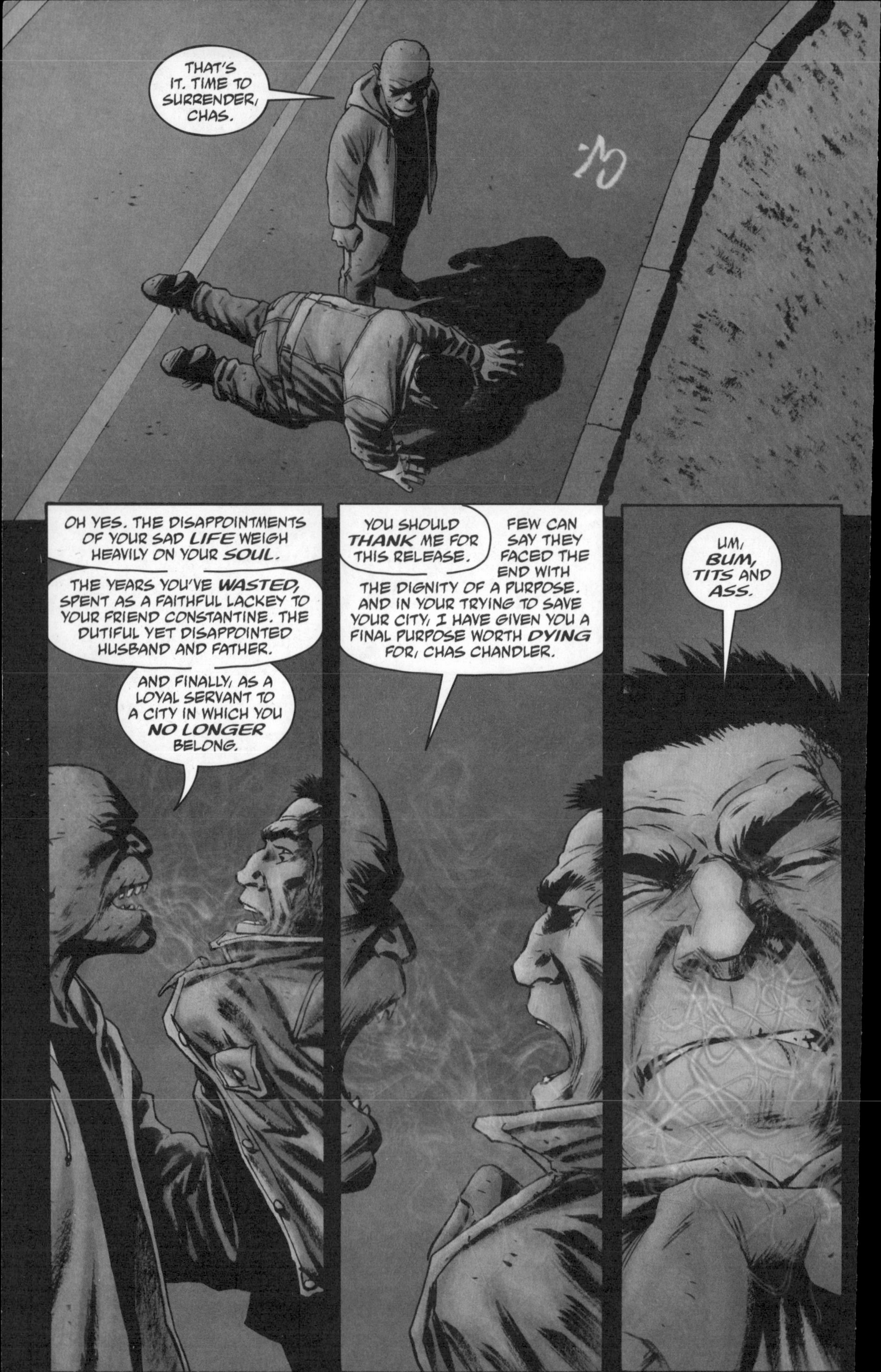
THAT'S IT. TIME TO SURRENDER, CHAS.
OH YES. THE DISAPPOINTMENTS OF YOUR SAD LIFE WEIGH HEAVILY ON YOUR SOUL.
THE YEARS YOU'VE WASTED, SPENT AS A FAITHFUL LACKEY TO YOUR FRIEND CONSTANTINE. THE DUTIFUL YET DISAPPOINTED HUSBAND AND FATHER.
AND FINALLY, AS A LOYAL SERVANT TO A CITY IN WHICH YOU NO LONGER BELONG.
YOU SHOULD THANK ME FOR THIS RELEASE.
FEW CAN SAY THEY FACED THE END WITH THE DIGNITY OF A PURPOSE. AND IN YOUR TRYING TO SAVE YOUR CITY, I HAVE GIVEN YOU A FINAL PURPOSE WORTH DYING FOR, CHAS CHANDLER.
UM, BUM, TITS AND ASS.

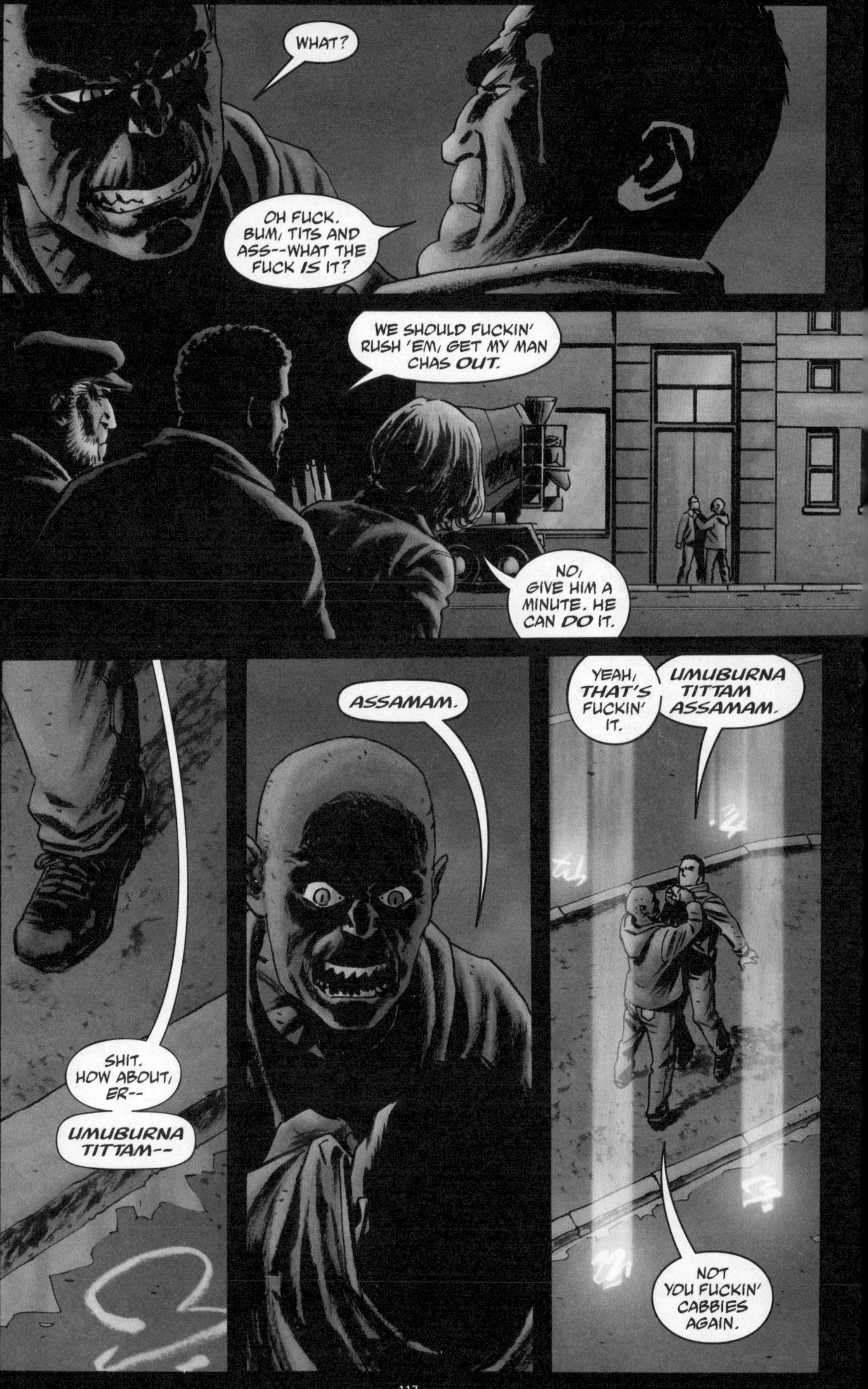
WHAT?
OH FUCK. BUM, TITS AND ASS--WHAT THE FUCK *IS* IT?
WE SHOULD FUCKIN' RUSH 'EM, GET MY MAN CHAS *OUT*.
NO, GIVE HIM A MINUTE. HE CAN *DO* IT.
SHIT. HOW ABOUT, ER--
UMUBURNA TITTAM--
ASSAMAM.
YEAH, *THAT'S* FUCKIN' IT.
UMUBURNA TITTAM ASSAMAM.
NOT YOU FUCKIN' CABBIES AGAIN.

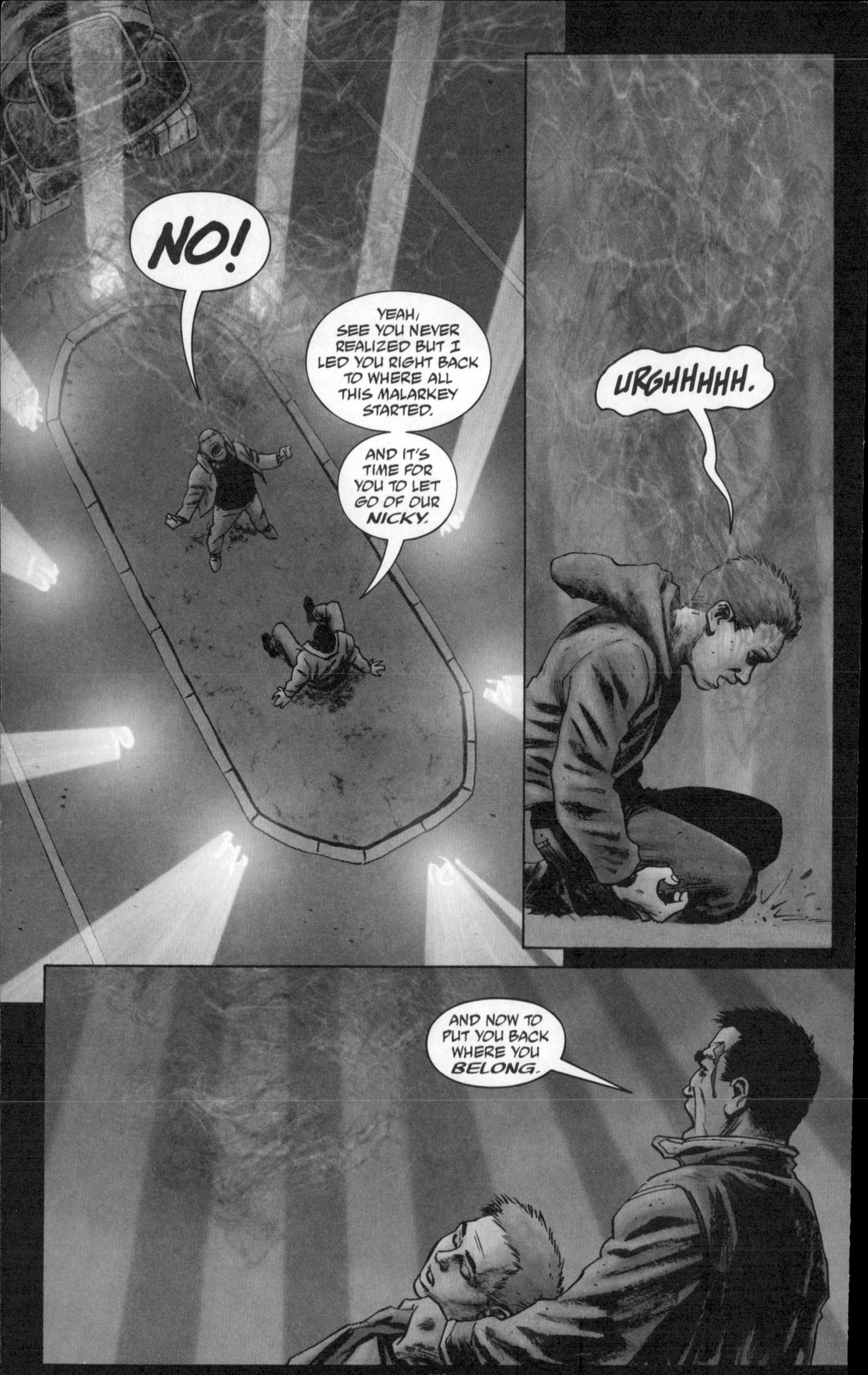
NO!
YEAH, SEE YOU NEVER REALIZED BUT I LED YOU RIGHT BACK TO WHERE ALL THIS MALARKEY STARTED.
AND IT'S TIME FOR YOU TO LET GO OF OUR *NICKY*.
URGHHHHH.
AND NOW TO PUT YOU BACK WHERE YOU *BELONG*.

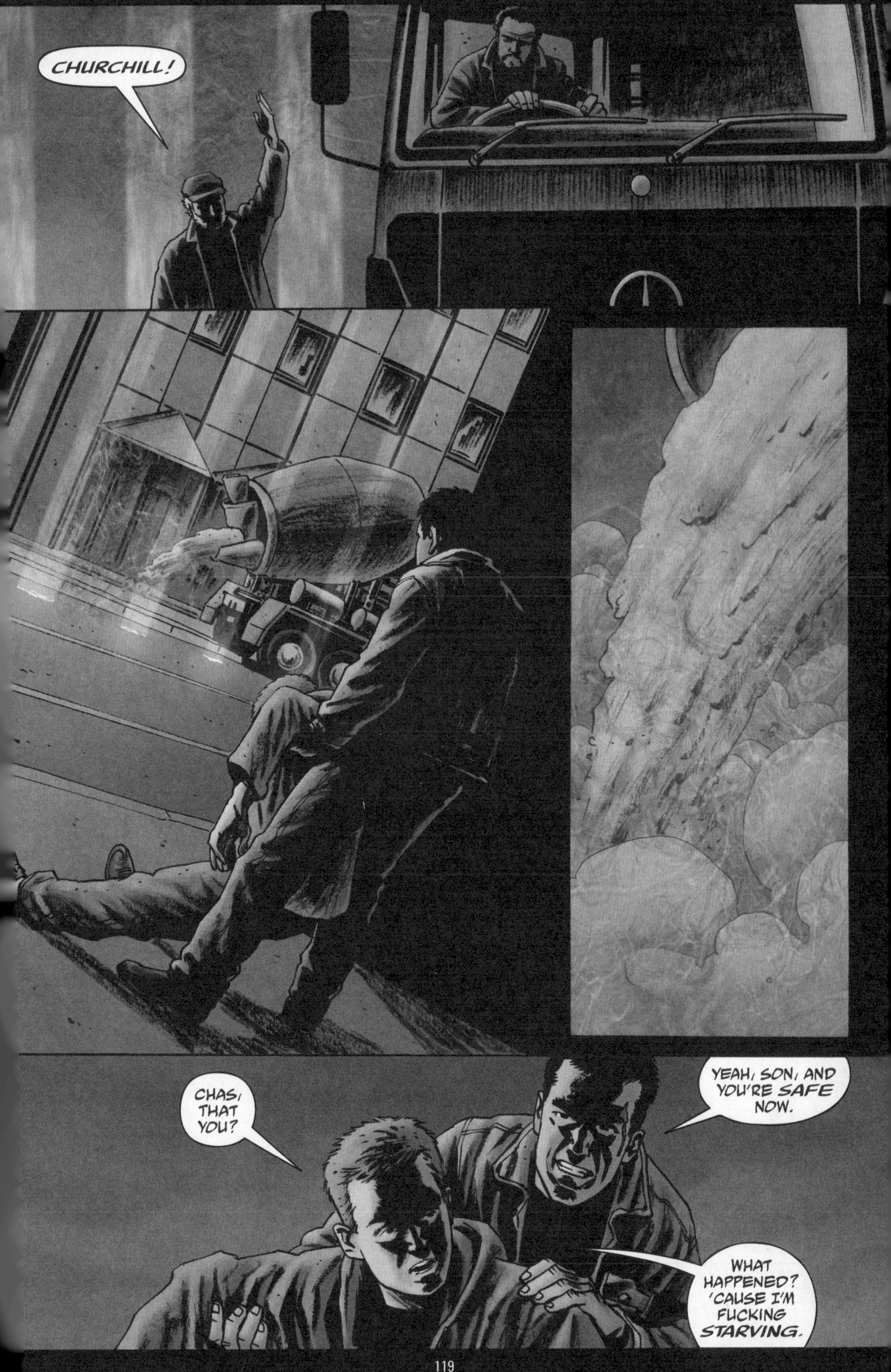
CHURCHILL!
CHAS, THAT YOU?
YEAH, SON, AND YOU'RE SAFE NOW.
WHAT HAPPENED? 'CAUSE I'M FUCKING STARVING.

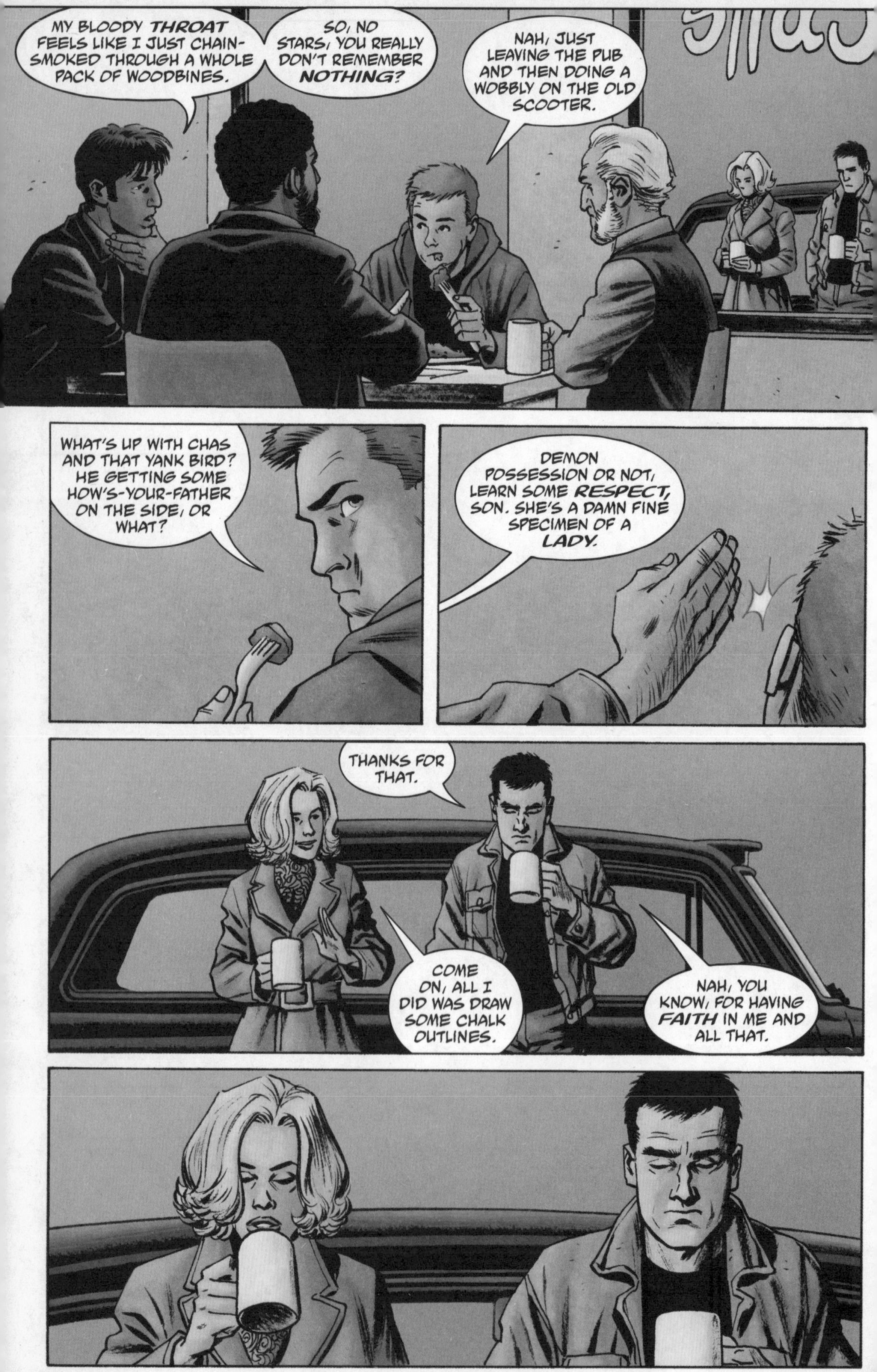
MY BLOODY THROAT FEELS LIKE I JUST CHAIN-SMOKED THROUGH A WHOLE PACK OF WOODBINES.
SO, NO STARS, YOU REALLY DON'T REMEMBER NOTHING?
NAH, JUST LEAVING THE PUB AND THEN DOING A WOBBLY ON THE OLD SCOOTER.
WHAT'S UP WITH CHAS AND THAT YANK BIRD? HE GETTING SOME HOW'S-YOUR-FATHER ON THE SIDE, OR WHAT?
DEMON POSSESSION OR NOT, LEARN SOME RESPECT, SON. SHE'S A DAMN FINE SPECIMEN OF A LADY.
THANKS FOR THAT.
COME ON, ALL I DID WAS DRAW SOME CHALK OUTLINES.
NAH, YOU KNOW, FOR HAVING FAITH IN ME AND ALL THAT.

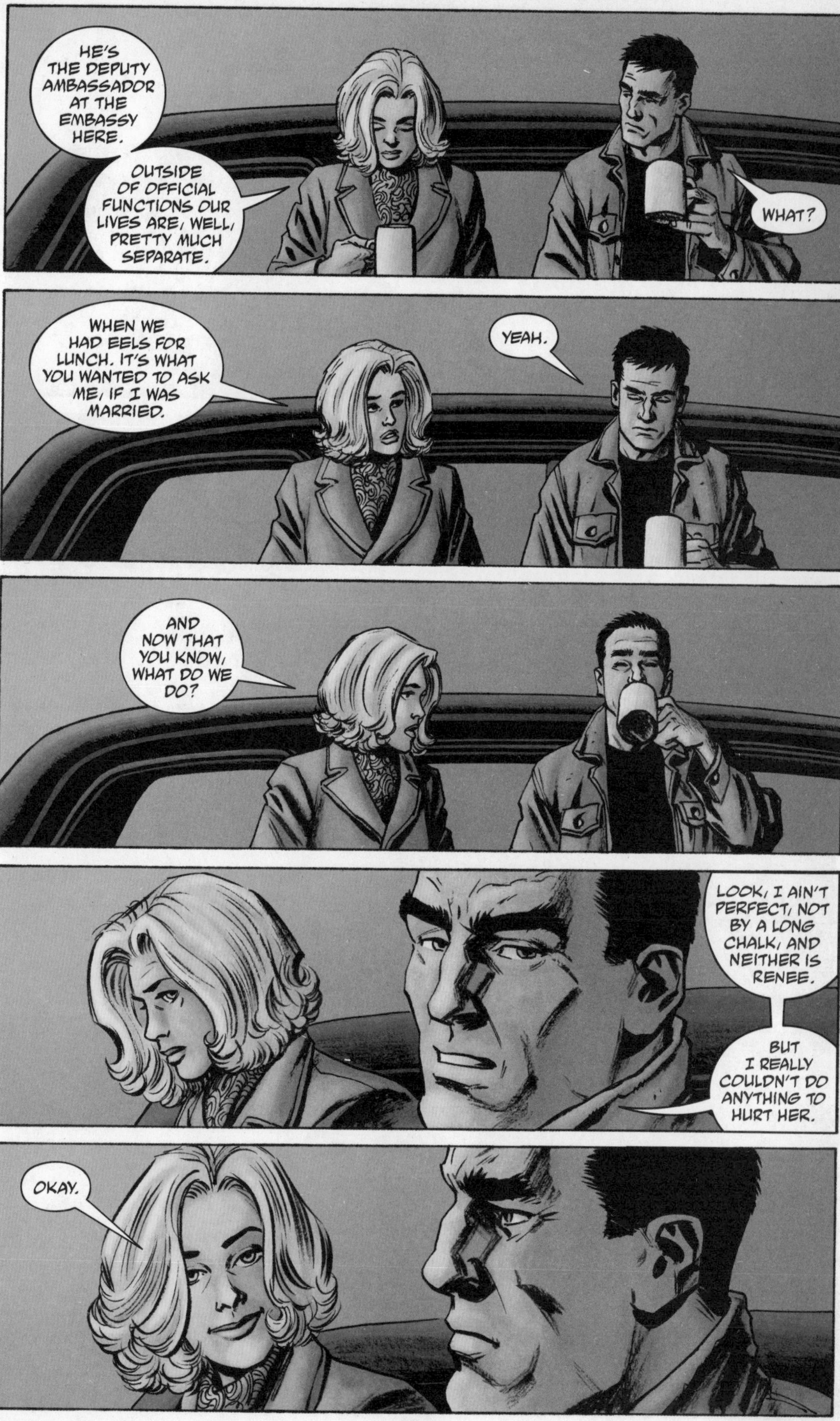
HE'S THE DEPUTY AMBASSADOR AT THE EMBASSY HERE.
OUTSIDE OF OFFICIAL FUNCTIONS OUR LIVES ARE, WELL, PRETTY MUCH SEPARATE.
WHAT?
WHEN WE HAD EELS FOR LUNCH. IT'S WHAT YOU WANTED TO ASK ME, IF I WAS MARRIED.
YEAH.
AND NOW THAT YOU KNOW, WHAT DO WE DO?
LOOK, I AIN'T PERFECT, NOT BY A LONG CHALK, AND NEITHER IS RENEE.
BUT I REALLY COULDN'T DO ANYTHING TO HURT HER.
OKAY.

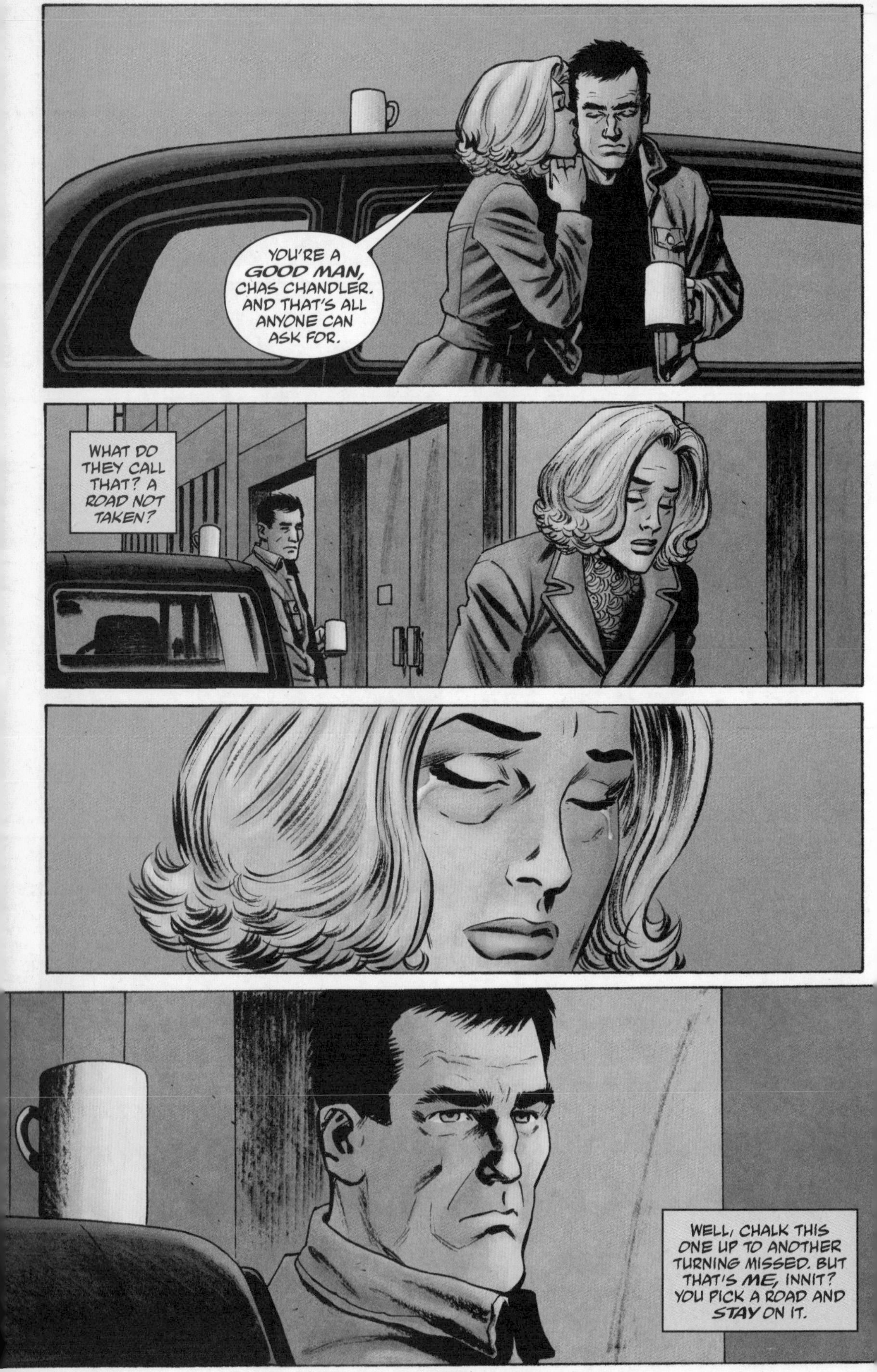

YOU'RE A GOOD MAN, CHAS CHANDLER. AND THAT'S ALL ANYONE CAN ASK FOR.
WHAT DO THEY CALL THAT? A ROAD NOT TAKEN?
WELL, CHALK THIS ONE UP TO ANOTHER TURNING MISSED. BUT THAT'S ME, INNIT? YOU PICK A ROAD AND STAY ON IT.

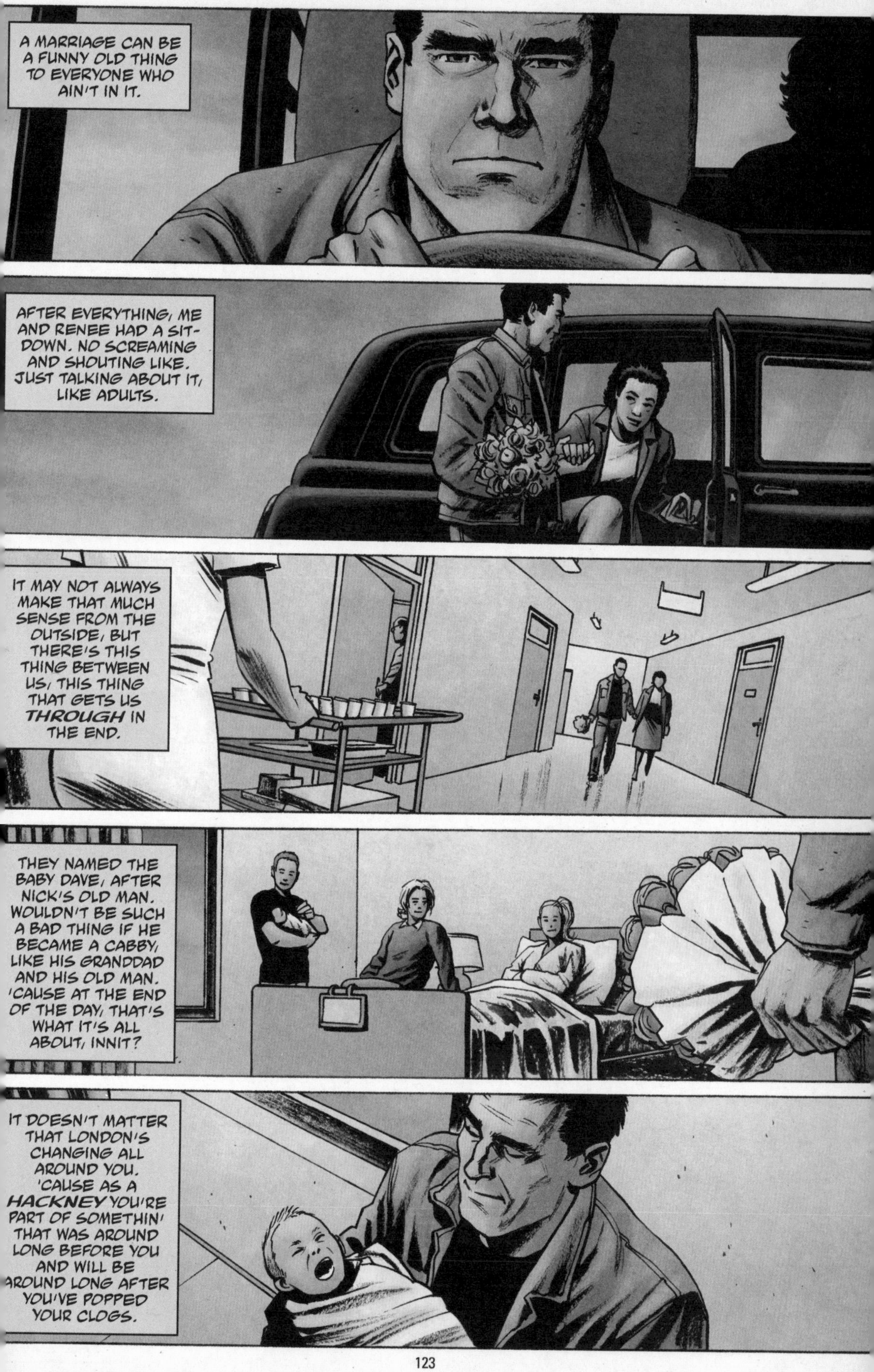
A MARRIAGE CAN BE A FUNNY OLD THING TO EVERYONE WHO AIN'T IN IT.
AFTER EVERYTHING, ME AND RENEE HAD A SIT-DOWN. NO SCREAMING AND SHOUTING LIKE. JUST TALKING ABOUT IT, LIKE ADULTS.
IT MAY NOT ALWAYS MAKE THAT MUCH SENSE FROM THE OUTSIDE, BUT THERE'S THIS THING BETWEEN US, THIS THING THAT GETS US *THROUGH* IN THE END.
THEY NAMED THE BABY DAVE, AFTER NICK'S OLD MAN. WOULDN'T BE SUCH A BAD THING IF HE BECAME A CABBY, LIKE HIS GRANDDAD AND HIS OLD MAN. 'CAUSE AT THE END OF THE DAY, THAT'S WHAT IT'S ALL ABOUT, INNIT?
IT DOESN'T MATTER THAT LONDON'S CHANGING ALL AROUND YOU. 'CAUSE AS A *HACKNEY* YOU'RE PART OF SOMETHIN' THAT WAS AROUND LONG BEFORE YOU AND WILL BE AROUND LONG AFTER YOU'VE POPPED YOUR CLOGS.

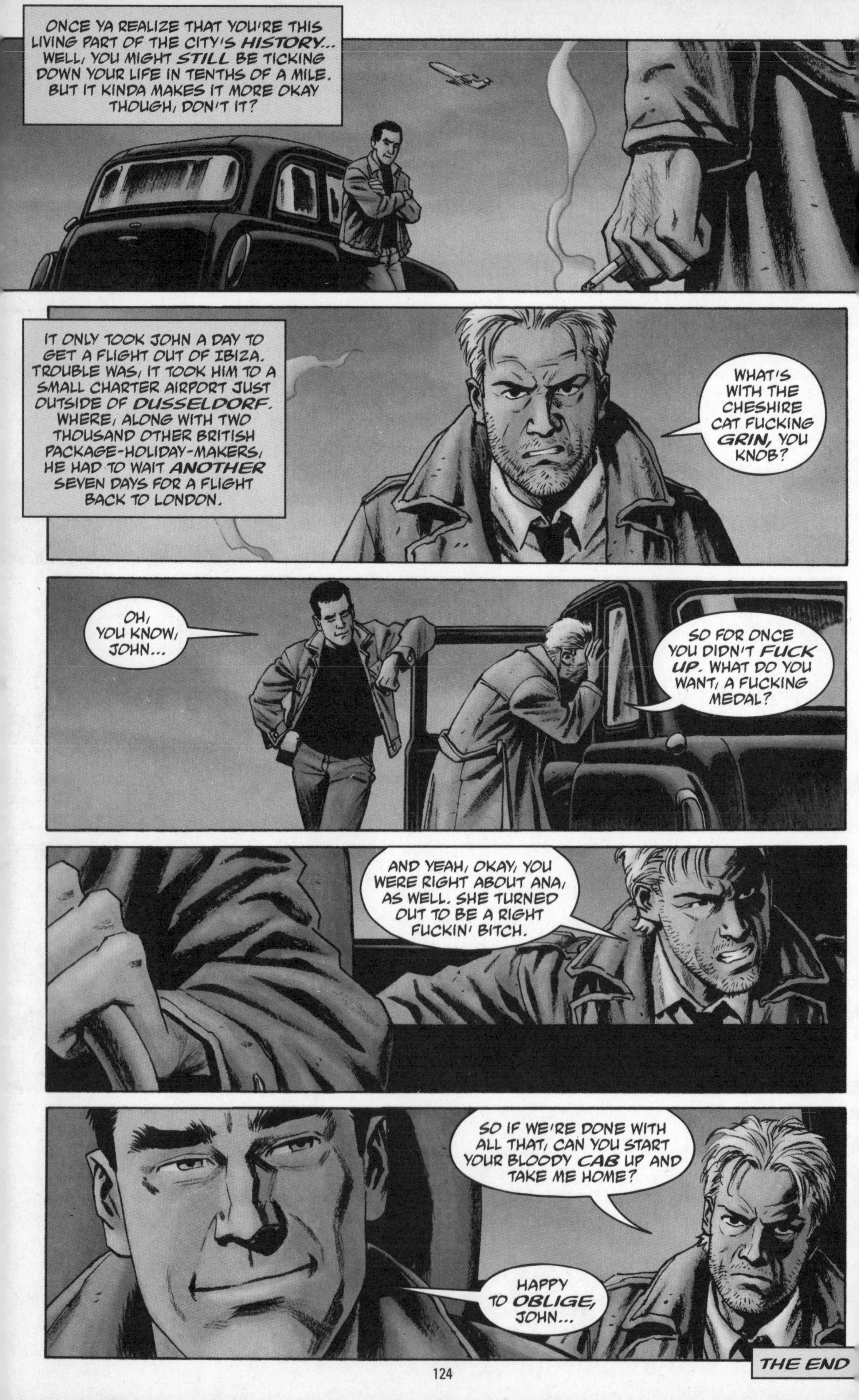
ONCE YA REALIZE THAT YOU'RE THIS LIVING PART OF THE CITY'S HISTORY... WELL, YOU MIGHT STILL BE TICKING DOWN YOUR LIFE IN TENTHS OF A MILE. BUT IT KINDA MAKES IT MORE OKAY THOUGH, DON'T IT?
IT ONLY TOOK JOHN A DAY TO GET A FLIGHT OUT OF IBIZA. TROUBLE WAS, IT TOOK HIM TO A SMALL CHARTER AIRPORT JUST OUTSIDE OF DUSSELDORF. WHERE, ALONG WITH TWO THOUSAND OTHER BRITISH PACKAGE-HOLIDAY-MAKERS, HE HAD TO WAIT ANOTHER SEVEN DAYS FOR A FLIGHT BACK TO LONDON.
WHAT'S WITH THE CHESHIRE CAT FUCKING GRIN, YOU KNOB?
OH, YOU KNOW, JOHN...
SO FOR ONCE YOU DIDN'T FUCK UP. WHAT DO YOU WANT, A FUCKING MEDAL?
AND YEAH, OKAY, YOU WERE RIGHT ABOUT ANA, AS WELL. SHE TURNED OUT TO BE A RIGHT FUCKIN' BITCH.
SO IF WE'RE DONE WITH ALL THAT, CAN YOU START YOUR BLOODY CAB UP AND TAKE ME HOME?
HAPPY TO OBLIGE, JOHN...
THE END

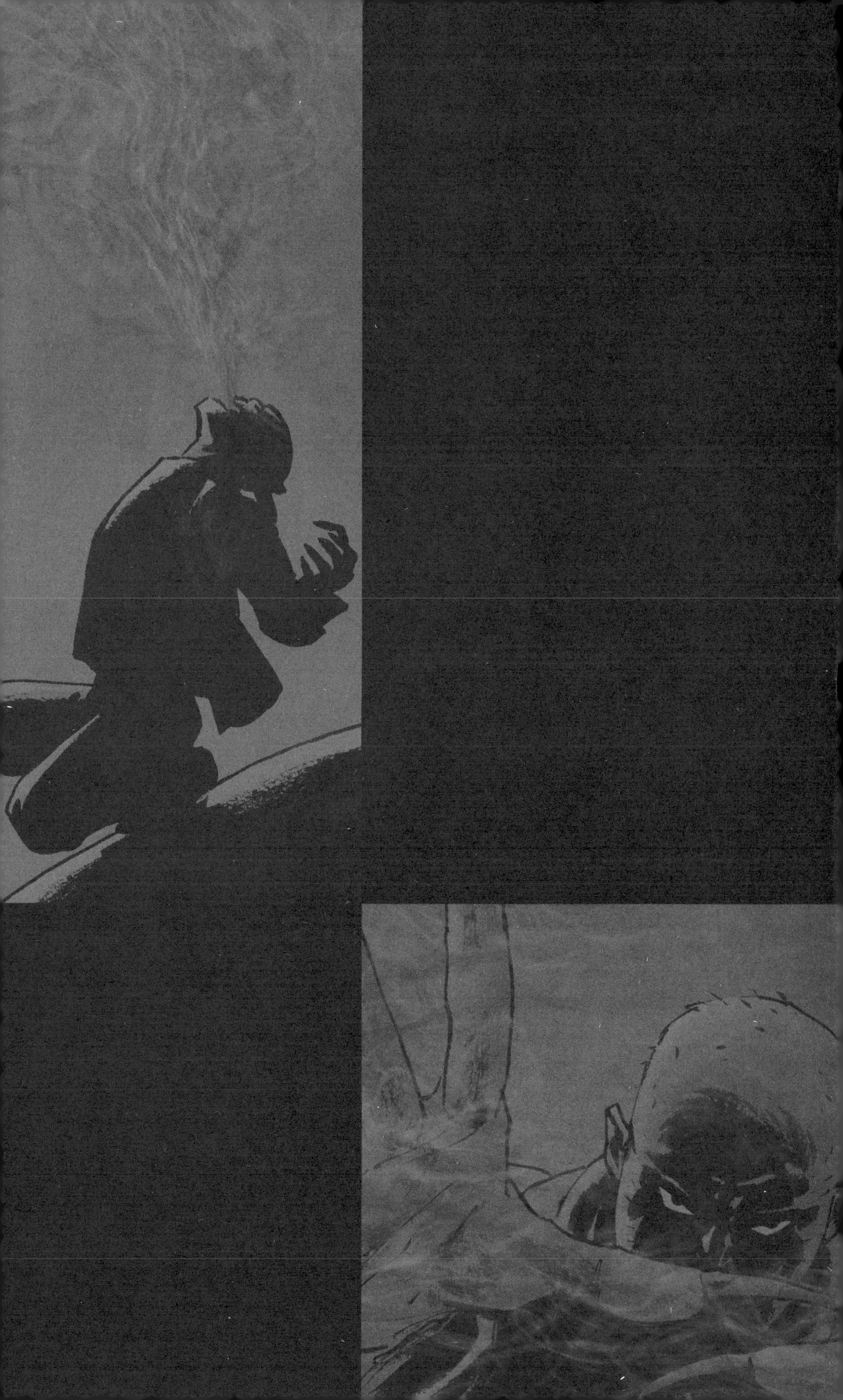

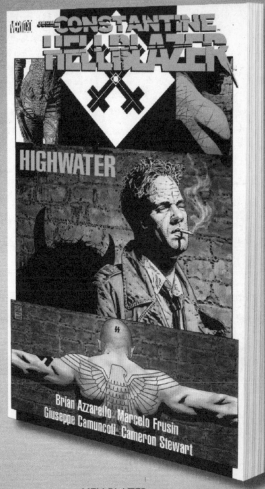

FROM THE WRITER OF
PREACHER

GARTH ENNIS

HELLBLAZER: DANGEROUS HABITS

HELLBLAZER: BLOODLINES

HELLBLAZER: FEAR AND LOATHING

HELLBLAZER: TAINTED LOVE

HELLBLAZER: DAMNATION'S FLAME

HELLBLAZER: RAKE AT THE GATES OF HELL

HELLBLAZER: SON OF MAN

VERTIGO
JOHN CONSTANTINE
HELLBLAZER
DANGEROUS HABITS
Garth Ennis William Simpson
Mark Pennington Tom Sutton Malcolm Jones III

HELLBLAZER:
RAKE AT THE GATES OF HELL

VERTIGO
JOHN CONSTANTINE
HELLBLAZER
RAKE at the GATES of HELL
Garth Ennis
Steve Dillon

with
STEVE DILLON

HELLBLAZER:
BLOODLINES

JOHN CONSTANTINE
HELLBLAZER
BLOODLINES
Garth Ennis
Will Simpson
Steve Dillon
Mike Hoffman
VERTIGO

with
STEVE DILLON

HELLBLAZER:
SON OF MAN

VERTIGO
JOHN CONSTANTINE
HELLBLAZER
SON of MAN
Garth Ennis
John Higgins

with
JOHN HIGGINS

GO TO
VERTIGOBOOKS.COM
FOR FREE SAMPLES OF THE FIRST ISSUES OF OUR GRAPHIC NOVELS

Suggested for Mature Readers

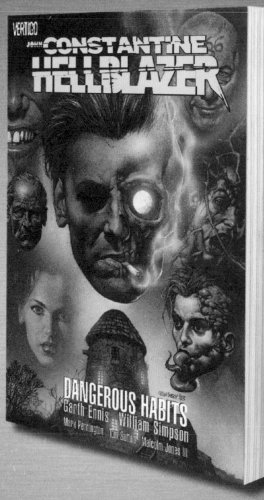

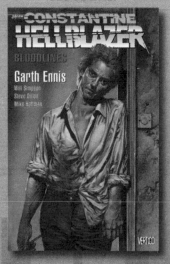